Learn HTML

Sunrise Midday Sunset

In a Weekend

Sunset Sunrise

Evening Sunrise

Revised Edition

STEVEN E. CALLIHAN

PRIMA TECH

A DIVISION OF PRIMA PUBLISHING

A Division of Prima Publishing

Prima Publishing, In a Weekend, and colophon are registered trademarks of Prima Communications, Inc., Prima Publishing, Rocklin, California 95677.

Publisher: Matthew H. Carleson
Managing Editor: Dan J. Foster
Senior Acquisitions Editor: Deborah F. Abshier
Project Editor: Kevin Harreld
Technical Reviewer: Jan Snyder
Copy Editor: Barton Reed
Interior Layout: Marian Hartsough
Cover Design: Prima Design Team
Indexer: Katherine Stimson

Microsoft, Windows, Windows NT, Internet Explorer, Notepad, and FrontPage are trademarks or registered trademarks of Microsoft Corporation. Netscape is a registered trademark of Netscape Communications Corporation. LVIEW is © 1998 Leonard Haddad Loureiro. All rights reserved.

Important: Prima Publishing cannot provide software support. Please contact the appropriate software manufacturer's technical support line or Web site for assistance.

Prima Publishing and the author have attempted throughout this book to distinguish proprietary trademarks from descriptive terms by following the capitalization style used by the manufacturer.

Information contained in this book has been obtained by Prima Publishing from sources believed to be reliable. However, because of the possibility of human or mechanical error by our sources, Prima Publishing, or others, the Publisher does not guarantee the accuracy, adequacy, or completeness of any information and is not responsible for any errors or omissions or the results obtained from the use of such information. Readers should be particularly aware of the fact that the Internet is an ever-changing entity. Some facts may have changed since this book went to press.

ISBN: 0-7615-1800-2
Library of Congress Catalog Card Number: 98-67613
Printed in the United States of America

99 00 01 02 II 10 9 8 7 6 5 4 3

To Jensen and Elizabeth

CONTENTS AT A GLANCE

CONTENTS

ACKNOWLEDGMENTS

Thanks to Kevin Harreld, Jan Snyder, and Bart Reed for helping to make the updating of this Revised Edition a relatively pain-free experience.

ABOUT THE AUTHOR

Steve Callihan is a freelance and technical writer from Seattle. He is also the author of *Create Your First Web Page In a Weekend* and a soon-to-be-released book, *Create Web Animations In a Weekend (with Microsoft Liquid Motion)*, both published by Prima Publishing.

INTRODUCTION

Probably one of the most common questions in job interviews these days is "Do you know HTML?" Knowing some HTML is rapidly becoming a requirement not only for computer professionals, but for anyone who works with a computer and a modem. A friend of mine recently told me of a job ad for an executive secretarial position that listed knowing HTML as a requirement! Becoming "functionally literate" in HTML is fast becoming one of the keys to future success in all sorts of fields.

The Web is a cooperative and participatory affair: You read my stuff, I'll read yours. If you want to publish effectively on the Web, you need to know at least some HTML.

If you decide to use a tool such as Microsoft FrontPage 98 (which will create much of your Web page for you), a solid understanding of HTML on the code level can only enhance your Web publishing efforts. You'll know what a particular element is and how it should work, which will help you maximize your results and efficiently correct problems, should they arise.

Who Should Read This Book

The good news is that you don't have to become an expert to take advantage of the benefits of HTML. One assumption this book makes is that you have interests that complement your computer skills. The computer is a tool that enables people to do stuff, not an end in itself. So, also, should be the Web and HTML. The Web, via HTML, should serve as an extension of your interests and purposes. What tends to get in the way is that many people think they need to know more than is really necessary. Don't make the mistake of thinking HTML is only for computer professionals and programmers. HTML is for everyone.

Also, HTML isn't something you learn first and do later. It's more like riding a bicycle, because you'll learn by doing. Don't worry about making mistakes. Mistakes are just experimental results by another name. Play around with it, experiment, and try new and different things. That's the only way you're going to truly learn.

What You Can Do in a Weekend

I can't promise that you'll be able to learn everything included in this book in a single weekend. I do promise that if you make the minimum effort required, by the end of the weekend, you'll be able to say with confidence, "I know HTML!"

A basic understanding of HTML is all that's required to create many of the Web pages you've visited while surfing the Web. The point is that you don't need to know a lot about HTML to get started actually using it. In other words, you don't need to know *everything* first! The more you learn, of course, the more you'll be able to do, and the more sophisticated the Web pages you create will be.

This book takes a graduated approach to learning HTML by dividing the process into easily achievable steps:

✪ Complete just the Basic HTML Tutorial (Saturday Morning) and you'll learn everything you need to know to create fairly sophisticated Web pages that include inline images, lists, hypertext links, image links, and more. Take the whole weekend to do just this one tutorial if you want. You'll still be able to say, "I know HTML!" All the remaining tutorials build on the foundation established by this one.

✪ Complete the Intermediate HTML Tutorial (Saturday Afternoon) as well, and you'll learn all you need to know to create even more sophisticated Web pages, including aligning headings and paragraphs, wrapping text around images, using fancy 3-D icon bullet lists, changing

font size and color, setting background colors, inserting images, and more. After this tutorial, you'll definitely be able to say, "I know HTML!"

✪ Complete the Tables, Frames, Forms, and Graphics Tutorials (Saturday Evening through Sunday Evening) and you'll learn everything you need to know to build all but the most sophisticated Web pages. In these tutorials, you'll learn to create fancy tabular layouts, multiframe Web sites, interactive forms, transparent banner graphics, image maps, GIF animations, and more. You'll absolutely for sure be able to say, "I know HTML!"

How much you'll be able to complete this weekend depends on your learning style and the effort you put forth. By investing a minimum amount of time and energy, you should be able to learn enough HTML to begin creating fairly sophisticated Web pages before the weekend is over.

What You Need to Begin

The examples and techniques shown in this book have all been tested using Windows 95, Windows 98, or Windows 3.1. I haven't tested them out in Windows NT, but it should work the same as Windows 95/98. You don't absolutely have to be a Microsoft Windows user to do the Basic and Intermediate HTML Tutorials, but Windows is required if you want to do any of the software tutorials or make use of any of the software tools included on the CD-ROM.

Although most of the illustrations come from Windows 98, the examples and techniques almost all apply equally to both Windows 3.1 and Windows 95, as well. Certain software tools and capabilities, however, may be available for Windows 95/98 that are not available for Windows 3.1. These cases are pointed out as you go along.

Besides a computer, of course, you only need three things to learn HTML using this book:

✪ **A graphical Web browser connected to the Internet**. You can do the Basic HTML Tutorial (Saturday Morning) with any fairly current graphical Web browser. To do the other tutorials in the book, however, you should use either Netscape Navigator (version 3.0 or higher) or

Microsoft Internet Explorer (version 3.0 or higher). The illustrations in this book feature mainly Navigator 4.0 and Internet Explorer 4.0. Ultimately, you'll probably want to download and install the latest versions of both of the major Web browsers. You can download the latest versions of Netscape Navigator or Microsoft Internet Explorer from their respective Web sites at **http://home.netscape.com/** and **http://www.microsoft.com/**.

- ✿ **A text editor.** I strongly recommend using Windows Notepad, which comes with both Windows 3.1 and Windows 95, rather than a word processor or an HTML editor. Notepad is perfectly suited for creating HTML files and offers several advantages over larger, more cumbersome programs. Many professional HTML coders prefer Notepad. A couple other Notepad-like HTML editors, HTML Notepad and Gomer HTML Editor, are also well suited for HTML coding. Avoid starting out with one of the WYSIWYG-type HTML editors. Learn some HTML first and then try out some of the fancier tools (a large selection of which are also included on the CD-ROM).

- ✿ **A graphics editor capable of creating GIF graphic files**. Any of the commercial draw or photo-paint programs can create GIF files; however, some excellent graphics programs for creating and working with GIF files are also available on the Web. You'll be using Paint Shop Pro 5, included on the CD-ROM, in the Graphics Tutorial (scheduled for Sunday evening). I highly recommend using Paint Shop Pro 5 as your main graphics editor.

You don't need to be a techie or a computer nerd to use this book, but you should have a working knowledge of basic Windows operations (3.1 or 95). The book is written with the assumption that you already know how to use a Web browser and navigate on the Web. It mentions quite a few resources available on the Web; therefore, you should know how to download a file or program from the Web. Because many programs on the Web are in compressed format—ZIP or TAR, for instance—you should know how to decompress files using utilities such as WinZip or PKUNZIP.

This book doesn't tell you how to use your computer, run Windows, sign up with an ISP (Internet Service Provider), install your Web browser, log on to the Internet, surf the Web, download files, and so on. If you need to learn about these tasks, plenty of other books are available in your local bookstore. This book only covers learning HTML to create Web pages.

This book also does not cover uploading your finished HTML files up onto a Web server. At the Web site for the book, however, you'll find an online tutorial for using WS-FTP LE (included on the CD-ROM) to upload your Web pages up to your server.

How This Book Is Organized

The book is divided into seven sessions, beginning on Friday evening and continuing into Sunday evening. Each session should take no more than two to four hours to complete. The following overview details each session's highlights:

- **Friday Evening: Getting Started**. Covers essential background information and the minimum requirements necessary to do the two Saturday HTML tutorials. This session also teaches you how to run your browser offline and includes an optional section on tools and resources that can help you apply HTML in the creation of Web pages.

- **Saturday Morning: The Basic HTML Tutorial.** This is a step-by-step tutorial that covers the basic HTML codes most commonly used to create Web pages. It's organized according to function to teach you what each code does and to give you an overall view of HTML and how it works. Although this tutorial is slated for Saturday Morning, feel free to go ahead and take all day.

- **Saturday Afternoon: The Intermediate HTML Tutorial**. This optional tutorial covers intermediate HTML, which is largely composed of codes originally introduced as "Netscape extensions" that have since been incorporated into HTML 3.2 and HTML 4.0. However, you don't need to know these codes to create your first Web pages. This session will teach you how to create more appealing, attractive, and effective Web pages. You should complete this tutorial prior to doing the more advanced tutorials.

- **Saturday Evening: The Tables Tutorial**. The evening sessions are bonus sessions. The Tables Tutorial will teach you to begin using tables in your Web pages, including how to create captions and headings, cells that span rows and/or columns, borders and margins, as

ON THE

CD

This marks resources or tools located on the CD-ROM that may be helpful to you in your Web publishing endeavors.

➡This code continuation character is used when one line of code is too long to fit on one line of the book. Here's an example:

```
<P>In <EM>Porgy and Bess</EM>, in the song "Summertime," George
➡Gershwin evokes the hazy, lazy days of a Southern summer.
```

When typing these lines, you would type them as one long line without the code continuation character.

Visit This Book's Web Site

I have set up the *Learn HTML in a Weekend (Revised Edition)* Web site at **http://www.callihan.com/learn2/**. If you don't have a CD-ROM drive, all the example graphics and files used in the tutorials can be downloaded from the book's Web site. You'll also find information and guidance on finding a Web host for your Web pages, an online tutorial on using WS-FTP LE to upload your HTML files up onto your Web server, additional software tools and utilities to assist you in Web publishing, information and resources on just about everything you might want to know about HTML and Web publishing. What's more, if you have any questions that this book doesn't answer, I've included an e-mail link so you can query the author.

Getting Started

- ✿ What is the Internet and the World Wide Web?
- ✿ What is a Web page?
- ✿ Where's HTML going?
- ✿ Getting ready for the tutorials

It's Friday evening—at least if you're following the schedule. Yes, for the purposes of this book, Friday evening constitutes part of the weekend. Okay, maybe that is fudging a bit, but if you're going to learn HTML in a weekend, you need to get this little reading assignment out of the way first.

The first section of this Friday evening session includes general background information on the Internet, the World Wide Web, HTML, and Web pages. You really should have some grounding in the medium before you start the HTML tutorials on Saturday or begin to try the software tutorials on Sunday. Of course, if you're already familiar with something covered in this session, feel free to skip or merely skim it.

The second section, "Getting Ready," covers selecting and setting up the tools you'll need to complete the HTML tutorials on Saturday and the software tutorials on Sunday. This includes selecting a Web browser, a text or HTML editor, and a graphics editor for creating custom graphics for your first Web page.

What Is the Internet?

It could be said that the Internet is the most valuable legacy left over from the Cold War. It originally came into being as the *ARPANet*, which was founded by the U.S. Defense Department's Advanced Research Projects Agency (ARPA) to link academic research centers involved in military research.

Today's Internet has grown far beyond its original conception. Originally linking just four university research centers, the Internet has become an international and global system consisting of hundreds of thousands of *nodes* (servers). In many ways, it has become what Marshall McLuhan called "the global village," in that every node is functionally right next door. You can just as easily communicate with someone in Australia as you can with someone two blocks down the street—and if the person down the street isn't on the Internet, it's actually easier to communicate with the bloke in Australia. That's the premise, even if the original founders didn't realize it, and today it has become an increasingly pervasive reality.

◄◄◄◄◄◄◄◄◄◄◄◄◄◄◄◄◄◄◄◄◄◄◄◄◄◄◄◄◄◄◄◄◄◄◄◄◄◄

A *client* is a computer that requests something from another computer. A *server* is a computer that responds to requests for service from clients.

◄◄◄◄◄◄◄◄◄◄◄◄◄◄◄◄◄◄◄◄◄◄◄◄◄◄◄◄◄◄◄◄◄◄◄◄◄◄

◄◄◄◄◄◄◄◄◄◄◄◄◄◄◄◄◄◄◄◄◄◄◄◄◄◄◄◄◄◄◄◄◄◄◄◄◄◄

An *internet* is a network of networks—a kind of *meta-network*. Simply put, the Internet is a set of protocols (rules) for transmitting and exchanging data among networks. In a broader sense, however, it's a worldwide community, a global village, and a repository of global information resources.

◄◄◄◄◄◄◄◄◄◄◄◄◄◄◄◄◄◄◄◄◄◄◄◄◄◄◄◄◄◄◄◄◄◄◄◄◄◄

◄◄◄◄◄◄◄◄◄◄◄◄◄◄◄◄◄◄◄◄◄◄◄◄◄◄◄◄◄◄◄◄◄◄◄◄◄◄

TCP/IP (Transmission Control Protocol/Internet Protocol) is the standard rule set for Internet communication. The essence of the Internet is not the wire, but the means for sending and receiving information across the wire. It doesn't matter what type of systems are connected to the Internet, be they mainframes, minicomputers, or Unix, Macintosh, or MS-DOS computers. All that matters is that they all use the same protocol, TCP/IP, to communicate with each other.

◄◄◄◄◄◄◄◄◄◄◄◄◄◄◄◄◄◄◄◄◄◄◄◄◄◄◄◄◄◄◄◄◄◄◄◄◄◄

What Is the World Wide Web?

The World Wide Web (also called the *WWW*, *W3*, or simply the *Web*) dates back to 1989, when it was proposed by Tim Berners-Lee, often called "the inventor of the World Wide Web." Many others have been critically involved, but Berners-Lee gets the credit for originally proposing and evangelizing the idea as a way to facilitate collaboration between scientists over the Internet.

On the original Web page for the World Wide Web Project, posted on the CERN (the European Laboratory of Particle Physics, birth place of the World Wide Web) server in 1992, Tim Berners-Lee described the World Wide Web as "a wide-area hypermedia information retrieval initiative aiming to give universal access to a large universe of documents." Today he's more liable to describe the Web as the "universal space of all network-accessible information." Ted Nelson, inventor of the concept of hypertext, wrapped all this up in a wonderfully apt term, describing the Word Wide Web as a "docuverse."

Like the Internet, the Web is essentially defined by a set of protocols:

- **HTTP (HyperText Transfer Protocol).** Used to exchange Web documents across the Internet. When you request a Web document from a server, the protocol used for the request is HTTP.

- **HTML (HyperText Markup Language).** Enables users to present information over the Web in a structured and uniform fashion. HTML is used to mark up documents so that a Web browser can interpret and then display them. See "What Is HTML?" later in this session for more information.

- **URLs (Uniform Resource Locators).** Addresses that identify a server, a directory, or a specific file. HTTP URLs, or *Web addresses*, are only one type of address on the Web. FTP, Gopher, and WAIS are other types of addresses you'll find fairly often on the Web as well. In fact, until fairly recently, more FTP and Gopher servers existed on the Internet than HTTP servers. See "What Is a URL?" later in this session for additional related information.

- **CGI (Common Gateway Interface).** Serves as an interface to execute local programs through a gateway between the HTTP server software and the host computer. Therefore, you can include a hypertext link in a Web document that will run a server program or script, for example, to process input from a customer request form.

Although other mediums of exchange on the Internet share the same cyberspace, the Web has come to epitomize the new paradigm. In fact, Web browsers can access not only Web or HTML documents, but the entirety of the Internet, including Gopher, FTP, Archie, Telnet, and WAIS, as well as mail and news servers. The Web's tendency to embrace and incorporate all other mediums, thus operating as a universal medium, is its most revolutionary characteristic.

A LITTLE HISTORY

The beginnings of the Internet go back at least as far as 1957, to the founding of the Defense Department's Advanced Research Projects Agency (ARPA) in response to the Soviet Union launching *Sputnik.* In 1963, ARPA asked the Rand Corporation to ponder how to form a command-and-control network capable of surviving attack by atomic bombs. The Rand Corporation's response (made public in 1964) was that the network would "have no central authority" and would be "designed from the beginning to operate while in tatters." These two basic concepts became the defining characteristics of what would eventually become the Internet. The Internet was conceptualized as having no central authority and as being able to operate in a condition of assumed unreliability (bombed-out cities, downed telephone lines). In other words, it would have maximum redundancy. All nodes would be coequal in status, each with authority to originate, relay, and receive messages.

What happened between this first military initiative and the Internet we know today? Plenty. Here are some of the highlights:

1965: Ted Nelson invents the concept of and coins the term *hypertext.*

1969: ARPANet, the forerunner of the Internet, is commissioned by the Department of Defense. Nodes at UCLA, Stanford, UC Santa Barbara, and the University of Utah are linked. Within two years, the number of nodes is increased to 15 to include MIT, Harvard, and NASA/Ames.

1972: Telnet is introduced.

1973: The first international connections to the ARPANet occur from England and Norway. FTP (File Transfer Protocol) is introduced.

1977: E-mail is introduced.

1979: Newsgroups (USENET) are introduced.

1982: ARPANet adopts TCP/IP (Transmission Control Protocol/Internet Protocol), the real beginning of the Internet.

1984: Domain Name Server (DNS) is implemented, allocating addresses among six basic "domains": gov, mil, edu, net, com, and org (for government, military, educational, network, commercial, and noncommercial hosts, respectively).

1986: NSFNet is formed by the National Science Foundation (NSF) using five supercomputing centers to form the first high-speed "backbone," running at 56Kbps. Unlike ARPANet, which is focused on military and government research, NSFNet is available to all forms of academic research.

1987: Ten thousand hosts make up the Web.

1988: The Web backbone is upgraded to T1 (1.544Mbps).

1989: Tim Berners-Lee proposes the invention of the Web, leading to the creation of the World Wide Web.

1990: ARPANet closes down. Archie is introduced on the Web. The World (world.std.com) becomes the first commercial provider of dial-up access to the Internet.

1991: Gopher is introduced. The World Wide Web is released at CERN (European Laboratory for Particle Physics) in Switzerland. The Web's backbone is upgraded to T3 (44.736Mbps).

1992: The Internet Society (ISOC) is formed. Viola, the first English-language graphical Web browser is released. Veronica is introduced to the Web. One million hosts are present on the Web.

1993: Marc Andreesen's Mosaic for X (X-Windows, a Unix GUI) is released by NCSA, followed shortly by versions for PC/Windows and

Macintosh. The White House goes online. The HTML 1.0 draft proposal is published.

1994: Mosaic Communications, later to become Netscape Communications, is formed by Marc Andreesen and James Clark, ex-president of Silicon Graphics. The first meeting of the W3 Consortium is held at MIT. The first cybermalls form. The HTML 2.0 draft proposal is published.

1995: Netscape goes public. NSFNet is replaced by a network of providers for carrying U.S. backbone traffic. NSFNet reverts to a research network.

1996: Bill Gates and Microsoft jump into the game with the Internet Explorer browser. Proposed recommendation for HTML 3.2 is released in May by the W3C (World Wide Web Consortium). The recommendation for Cascading Style Sheets, level 1 (CSS1) is released in December.

1997: The final recommendation for HTML 3.2 is released in January. The working draft for the Document Object Model (DOM), a key element in the future direction of Dynamic HTML, is released in September. The final recommendation for HTML 4.0 is released in December.

1998: Proposed recommendation (the last step before final release) for MathML (Mathematical Markup Language) and the final recommendation for XML 1.0 (Extensible Markup Language) are released in February. Proposed recommendation for Cascading Style Sheets, level 2 (CSS2) and an updated working draft for the Document Object Model (DOM) are released in March. Total users of the Web is estimated at between 35 and 50 million.

What Is Hypertext?

You could say the Web is a graphical, platform-independent, distributed, decentralized, multiformatted, interactive, dynamic, nonlinear, immediate, two-way communication medium. The basic mechanism that enables all this is actually quite simple—the *hypertext link*. It's a kind of "jump point" that allows a visitor to jump from a place in a Web page to any other Web page, document, or binary data object (a script, graphic, video, and so on) on the Web. Not only can you jump to another Web page, but you can jump to another place, either in the same Web page or another Web page. If you've ever clicked a link and then jumped to a place in the middle of either the same or another Web page, you've seen this capability in action. A link can connect anything, anywhere that has an address (or URL) on the Net. When Ted Nelson originally coined the term *hypertext* in 1965, he conceptualized it simply as "nonsequential writing." In other words, any link can go to any object anywhere (anything with an address) within the *docuverse*, or "universal space of all network-accessible information," as Tim Berners-Lee puts it. See Figure 1.1 for a general representation of how hypertext links work.

Figure 1.2 illustrates some of the different kinds of data objects to which you can link from a Web page. Note the difference here between an inline image, which appears as part of the Web page, and other graphics, which your browser or viewer can link to and display separately.

A hypertext link, also referred to as an *anchor*, actually works much like a cross-reference in a book, except that you can immediately go to it simply by clicking the link, whether it's a link within the same document or to a page or document halfway around the world. You don't have to thumb through the book or go down to the local library to find the reference. Anything that

Figure 1.1

Using hypertext links, you can jump from one Web page to another Web page.

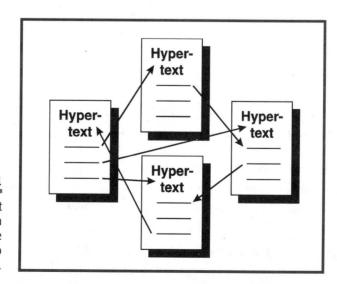

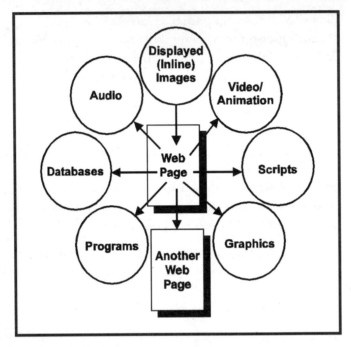

Figure 1.2

A Web page can link to many other kinds of data objects besides just other Web pages.

has an address on the Web can be linked, including Gopher documents, FTP files, and newsgroup articles.

What Is Hypermedia?

Given that hypertext linking occurs within and between documents, it makes sense that *hypermedia* (a term also coined by Ted Nelson) refers to connecting with and between other nontext (binary) media, such as graphics, audio, animation, video, and software programs. Many pages on the Web are now generated on the fly from scripts, programs, and database queries. Increasingly, Java applets are being used to generate dynamically interactive Web sites. (Hypermedia might be, for instance, another term for *Dynamic HTML*.) Over time, the Web will naturally evolve from a system predominantly composed of primarily static hypertext Web pages to one predominantly composed of dynamically interlinked hypermedia, within which text is just another medium.

For now, though, the Web still mainly consists of documents, or *pages*, and you can still think of hypermedia as a subcategory of hypertext.

What Is HTML?

HTML (HyperText Markup Language) was originally intended as a subset of SGML (Standard Generalized Markup Language). SGML was developed to standardize the markup, or *preparation for typesetting*, of computer-generated documents. HTML, on the other hand, was specifically developed to mark up, or *encode*, hypertext documents for display on the World Wide Web. Due to the many *ad hoc* extensions that have been added to it, however, HTML can no longer be said to be merely a subset of SGML (unless you want to think of it as a misbehaving subset).

An HTML document is a plain text file (or what is often called an *ASCII file*) with codes (called *tags*) inserted in the text to define elements in the document. HTML tags generally have two parts—an on-code and an off-code—which contain the text to be defined. A few tags don't require off-codes (I'll note these when I cover them). You can represent a tag in the following way, where the ellipsis (...) represents the text you want to tag:

```
<Tagname> ... </Tagname>
```

For instance, the following is the tag for a Level 1 heading in a Web document:

```
<H1>This is a Level 1 heading</H1>
```

The most important thing to keep in mind about HTML is that its purpose isn't to specify the exact formatting or layout of a Web page, but to define and specify the specific elements that make up a page—the body of the text, headings, paragraphs, line breaks, text elements, and so on. You use HTML to define the composition of a Web page, not its appearance. The particular Web browser you use to view the page controls the display of the Web page. For instance, you can define a line using the <H1> ... </H1> tag, but the browser defines the appearance of a first-level header line. One browser might show H1 lines as 18-point Times Roman text, whereas another might show H1 lines in a totally different font and size.

To understand why this is the way it is, you need to understand how HTML-coded Web pages and Web browsers work together. To display a Web page on your computer, a Web browser must first download it and any graphics displayed on the page to your computer. If the Web page were to specify all the formatting and display details, it would increase the amount of data to be transmitted, the size of the file, and the amount of time it takes to transfer. Leaving all the formatting and display details to the Web browser means that the size of HTML documents sent over the Web can remain relatively small, because they're just regular ASCII text files. It's rare to have an HTML file that exceeds 30KB (not counting any graphics it may contain).

However, this means that every Web browser may have its own idea about how to best display a particular Web page. Your Web page may look different in Netscape Navigator than it does in NCSA Mosaic. That's why you'll want to test your completed page on more than just one browser. Some Web browsers now support the display of tables, which was part of the proposed HTML 3.0 standard and has since been incorporated into HTML 3.2, but some don't. HTML 3.2 gives the official stamp of approval to most of the Netscape extensions to HTML. However, none of the Microsoft extensions to HTML were so favored.

Most current graphical Web browsers—not just Navigator and Internet Explorer—now support HTML 3.2. In the Intermediate HTML Tutorial, scheduled for Saturday afternoon, I'll show you how to effectively incorporate HTML 3.2 features into your Web pages.

The advent of the new HTML 4.0 specification adds more complications to the mix. At the time of this writing, the current versions of Netscape Navigator and Internet Explorer already support parts of but by no means all of what's included in HTML 4.0. Also, the latest version of Internet Explorer seems to be fairly fully compliant with the Cascading Style Sheets, level 1 standard, but the latest version of Navigator seems to be lagging somewhat behind here. Neither browser has yet to support the latest proposed standard: Cascading Style Sheets, level 2. Add into that the other recent developments, such as the DOM (Document Object Model), XML (Extensible Markup Language), and MathML (Mathematical Markup Language), and it's clear that the two major browsers are currently playing "catch-up."

Most of HTML 4.0 should be supported fairly quickly, as well as most of the new Cascading Style Sheets standards (CSS1 and CSS2), especially where competitive pressures between the two main browsers dictate that they be entirely up-to-date. However, other aspects of HTML 4.0 for which there may not be the same degree of competitive demand may not be implemented as quickly. The appealing features, such as full support for Cascading Style

Sheets, should be implemented first, while less demanded features, such as some of the new form elements and attributes, may have to wait their turn. Anyway, trying to prognosticate the future of HTML is sort of like trying to guess the weather. Stay tuned for the nightly report, in other words, because that's exactly how fast things will be changing. On the other hand, remember that the more things change, the more they stay the same—most of what's being added to HTML now is frosting on the cake. The body of the "cake" is still composed almost entirely of HTML 2.0 and HTML 3.2 elements and attributes.

If you're concerned with compatibility with the vast majority of current graphical Web browsers, it may be wise for the time being to stick with HTML 3.2 elements and attributes, at least until HTML 4.0 is more fully supported—except possibly for frames (the FRAMESET element), which are supported by most current Web browsers. If you want to incorporate any of the new HTML 4.0 features, you should thoroughly check your pages out in both of the main Web browsers. Although other Web browsers, or earlier versions of Navigator and Internet Explorer, simply ignore unrecognized tags, you should be aware that a Web page that looks fantastic in a Web browser supporting HTML 4.0 may look pretty crummy in one that doesn't. It's probably not a bad idea to keep an older Web browser installed on your system so you can check and make sure your pages display acceptably in browsers that don't support HTML 4.0.

NOTE

As HTML has evolved, both officially and in an *ad hoc* manner (via browsers having their own extensions), it has become more descriptive, thus allowing you more freedom to "design" your page rather than simply "schematicize" it. The more attention you give to designing your page's particular appearance, however, the less likely it is that all browsers will display your page consistently and accurately. The Basic and Intermediate HTML Tutorials show you how different browsers can display the same element. Also, many of the "designer" features that have been added to HTML require an up-to-date Web browser to display them.

In this book, the discussion of HTML falls into three categories: Basic HTML, Intermediate HTML, and Advanced HTML. These divisions are in no way official—they're just an attempt to pare down the material into more serviceable chunks.

Basic HTML encompasses most but not all of what was HTML 2.0 (the HTML standard prior to HTML 3.2). I cover this level of HTML in the Basic HTML Tutorial (Saturday Morning). Most graphical Web browsers, both old and new, should support this level of HTML.

Intermediate HTML encompasses most of what's included in HTML 3.2, as well as a few tidbits from HTML 4.0. I cover this level of HTML in the Intermediate HTML Tutorial (Saturday Afternoon) and the Tables Tutorial (Saturday Evening). Most current graphical Web browsers should fully support HTML 3.2, but support from earlier browser versions may be a bit sketchy (HTML 3.2 is largely a pastiche of what were previously called *Netscape extensions* and previously proposed elements that were originally to be included in the failed HTML 3.0 proposal).

Advanced HTML includes HTML 2.0, HTML 3.2, and HTML 4.0 tags, as well as other advanced features, such as Cascading Style Sheets and Dynamic HTML. To attempt to teach you everything that's included in Advanced HTML in a single weekend simply is not possible. Instead, the approach I've taken with this book is to provide a series of software tutorials that will show you how to use readily available software tools (included on the CD-ROM) to incorporate more advanced HTML features, such as frames, forms, and image maps, in your Web pages. You'll also find all the HTML 4.0 tags and attributes covered in Appendix A, "HTML Quick Reference." Although I don't provide any in-depth coverage of Cascading Style Sheets and Dynamic HTML in this book (they would require books of their own), you will find software tools on the CD-ROM that can assist you in adding these features to your Web pages.

I've also included a collection of Web page templates on the CD-ROM to assist you in creating many different kinds of Web pages, including Web pages using tables and frames. For more information on the Web page templates included on the CD-ROM, see Appendix D, "What's on the CD-ROM?"

If you want to include the latest HTML 4.0 and other recently introduced advanced features, you should keep in mind that even current Web browsers may not support everything included in the latest specifications and standards. Before making use of one of these features in a Web page, you should check and make sure it's supported by current Web browsers. You should also then check your page in one or more older browsers (such as NCSA Mosaic

2.0, for instance) to ensure against any unpleasant surprises. And if your page has any major display problems in older browsers, you might want to clearly label it as an "HTML 4.0 only" page, or create a front page that has links to HTML 4.0 and non-HTML 4.0 versions of your page.

What Is a URL?

A *URL* (*Uniform Resource Locator*) identifies the address, or location, of a resource on the Internet. Every Web page has its own unique URL. If you know the URL of a Web page and access is not restricted, you can connect to it and view it in your browser. Resources other than Web pages also have URLs, including FTP, Telnet, WAIS, Gopher, and newsgroups.

A URL may consist of the following parts:

- ✪ **Service.** This designator specifies the service being accessed: http (for WWW), ftp, gopher, wais, telnet, or news.

- ✪ **Host.** The host designator specifies the domain name of the server being accessed. For instance: **www.myserver.com**.

- ✪ **Port number.** The port number only needs to be specified if it's a nonstandard port number for the service being accessed. Most URLs don't require port numbers (the default port number is 80 for Web servers and 21 for FTP servers, for instance).

- ✪ **Resource path.** The resource path specifies the directory path and often the file name of the resource being accessed. At minimum, you should probably include a backslash (/) here to indicate the root directory of a domain (although most Web browsers let you get away with leaving this off following a domain name): for instance, **http://anywhere.com/** rather than **http://anywhere.com**. You can exclude the file name here if you use the default file name for index files specified by the server, which may be INDEX.HTML, INDEX.HTM, HOME.HTML, or DEFAULT.HTM, depending on the actual server. If you don't use the default file name for index files, you must include the actual file path and name of the Web page: for instance, **http://anywhere.com/myfolder/mypage.html**.

Figure 1.3 shows a diagram of a URL. Because most Web addresses don't use port numbers, this illustration leaves out the port number.

Figure 1.3

A Uniform Resource
Locator (URL) is
the address of a
resource on the
Internet.

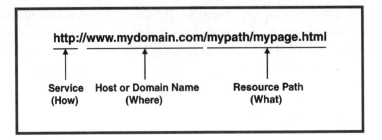

A URL is actually an instruction or request from an agent (such as a Web browser) to a server on the Internet that specifies the following three things:

- **How?** This is the protocol for the transaction. For Web pages, this is HTTP. Essentially, the protocol tells the server what software it needs to run to manage the transaction. More than one server can reside on the same computer—for instance, a single computer can function both as an FTP server and as an HTTP (or Web) server.

- **Where?** This is the address where the transaction is to take place. For instance, **www.mydomain.com/mypath/** specifies the domain name and the location within that domain of what is to be transacted.

- **What?** This is the name of what is to be transacted. For instance, **mypage.html** specifies the actual HTML document, or Web page, as the subject of the transaction.

NOTE If you link to a file or data object that resides within the same directory structure as the referring page, you don't have to supply the full URL for it, just as you don't have to dial the area code for a local phone call. When a link is local (**pages/mypage.htm**, for instance), it's known as a *relative URL*, whereas a full URL is known as an *absolute URL* (**http://www.myserver.com/pages/mypage.htm**, for instance). The biggest advantage of using relative rather than absolute URLs is that you don't have to change them when you load your pages up on your server, as long as your local and remote folder structures are the same. You can also move your Web pages and attendant files to a new server, or to a new folder structure on the same server, without having to change your relative links. See "Using Relative URLs" in the Basic HTML Tutorial.

CAUTION ◆

Most Web pages reside on Unix servers. Unlike MS-DOS and Windows systems, Unix systems use case-sensitive file paths and names. Therefore, if you see a path and file name like **MySite/HOMEPAGE.html**, you should type it exactly as it appears. Changing the capitalization to "Mysite" may put you somewhere else entirely or nowhere at all.

◆ ◆

What Is a Domain Name?

Every Internet server has a numerical IP (Internet Protocol) address, which usually consists of four numbers between 0 and 255, separated by periods (something like 185.35.117.0, for instance). Computers prefer numeric addresses of this type because they're precise. Unfortunately, humans have trouble remembering numbers—we prefer meaningful text addresses such as **www.mysite.com.** That's what a domain name is: a text alternative to an IP address. You can usually use the two interchangeably. The point is that if you know the domain name, you don't have to know anything about the IP address. You will, however, sometimes run into an odd URL on the Web that specifies the IP address rather than the domain name (and nothing forbids a server from having an IP address but no domain address).

Most servers have applied for and received a domain name from the Inter-NIC (the *Internet Network Information Center*), which handles domain name registrations. As long as your Web pages are located on a server that has a domain name, you can use that domain name in the addresses, or URLs, for those Web pages. You don't have to have your own server to have your own domain name. You can also set up a Web site on someone else's server and use your own domain name in what is often referred to as a *virtual host* arrangement—to the outside world, you appear to have your own server (**www.yourname.com**, for instance) when in reality, you don't.

NOTE Registering domain names used to be free, but this led to a free-for-all somewhat similar to the Oklahoma Land Rush, as companies and individuals scrambled to grab up domain names before anyone else could claim them. Because an organization or individual could claim an unlimited number of domain names, speculative trading (in other words, scalping) in domain names evolved. For these reasons, as well as to help fund the costs of registering rapidly increasing domain name requests, as of September, 1995, the InterNIC started charging a fee for registering and maintaining a domain name—$70 for the first two years; $35 a year thereafter. Even so, one company still forked out the $70 to grab up as many "last names" (smith.com, jones.com, etc.) as they could, so they could resell them for Web-based e-mail addresses (luckily, I got mine, callihan.com, before they started doing this).

A domain name represents a hierarchy, starting with the most general word on the right and moving to the most specific word on the left. It can include a country code, an organization code, and a site name. For instance, **myname.com.au**, reading from right to left, specifies the name of a site in Australia (au) in the commercial (com) subcategory, called "myname." Every country connected to the Internet has its own code: "uk" (United Kingdom), "ca" (Canada), "fr" (France), "nz" (New Zealand), and so forth. The country code for the United States is "us." Most sites in the United States don't include the country code, however, because the Internet began in the United States and the country codes were created later, after the Internet went international. Here's a list of the organization codes:

- **EDU for *education*.** Schools and universities, for instance, use this organization code.
- **GOV for *government*.** Various governmental departments and agencies use this organization code.
- **MIL for *military*.** The Internet was, after all, originally a U.S. Defense Department initiative (the ARPANet).
- **NET for *network*.** Refers to a network connected to the Internet. In practice, you usually run into this organization code with ISPs (Internet Service Providers) offering public access to the Internet.
- **COM for *commercial*.** This code was created to accommodate commercial usage of the Internet by business enterprises.

Figure 1.4

Internet domains can be organized in general categories, such as COM or EDU, or they can be organized in "international" categories, such as CA (for Canada) or UK (for the United Kingdom).

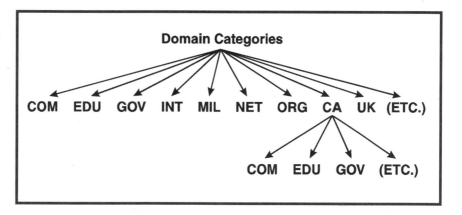

- **ORG for *organization*.** This code is for noncommercial, nonprofit organizations.

Figure 1.4 gives you a graphical representation of the domain name system.

NOTE A number of initiatives are in place to add new top-level domain name categories. The most likely candidates are ".firm," ".shop," ".web," ".arts," ".rec," ".info," and ".nom." How soon these new domain categories will become available is anyone's guess. The U.S. Government is currently in charge of the domain hierarchy, a vestige of the beginnings of the Internet as a U.S. Defense Department initiative (the ARPANet). It wants to hand this responsibility off to an international standards body. The hold-up has been over deciding which standards body should be responsible for this.

What Is a Web Page?

A *Web page* is a hypertext (HTML) document contained in a single file. To have more than one Web page, you must have more than one file. Despite the connotation of the word *page*, a Web page can be any length, although display of most Web pages extends to no more than two or three screens.

A Web page is simply a plain text document. All codes are entered into the document as ordinary text, with none of the binary-level formatting a word processor would embed in it. When you mark some text as italic in a word processing document, you don't see the actual computer code that causes the text to appear or print in italics. In HTML, you have to do it all yourself. There's no underlying program code to translate what you type as you go. You type in `<I>` where you want the browser to turn on italics and `</I>` where you want it to turn them off. This cuts down on the computer overhead, allowing Web pages to remain small but still pack quite a punch.

When a browser displays a Web page, the page may appear to contain special graphical elements such as logos or buttons. These graphics don't reside in the HTML file itself; they're separate files that the HTML file references. For instance, you might see a line like this in the HTML file:

```
<IMG SRC="mylogo.gif">
```

The code places the graphic into the version of the page that a browser displays. When a browser displays the page, the reference opens and inserts the graphic in the specified spot. You can include a banner or logo, buttons, icons, separator bars, navigational icons, and more. See Figure 1.5 for a graphical representation of a Web page that contains these different kinds of elements.

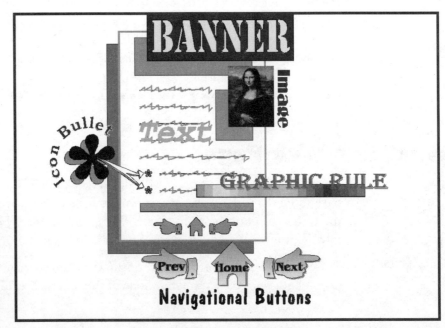

Figure 1.5

Graphic elements are actually separate files linked to and displayed as part of your Web page.

What Is a Web Site?

The term *Web site* has a couple different (although analogous) meanings. Servers are often called Web sites (sites on the Web), but any grouping of related and linked Web pages sharing a common theme or subject matter may also be called a Web site. To avoid confusion, in this book, I'll always refer to a collection of related Web pages as a *Web site*. I'll refer to a Web server as simply that: a *Web server*, or, alternatively, as a *Web host* (a Web server that "hosts" Web sites).

Your access provider (the company or organization that provides you access to the Internet) may give you space for a personal, noncommercial Web site at little or no cost. If you're a student, you may be able to have your pages hosted by your school's server. Many online services, such as CompuServe and America Online, also host Web pages at a reasonable cost. If you want to create a commercial Web site that offers a product or service or you want to create a more sophisticated Web site that requires more space, higher traffic allowances, more technical support, and a wider range of features than your access provider will give you, you may need to rent your Web space from what is commonly called a *presence provider*. A presence provider focuses on or specializes in providing Web space and can offer a fuller menu of services aimed specifically at Web publishers. A presence provider also can register and maintain a domain name for you, usually at a reasonable cost, making it look to the outside world as if you own your own server (rather than merely as a tenant renting space).

A Web site is simply a collection of allied Web pages, similar to the chapters in a book, tied and linked together, usually through a home page (sometimes also called an "index page") that serves as the directory to the rest of the Web site. The different Web pages that compose the site are interlinked and related to each other as parts of a whole. Dissimilar Web pages that are unlinked (that is, *unrelated*) to each other, on the other hand, don't form a Web site, even if they're stored in the same directory on the same server.

What Is a Home Page?

The term *home page* can have a number of different meanings. When you start your browser, it loads whatever Web page you designate as its home page (which can be a Web page up on the Internet or even a page on your own hard drive). Most browsers have a Home button or command that takes you back to the page designated as the browser's home page. This page may vary according to the browser or access provider you're using—it could be Netscape's Netcenter Web site or Microsoft's Web site if you're using either of their browsers, or it could be the home page of your access provider (AOL, MCI Internet, and so on). You can, however, specify whichever page you want as your browser's home page. This is also sometimes referred to as a *start page*.

The term *home page* can also refer to an entry point (or *front door*) to a Web site or a group of linked and related Web pages. It can also designate any Web page that stands on its own (in keeping with the front door comparison, you could think of a standalone Web page as a one-room shack). The diagram in Figure 1.6 shows the relationship between home and Web pages.

Most servers let you create a default home page (most often named INDEX.HTML) that loads automatically without the file name having to be specified in the URL. This allows you, for example, to have **http://www.myserver.com/mydirectory/** as your URL rather than **http://www.myserver.com/mydirectory/index.html**. This is often also referred to as an *index page*.

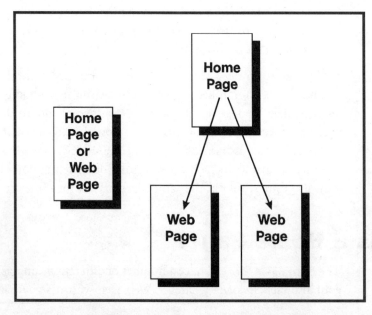

Figure 1.6

A home page can be either a standalone Web page or an entry point to a Web site.

Home pages used as entryways are generally kept small, often serving simply as menus or directories to the Web pages that make up the rest of the Web site. The idea here is that a viewer needs only to display the home page, which is relatively small, and then decide what else to view in the remainder of the Web site.

Having a Web site go deeper than three or four levels is rare, but the number of levels of Web pages you might want to have appended as *subpages* off of your home page is technically unlimited. The deeper a Web page is (a subpage of a subpage of a subpage of your home page), the less accessible it will be to the visitors of your site. The main idea is that pages you want to be the most readily accessible to visitors of your site should be prominently linked from its home page or from a subpage of its home page. See Figure 1.7 for an illustration of a multilevel Web site.

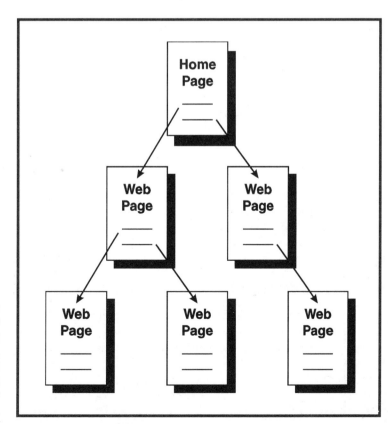

Figure 1.7

A Web site can have several levels, although you should keep it to three or fewer levels.

You can also create a home page that links together multiple home pages. You might, for instance, have a series of Web sites that are relatively autonomous, share a common theme, are produced by the same department, or are part of a larger project. Also, you may simply want to link pages together to get increased visibility on the Web—as is the case with the various cybermalls prevalent on the Web.

Take a Break

You might want to take the opportunity at this juncture to take a break. Relax and stretch a bit. Fix a cup of tea or get yourself a glass of juice. I'll see you back in five minutes or so for the remainder of this session.

If you're short on time, feel free to skip ahead to the "Getting Ready" section later in this session. You don't need to read the "Where's HTML Going?" section that follows to do the HTML tutorials on Saturday or the software tutorials on Sunday. Therefore, if the midnight chimes are starting to ring, feel free to skip ahead now. You can come back and read the "Where's HTML Going?" section later.

Where's HTML Going?

To understand where HTML is going, you have to have some idea of where it's been. The following is a brief rundown on what has lead up to the current state of affairs, and what is likely to happen in the future.

HTML 1.0 and HTML 2.0

HTML 1.0 and 2.0 were the two earliest versions of HTML. In this book, the Basic HTML Tutorial (Saturday Morning) focuses exclusively on these versions of HTML. HTML, however, is in many ways like the layers of an onion, with the earlier versions still surviving as the inner layers of later versions. Some of the features that date back to these first versions of HTML include inline images, bullet and numbered lists, definition lists (glossaries), and input forms.

Netscape and Microsoft Extensions

Both Netscape and Microsoft developed their own special extensions to HTML for use in their browsers. These can be used in any Web document, but they translate into special formatting only when a user views the Web page in the particular browser for which they were created (unless the other browser's manufacturer provides support for the extensions, too).

Most of the extensions to HTML that Netscape pioneered have been incorporated into either HTML 3.2 or 4.0. The only purely "Microsoft extension" to be included in HTML 4.0 is the FACE attribute for the FONT tag, although Microsoft supported a number of proposed HTML 4.0 elements in its Internet Explorer 3.0 browser prior to the release of HTML 4.0. Some extensions, both old and new, such as Microsoft's MARQUEE tag and Netscape's BLINK tag can only be displayed in one or the other of these browsers, but not both. Unless everybody in your target audience uses the same browser, you should avoid using HTML that will only work in one browser. Preferably, you want your HTML to work in *all* browsers.

Probably the most noteworthy of Netscape's recent innovations is frames (using the FRAMESET and FRAME tags). The use of frames is rapidly proliferating on the Web, compelling other Web browsers to follow suit and incorporate the display of frames in their repertoire. Frames have since been incorporated into HTML 4.0, despite a certain amount of controversy. Although some people hate them, others swear by them. As usual on the Web, what Web publishers use is what matters, and on that score the vote is in: a qualified thumbs up. The primary objections to frames are two fold: a "formal" objection that they violate the spirit of SGML (of which HTML is supposed to be a subset) and a "functional" objection that they make it difficult to link into a subpage within a frameset (meaning that a bookmark, for instance, would return you not to the subpage where you were at, but only to the initial "front" page defined in the frameset).

◄◄◄

A page using frames is defined using the FRAMESET tag, so a collection of Web pages defined by a FRAMESET tag is often referred to as a *frameset*. Every Web page that uses frames starts from an initial frameset, although further framesets may be nested inside of the initial frameset.

◄◄◄

Microsoft has introduced a number of extensions to HTML that have remained unique to its Web browser, Internet Explorer. These include the capability to automatically play background sounds using the BGSOUND tag (you can add background sounds to Navigator, but only by using an entirely different method). Microsoft has introduced scrollable background images (when you scroll down through the text, the background image remains fixed). This same effect, however, can now be done using Cascading Style Sheets. Microsoft's addition of the FACE attribute to the FONT tag, on the other hand, has since been supported in Navigator 4.0 and has been included in HTML 4.0.

HTML 3.0

HTML 3.0 was proposed as the next standard for HTML following HTML 2.0. However, the ambitiousness of HTML 3.0 ultimately proved its downfall—coming to an agreement of how to implement it simply was impossible. Ultimately, the W3C (World Wide Web Consortium) abandoned HTML 3.0 in favor of a much more modest proposal, HTML 3.2.

A number of HTML 3.0 features, however, found support in Web browsers—the most notable of which is tables. Other proposed HTML 3.0 elements that gained the favor of Web browsers to one degree or another include superscripts and subscripts, font size changing (with the BIG and SMALL tags), and underlining. Those parts of the proposed HTML 3.0 standard that have been most widely implemented in current Web browsers have since been incorporated into HTML 3.2. Additionally, even more tags proposed for inclusion in HTML 3.0 have been included in HTML 4.0, including tags for marking insertions and deletions, acronyms, and quotations.

HTML 3.2

In May, 1996, the W3C announced HTML 3.2 as its new specification for HTML. The final recommendation for the HTML 3.2 specification was delivered in January, 1997. HTML 3.0, which was the previous draft proposal for the next HTML standard, was abandoned, largely because the differences between HTML 2.0 and HTML 3.0 were too large to achieve consensus and agreement. HTML 3.2 was a much more modest step up from HTML 2.0 and had been carefully crafted and developed in cooperation with industry leaders, including IBM, Microsoft, Netscape, Sun Microsystems, and others. Here are some of the primary features included in the HTML 3.2 standard:

○ Tables
○ Applets (for Java and JavaScript)
○ Background images
○ Background, text, and link colors
○ Font sizes and colors
○ Flowing of text around images
○ Image borders
○ Height and width attributes for images
○ Alignment (left, center, or right) of paragraphs, headings, and horizontal rules (the CENTER tag)
○ Superscripts and subscripts (the SUP and SUB tags)
○ Strikethroughs (the STRIKE tag)
○ Document divisions (the DIV tag)
○ Client-side image maps (the MAP tag)
○ Provisions for style sheets (the STYLE tag), left otherwise undefined

A large part of the HTML 3.2 specification is a rubber stamping of what originally were Netscape's unofficial and *ad hoc* extensions to HTML. The rest of the HTML 3.2 specification covers features of HTML 3.0 that already gained wide acceptance and implementation (tables, for instance). HTML 3.2 really offered little that hadn't already been widely implemented.

HTML 4.0

As of December, 1997, HTML 4.0 is the officially recommended specification for HTML. Like HTML 3.2, HTML 4.0 is a mix of both the old and the new. Included in it are elements that were previously either Netscape or Microsoft extensions (frames and font face changes), as well as a number of entirely new elements and capabilities. Here are some of the primary features included in HTML 4.0:

○ Frames, including inline frames

- Cascading Style Sheets, level 1 (CSS1)
- New form elements, including the BUTTON element, which allows the creation of graphical form buttons
- New table elements, including the ability to apply formatting to column and row groups
- New text-markup elements, including the INS (insert), DEL (delete), Q (quote), S (strikeout), and SPAN elements
- Microsoft's FACE attribute, which allows you to specify font faces that can be used when displaying text marked by the FONT element
- New universal attributes (ID and CLASS) that can be used to apply styles to individual instances of tag elements, as well as additional "intrinsic event" attribute handles that can trigger the activation of scripts from events such as passing the mouse over an element, clicking an element, and so on

At the time of this writing, full browser support for HTML 4.0 had yet to become a reality. Full agreement on how Cascading Style Sheets should be displayed has yet to be achieved—the same style sheet may have radically different results depending on whether it's displayed in Navigator or Internet Explorer. Also, a number of the new tags in HTML 4.0 have yet to be supported by either major browser. Before using a particular HTML element, you should at least check to see if it's supported yet by current Web browsers. Also, be aware that older Web browsers may not support them at all.

Here are some of the current initiatives afoot to expand and extend HTML:

- The recommendation for Cascading Style Sheets, level 2 (CSS2) was released in May, 1998. CSS2 style sheets allow you to specify fonts on the Web that can be downloaded with a Web page, create rectangular regions containing other elements that can overlap and be positioned anywhere on a Web page, and define multiple style sheets for a single Web page that can be used by different media types (such as speech synthesizers, Braille printers, handheld devices, and so on).
- The Dynamic Object Model (DOM) is the keystone for the full implementation and development of Dynamic HTML, allowing the dynamic addressing of any "objects" in a Web page via scripts or programs. It allows much more interactivity (that is, the dynamic

updating and accessing of Web page content in response to user actions). Right now, Netscape and Microsoft are supporting different versions of the DOM and Dynamic HTML, but they have agreed to standardize on the same DOM in their next generation of browsers.

✿ Mathematical Markup Language (MathML) provides complex formatting capabilities for equations and formulas.

I cover the most relevant new HTML 4.0 features in the Intermediate HTML Tutorial (Saturday Afternoon) and the Tables Tutorial (Saturday Evening). Frames, a new HTML 4.0 feature, although long supported by both major Web browsers, is covered in the Frames Tutorial (Sunday Morning). Also, you'll find a couple Web page templates on the CD-ROM that you can use to easily create a two-frame or a three-frame Web site, as well as some sample Cascading Style Sheets you can easily customize.

XML: The Next HTML?

The W3C has announced that its future development efforts will be concentrated on XML (Extensible Markup Language) rather than HTML. Some may be tempted to see this as the end of HTML, but that's hardly likely. The good news is that HTML proper (HTML 4.0) should remain stable into the future, with few if any new tags being introduced. The capabilities of HTML 4.0, through the development of Cascading Style Sheets (CSS1 and CSS2) and the Dynamic Object Model (DOM), will continue to evolve and change. These developments alone will ensure that the capabilities of HTML will continue to evolve for many years to come. The addition of new tags is unlikely. Also, millions of HTML documents are currently residing on the Web; therefore, any future Web browsers will have to maintain backward compatibility with all versions of HTML.

XML represents an attempt to create what HTML was originally intended to be: a true subset of SGML (Standard Generalized Markup Language). XML is described as a meta-language, a kind of umbrella language, if you will, under which any number of other markup languages may conceivably be fashioned. HTML would be considered one of the markup languages included under the XML umbrella, as would also MathML, the proposed markup language for representing mathematics and equations on the Web. Conceivably, any interested group could create its own markup language, publish an SGML-conforming DTD (Document Type Definition) on the Web, and then have it instantly recognized by any XML-compatible Web browser. This would allow academic groups, for instance, to create their own markup language for displaying academic and scientific papers and articles, including footnotes, citations, bibliographies, figure captions, and so on.

XML will not, itself, determine how a Web document or object will be displayed. XML merely specifies the structural elements of a Web document (similar to the original intention of HTML). How a document will be displayed or formatted will be governed by which style sheet is attached to the document. Currently with HTML, two entirely separate sets of documents often need to be maintained—one for display online and the other for printing out in hard copy form. XML would allow a single set of documents to be used for both purposes—you only need to change the attached style sheet.

Even though XML has been dubbed the next Web standard by the W3C, it's still far from being a done deal. Many obstacles still need to be overcome before the full promise of XML can become a reality. Both Microsoft and Netscape are promising that the next generation of their Web browsers will be fully XML compliant. To what extent users will adopt it, however, is entirely undetermined. XML will probably be popular at first with larger organizations that have extensive document collections or databases that they want to publish on the Web yet still have available in other forms. Also, XML editors will undoubtedly be available that will allow any user to easily create his or her own XML documents. However, whether it will be as easy to hand-code an XML document as it is to hand-code an HTML document is doubtful. One of the real advantages of HTML is that you can create HTML documents using a straight text editor, such as Windows Notepad. The cost of future XML editors is currently unknown, but they probably won't be free or necessarily cheap.

The W3C (World Wide Web Consortium), the organization responsible for HTML and Web development, has committed itself to maintaining the character of HTML as a "language that the ordinary person can use" and its accessibility to individuals who "still find value in writing their own HTML from scratch." Such language is unlikely to be used to describe XML. For that reason, alone, I cannot help but feel that the future of HTML is quite secure. Although XML will undoubtedly be a valuable alternative to HTML for those who need or desire its particular capabilities, it's not likely to be HTML's replacement. In other words, you probably won't be able to learn it in a weekend.

Getting Ready

This section deals with a few issues you need to get out of the way before you start the HTML tutorials tomorrow morning. Included are the following topics:

- Minimum requirements
- Selecting your text editor
- Setting up for offline browsing

Minimum Requirements

The minimum requirements for doing the Basic HTML Tutorial and planning and creating your first Web page are simply that you have either Windows 3.1 or Windows 95/98 and a graphical Web browser already set up or installed. Everything else you'll need is provided on the accompanying CD-ROM (or can be downloaded from this book's Web site).

If you want to do all the examples in this book, you should use the latest version of either Netscape Navigator or Microsoft Internet Explorer as your browser.

ON THE
CD

If you don't yet have a browser, Opera 3.21, an excellent Web browser capable of handling pretty much everything that's covered in this book, has been included on the CD-ROM. Many people prefer it over Navigator or Internet Explorer, due to its smaller size and more sprightly performance. You're free to use it for 30 days before you need to register it.

If you're using an earlier browser, such as Navigator 2.0 or Internet Explorer 3.0, you should be able to do most but not all of the examples in this book.

Selecting Your Text Editor

You don't need anything fancy to create HTML files. Because HTML files are straight ASCII text files, any ordinary text editor will do. My recommendation, at least for the purposes of doing the tutorials in this book and planning and creating your first Web page, is that you stick to using Windows Notepad, which comes with Windows 95/98 and Windows 3.1, as your text editor.

Notepad has a number of advantages that make it the tool of choice for many professional Web publishers:

⚙ You already have it.

⚙ It's a small, efficient program, so it can easily remain in memory with your Web browser without hogging precious system resources. New Web browsers are known to be resource hogs.

⚙ Because Notepad is a text editor rather than a word processor, you can have an HTML file open in both Notepad and your Web browser at the same time. You can't do that with Write, Word, WordPerfect, and most other word processing programs.

Using an HTML Editor

You can also use an HTML editor, if you wish, to do the HTML tutorials and examples in this book. My recommendation, however, is that you don't get bogged down trying to learn the ins and outs of an HTML editing program when you need to focus on learning HTML. Learn HTML first and then investigate what HTML editing programs can do for you.

You also need to gain a code-level familiarity with HTML. Only then can you stick your head under the hood if something doesn't work right. That means typing in your HTML codes the old-fashioned way, and not just inserting them from a drop-down menu or toolbar.

Once you've learned some HTML, by all means feel free to experiment with some of the different HTML editors available. You'll find several HTML editors on the CD-ROM. For the time being, however, stick with Windows Notepad.

If you do decide to use an HTML editor, use one that will allow you to work the same way you would using Notepad. In other words, you should avoid using WSYWYG HTML editors that won't allow you to type in your own HTML from scratch.

ON THE

CD

Aardvark Pro and HTMLed32 are HTML editors available on the CD-ROM that allow you to create your HTML files just like you would with Windows Notepad—typing in the codes from scratch. As an added bonus, you don't have to turn on Word Wrap every time as you have to do with the Windows 3.1 and Windows 95 versions of Notepad (with the Windows 98 version, Word Wrap stays turned on until you turn it off).

Using a Word Processor

I don't recommend you use a word processing program for the tutorials in this book. You can't keep the same file open in both your word processor and your Web browser, which means you won't be able to dynamically debug your HTML files. Take it from me, do yourself a favor and don't bother trying to use a word processor for creating HTML files. Stick to Notepad or one of the Notepad-like HTML editors.

Setting Up for Offline Browsing

As I mentioned previously, you'll want to be able to switch back and forth between your text editor and your Web browser as you work through this book, updating the display of your Web page in your browser as you go. You'll want to do this offline so that you don't run up your Internet bill and hog bandwidth just to edit and preview local HTML files. Even if you have unlimited access to the Internet, hogging an Internet connection just to be able to preview local HTML files is both selfish and wasteful.

Offline Browsing in Windows 95/98

Offline browsing in Windows 95/98, using either Netscape Navigator or Microsoft Internet Explorer, is fairly simple.

Netscape Navigator

The following is the quick-and-dirty way to run either Navigator Gold 3.0+ or Navigator 4.0+ offline:

1. Start Navigator Gold 3.0+ or Navigator 4.0+.
2. If you've set your dialer to automatically connect to the Internet, it

will start to dial your ISP's access phone number. If it does this, click Cancel.

3. At the Connect To dialog box, which prompts you to make a dial-up connection to the Internet, click the Cancel button (to avoid connecting to the Internet).

NOTE If you're dialer has a Connect Automatically check box (not present on the original Windows 95 dialer), you may want to uncheck it if you are planning on editing local HTML files on more than just an occasional basis. Alternatively, you could also specify a local Web page or a blank page as your browser's start page.

4. You'll get an error message that reads "Netscape is unable to locate the server." This is just Navigator trying to tell you it tried to connect to the Internet but couldn't. Click the OK button.

5. Navigator will display a copy of its default home page if it can be loaded from the cache. Otherwise, it will display a blank page.

6. To open and display a local Web page (HTML file) from your hard drive in Navigator Gold 3.0+, choose File, Open File in Browser. In Navigator 4.0+, choose File, Open Page, Choose File.

NOTE You haven't actually created any HTML files yet, but if you want to test out loading a local HTML file into Navigator, you can use Navigator's bookmark file, BOOKMARK.HTM. The location of this file depends on your version of Navigator. To find where it's stored, just click the Start button on the Windows 95/98 Taskbar and then select Find, Files or Folders. Then perform a search for "BOOKMARK.HTM."

Microsoft Internet Explorer

If you're using a version of Internet Explorer earlier than version 3.02, you should download and install the latest version of Internet Explorer from Microsoft's Web site if you want to run it offline.

The following is the quick-and-dirty way to run Internet Explorer 3.02 or greater offline:

1. Start Microsoft Internet Explorer 3.02 or Internet Explorer 4.0 or greater.

2. If you've set your dialer to automatically connect to the Internet, it will start to dial your ISP's access phone number. If it does this, click Cancel.

3. At the Connect To dialog box, which prompts you to make a dial-up connection to the Internet (in version 4.0 or earlier), click the Cancel button. In Version 4.01 or greater, click the Work Offline button.

• •

 NOTE   If you're dialer has a Connect Automatically check box (not present on the original Windows 95 dialer), you may want to uncheck it if you are planning on editing local HTML files on more than just an occasional basis. Alternatively, you could also specify a local Web page or a blank page as your browser's start page.

• •

4. In versions 4.0 and earlier, the message "Internet Explorer cannot open the Internet site **http://home.microsoft.com**" is displayed. Just click the OK button. In version 4.01 or greater, the message "Unable to retrieve Web page in offline mode" is displayed in the browser window.

5. Internet Explorer version 4.0 and earlier will display its default start page if it can be loaded from the cache. If the default start page is not available in the cache, Internet Explorer version 4.0 and earlier will load a local blank HTML file. Version 4.01 simply displays the message quoted in step 3.

6. In all versions, to open and display a local Web page (HTML file) from your hard drive, select File, Open, Browse. Go to a folder where a local HTML file you want to use is stored and then double-click it to open it. Click OK to load the file into Internet Explorer.

• •

 NOTE   Unlike Netscape Navigator, Microsoft Internet Explorer does not conveniently create a bookmark file in HTML format that you can use to test loading a local HTML file. To actually test loading a local HTML file in Internet Explorer, you'll need to wait until you create and save your first HTML file tomorrow morning (that is, unless you've also got Netscape Navigator installed).

• •

Other Options for Offline Browsing in Windows 95/98

You can customize how Internet Explorer or Navigator will run offline in Windows 95/98. Both browsers allow you to set their preferences or options to specify a local or blank home page, which can save you some time when running your browser in offline mode.

Offline Browsing in Windows 3.1

Running your Web browser offline in Windows 3.1 is a good deal more problematic than in Windows 95/98. Go ahead and try the "quick-and-dirty" method described for Windows 95/98. If that doesn't work, your Winsock dialer will not allow you to run entirely offline. Instead, try the following "quasi-offline" method:

1. Log on to the Internet.

2. Run either Netscape Navigator or Microsoft Internet Explorer as you normally would.

3. Log off of the Internet. To do this, hold down the Alt key and then press the Tab key to select your Winsock "dialer" application. Then execute the commands you normally use to log off the Internet. (From now on, I'll refer to this type of action as "pressing Alt+Tab.")

4. Return to your Web browser (by pressing Alt+Tab to select your browser) and load a local HTML file. For Navigator versions earlier than 4.0, select File, Open File. For Navigator version 4.0 and higher, select File, Open Page, Choose File. For all Internet Explorer versions, select File, Open, Browse.

5. Before exiting either Navigator or Internet Explorer, use Alt+Tab to hop out to Program Manager and run your dialer to log on to the Internet again.

CAUTION   When you're using the quasi-offline browsing method, if you exit your Web browser before logging back on to the Internet, your Winsock "dialer" application may hang when you try to log off. If that happens, it's no big deal, but you'll need to rerun Windows before being able to log back on to the Internet.

Other Options for Offline Browsing in Windows 3.1

Microsoft has a version of Internet Explorer 3.02 available that includes a Winsock dialer that allows you to run your browser in offline mode in Windows 3.1. You can also use it to run Netscape Navigator offline.

FIND IT ON ▶
THE WEB

You can download Microsoft Internet Explorer With TCP/IP Stack & Dialer from the Tucows Web site. Go to **http://www.tucows.com/**, select a mirror site near where you're located, and then select Windows 3.x. Under the Connectivity heading, click Networking (TCP/IP).

Another option for running Netscape Navigator offline is to download and set up MOZOCK.DLL (available at the Web site for this book). To use it, you should copy MOZOCK.DLL to the same folder where NETSCAPE.EXE resides. Then rename it to WINSOCK.DLL. To get on the Web, you'll need to run your dialer and then run Netscape Navigator.

There are various ways that you can customize how Internet Explorer or Navigator will run offline in Windows 3.1. Both browsers allow you to set their preferences or options to specify a local or blank home page, which can save some time when running your browser in offline mode.

Running Other Browsers Offline

If you use a browser other than the ones discussed here, you need to check its documentation, help files, or online technical support for the preferred method of running it offline. In most cases, some version of the quick-and-dirty or quasi-offline browsing methods should work for almost any browser.

What's Next?

Having finished the first session, you should now have a good grounding in the basics of the Internet and the World Wide Web, and you should have a good grasp of URLs, hypertext, HTML, and Web pages. You should also have chosen the editor (Windows Notepad is recommended) you want to use to create your HTML files, and you should have some idea of how to run your browser offline.

Tomorrow morning, you'll be doing the Basic HTML Tutorial. Feel free to take all day, if you want, to do this tutorial. If you have the time, I've scheduled the Intermediate HTML Tutorial for tomorrow afternoon and the Tables Tutorial for tomorrow evening. Try to get a good night's sleep. I'll see you first thing in the morning for your first lesson in HTML!

SATURDAY MORNING

The Basic HTML Tutorial

- ✿ Anatomy of an HTML tag
- ✿ Headings, paragraphs, and line breaks
- ✿ Text highlighting (bold, italic, and monospace)
- ✿ Lists, hypertext links, and link lists
- ✿ Inline images and image links

Last night you read up on the Internet, the Web, hypertext, HTML fundamentals, and Web pages. You should now have a pretty good idea about what Web publishing is all about. Additionally, in the "Getting Ready" section, you chose the Web browser and text editor you're going to be using to do the Basic HTML Tutorial this morning and the Intermediate HTML Tutorial this afternoon. I recommend using the latest version of either Netscape Navigator or Microsoft Internet Explorer as your Web browser and Notepad as your text editor.

This morning's tutorial walks you through a top-down approach to learning HTML, organized according to function. Just start from the beginning and continue to the end. By then you'll know enough HTML to create a wide range of different kinds of Web pages.

HTML contains many more tags and attributes for defining document elements than most people could learn in an entire week, let alone in a weekend. But fear not. This book cuts it down to size. This tutorial covers "basic" HTML, which includes the most useful of the HTML 2.0 tags. All current graphical Web browsers fully support HTML 2.0, which until fairly recently was the standard for HTML.

HTML 2.0 is almost entirely included in (with only a very few minor exceptions) and forms the core of the later versions of HTML (HTML 3.2 and 4.0), so you don't need to be concerned that it will ever go out of style or become outmoded. As long as HTML exists, what counts for "basic" HTML will remain largely unchanged.

The optional Intermediate HTML Tutorial that's scheduled for this afternoon covers many of the HTML 3.2 tags, along with a few of the new HTML 4.0 tags.

Everyone has his or her own learning style and speed. Although the Basic HTML Tutorial was designed to be completed in a single morning, you may take more or less time to complete it. The most important thing is to work at your own speed without feeling rushed. If you want to take the whole day to do just this one tutorial, do so. So relax, sit back, and have some fun.

Creating a Working Folder

When you install the example files from the CD-ROM (see next section), a C:\HTML folder will be created to hold these files. You'll be using C:\HTML as the base working folder for all the tutorials in this book.

Installing the Example Files

On the CD-ROM, I've included example graphics and other files for you to use in this tutorial, as well as in all the other tutorials in this book. Just use Prima's CD-ROM interface to install these files to C:\HTML on your hard drive:

NOTE If you don't have a CD-ROM drive, you'll be glad to know that all the example files are available for download from this book's Web site: **http://www.callihan.com/learn2/**. Just create your working folder (C:\HTML), then unzip the files into it. If you don't have a program for unzipping ZIP files, see my Web Tools site at **http://www.callihan.com/webtools/** for a link to where you can download WinZip.

1. Insert the *Learn HTML in a Weekend* CD-ROM in your CD-ROM drive.

2. If you are using Windows 95/98, Prima's CD-ROM interface will automatically run, unless you have disabled Autorun. If the CD-ROM

interface does not automatically run, from the Start menu, select Run, then type **D:\prima.exe** (where D:\ is your CD-ROM's drive letter) and click OK.

3. If you are using Windows 3.1, select File, Run from Program Manager's menu bar, then type **D:\prima.exe** (where D:\ is your CD-ROM's drive letter). Click OK.

4. At the main window of Prima's CD-ROM interface, click Examples.

5. At the Examples window, click Tutorials, then select Install.

6. At the WinZip Self-Extractor window, click Unzip to unzip the example files to C:\HTML.

7. Click on OK when told the files have been unzipped, and then click the Close button.

A Quick Word About HTML

Before you begin to do the tutorial, a quick reminder about the nature of HTML might save you some unnecessary confusion. The philosophy behind HTML is to specify the framework of a page, not its actual appearance or display. Remember: The appearance of a Web page onscreen is determined by the browser used to view it.

Actually, you do have a good deal of control over how most browsers present your page. Today's graphical Web browsers allow you to include inline graphics as well as interlaced and transparent graphics, background images and colors, image maps, forms, tables, various font sizes, animation, streaming audio, and more.

Although most current graphical Web browsers now support most of these enhancements, HTML 2.0 specifies only some of them. Many facilities for more complete control over how your Web page will be displayed have been incorporated into HTML 3.2 and HTML 4.0, the latest versions of HTML. You should remember that many people still use older browsers that do not support the latest HTML developments (including those who are still using text-based browsers such as Lynx).

NOTE A very real concern in HTML is backward compatibility and universal access to one's documents. Old Web pages need to be displayed properly in new Web browsers, just as new Web pages, in most cases, should be coded in such a fashion that they won't break old browsers. Old browsers never go away—they just keep getting used. Every visitor is important, in other words.

Obviously, if you're creating a page, "Internet Explorer 4.0 Tips and Tricks," you only need to be concerned about people using Internet Explorer 4.0. If, however, you're putting up a page, "Genealogy Tips and Tricks," you would obviously not want to exclude someone from viewing your page simply because his or her browser isn't the same as yours. Even if someone were using Lynx, a text-based browser that's more like an HTML 1.0 browser, you would still want him or her to be able to access and read your page. In this afternoon's Intermediate HTML Tutorial, I'll show you how to use many of the new HTML 3.2 and HTML 4.0 features without breaking older browsers. When a feature is liable to have a deleterious effect on earlier browsers, I'll let you know.

The Basic HTML Tutorial sticks to HTML 2.0, which should be compatible with all Web browsers, old and new. In the Intermediate HTML Tutorial, scheduled for this afternoon, I'll show you how to use some stuff from the newer standards—HTML 3.2 and 4.0—to give your Web pages more of a designer look. However, if you don't have time to get to the Intermediate HTML Tutorial today, don't worry. The Basic HTML Tutorial covers everything you need to know to start creating Web pages. You can always come back and do the Intermediate HTML Tutorial and the Table Tutorial later if you don't have time to do them today.

Anatomy of a Tag

The word *tag* or *tag element* refers to the HTML code that defines the elements in an HTML file—the headings, images, paragraphs, lists, and whatnot. The two kinds of tags are *containers*, which bracket or contain text or other tag elements, and *empty tags*, which stand alone. A container tag element actually consists of two tags, a start tag and an end tag, which bracket the text they affect. An empty tag functions as a single standalone element within an HTML document and therefore doesn't bracket or contain anything else.

HTML tags are inserted into a document between lesser than (<) and greater than (>) symbols (also referred to as *left* and *right angle brackets*). For instance, a start tag of a container tag or an empty tag element looks like this:

```
<tagname>
```

You always precede an end tag of a container tag element with a forward slash (/) to distinguish it from a start tag:

```
</tagname>
```

To tag a section of text, you contain it within the start and end tags of a tag element. For instance, text contained in a level-one heading tag would look like this, where <H1> is the start tag and </H1> is the end tag:

```
<H1>This is a Level-One Heading</H1>
```

Whenever I refer to a *level-one heading tag*, I mean both the start and end tags. When I want to specifically refer to a start tag or an end tag, I'll say "the start tag" or "the end tag." Note, however, that a few tags look like empty tags, but actually are container tags that have implied end tags.

Typing tag names in all capital letters is somewhat conventional, although by no means required. This helps distinguish HTML tags from the remainder of the text being tagged. As a rule, this book presents tag names in all caps.

Tag Attributes

Attributes allow you to specify how Web browsers should treat a particular tag. An attribute is included within the actual tag (between the left and right angle brackets), either within a start tag or an empty (standalone) tag. End tags can't contain attributes. Most of the tags covered in this tutorial don't use attributes, but you'll use them to include images or hypertext links in a Web page toward the end of this tutorial.

Most attributes are combined with a value to allow you to specify different options for how a Web browser should treat the attribute. Here's the format for including an attribute value in a tag:

```
ATTRIBUTE="value"
```

For instance, to specify that the middle of an image should be aligned with the line of text it appears on, you would include the following attribute value inside the IMG tag:

```
ALIGN="middle"
```

Tag attributes are, by convention, usually typed in all caps, with any values assigned to them typed in lowercase. You don't have to do it this way, but this convention does make it easier to pick these elements out. Also, in most cases, you can get away with not placing values inside quotation marks. However, enough instances exist in which this won't work that it's a good idea to stick to adding the quotes.

Nesting HTML Tags

You should always *nest* HTML tags and never overlap them. For instance, always do this:

```
<B><I>Always nest tags inside each other.</I></B>
```

Notice that the <I>...</I> pair is nested within the <B>...</B> pair. Never overlap tags so that the outer tag ends before the inner tag:

```
<B><I>Don't overlap tags, like this.</B></I>
```

HTML operates in a hierarchical, top-down manner. A tag element may have other tag elements nested in it or it can be nested within other tag elements. If you overlap two tags, a browser can't tell what should fall inside of what, and it may not be able to display your file at all. Be kind to your browser as well as your potential readers: Don't overlap tag elements.

The Scratch Pad Model

The model that this tutorial employs resembles a "scratch pad" approach. Think of your text editor as a scratch pad. As you do the Basic HTML Tutorial, enter the suggested tags and text as though you were jotting them down on a paper; in other words, you don't have to clean the slate each time you move on to a new section. Just move on down the page, leaving everything

you've already done in place. Doing so also leaves you with a sample file to which you can return and reference later.

Starting Your HTML File

To start your HTML file, follow these steps:

1. Run Windows Notepad.

   In Windows 95, click the Start button and then select Programs, Accessories, Notepad.

   In Windows 3.1, double-click the Notepad program icon in the Accessories window.

2. Save a "scratch pad" file to use in this morning's tutorial. In Notepad, select File, Save As. Save your file to the C:\HTML folder and name it SCRATCH.HTM.

NOTE When you first open Notepad in Windows 3.1 or 95, Word Wrap is not turned on. If you type a line of text without hitting Enter, it will just keep right on going without wrapping. To turn on Word Wrap, just select Edit, Word Wrap (so that it's checked). Unfortunately, you must reset this option every time you use Notepad if you want Word Wrap on.

When you turn Word Wrap on in Notepad in Windows 98, it will stay turned on for future Notepad sessions (that is, until you turn it back off).

Starting Your Page: Document Tags

All HTML files should include at least these tags:

- The HTML tag
- The HEAD tag
- The TITLE tag
- The BODY tag

The following sections discuss each of these tags.

> **TYPOGRAPHY LEGEND**
>
> In the tutorials in this book, words and code that you should type are formatted as `bolded` and `monospaced` text.
>
> Text that shouldn't be typed in by you (that is, text that's shown for the purpose of an example) or text that you've already typed is formatted as `monospaced` text.
>
> *Italicized text* in the input examples does not represent actual typed text. Instead, it indicates what should be typed. *Your Name*, for instance, would indicate that your actual name should be typed.
>
> File and folder names are referenced in all uppercase purely for the sake of readability, except when you're asked to type in a file name (such as when saving your HTML file), in which case the file name will be presented as text to be typed.

The HTML Tag

Recall that a tag defines a structural element within an HTML document. The HTML tag defines the topmost element—the HTML document itself—as an HTML document rather than some other kind of document. The HTML tag is a container tag that has a start and an end. All other text and tags are nested within it. Here's an example:

```
<HTML>
Your HTML document's contents and all other tags . . .
</HTML>
```

In your scratch-pad file in Notepad (or other text editor), type the start and end HTML tags, putting a single hard return between them, like this:

```
<HTML>
</HTML>
```

NOTE Remember that the HTML start tag (<HTML>) must remain at the very top of your file, whereas the HTML end tag (</HTML>) must remain at the very bottom of your file. Everything else must fall between these two tags.

The HEAD Tag

The HEAD tag contains information about your HTML file. It also may contain other tags that help to identify your HTML file to the outside world. The HEAD tag is nested within the HTML tag. Type the HEAD tag inside the HTML tag now, like this:

```
<HTML>
<HEAD>
</HEAD>
</HTML>
```

Usually, the only tag contained within the HEAD tag is the TITLE tag. Other tags can also be contained within the HEAD tag, but of these, only the META, BASE, LINK, and SCRIPT tags are very useful. I cover the TITLE tag in this tutorial, and show you a couple examples of using the SCRIPT tag in both the Intermediate HTML and Tables Tutorials. For information on how to use the META, BASE, and LINK tags, as well as other elements that can be nested in the HEAD tag, see Appendix A, "Quick HTML Reference."

The TITLE Tag

The TITLE tag is nested inside of the HEAD tag. It identifies your page to the rest of the world. For instance, a search engine such as Yahoo! or WebCrawler might display the text included in your TITLE tag as a link to your page. The tag also displays on your browser's title bar, but it doesn't appear as part of the page. Make the title descriptive, but keep it under 50 characters, if possible. Try to use a short title followed by a brief description. Someone else should be able to tell what your page is about simply by looking at the title. Think of it as your welcome mat. Now, type the TITLE tag inside the HEAD tag:

```
<HTML>
<HEAD>
<TITLE>Your Title: Describe Your Title</TITLE>
</HEAD>
</HTML>
```

NOTE Feel free to substitute a title here of your own choosing. This is just for practice, however, so don't spend all day trying to think up a good one.

Officially, the TITLE tag is a required element that you should include in each HTML document. In practice, however, most Web browsers let you get away with not including a TITLE tag. Still, you should include a TITLE tag in your HTML document. If you don't include a title, the title of your page appears in some browsers as "Untitled." In others, the URL for the page appears on the browser's title bar. Also, if your page doesn't have a title, anybody who book-marks your page in Navigator, for instance, will end up with a blank bookmark entry in their bookmark list. If you want the page to show up without a title, nothing stops you from including a TITLE tag and leaving it blank. However, that defeats the whole purpose of including the tag in the first place.

The BODY Tag

The BODY tag is the complement of the HEAD tag; it contains all the tags, or elements, that a browser actually displays as the body of your HTML document. Both the HEAD tag and the BODY tag are nested inside the HTML tag. Note, however, that the BODY tag comes after the HEAD tag; they denote separate parts of the HTML document.

NOTE The HEAD and BODY tags are the only tags that are nested directly inside the HTML tag. Other than the TITLE tag, which you inserted within the HEAD tag for this example, you should nest all text and tags you enter in this tutorial inside the BODY tag. Be sure to keep both </BODY> and </HTML> end tags at the bottom of your HTML file.

Type the BODY tag after the HEAD tag but inside the HTML tag, like this:

```
<HTML>
<HEAD>
<TITLE>Your Title: Describe Your Title</TITLE>
</HEAD>
<BODY>
</BODY>
</HTML>
```

You've officially started your HTML file. All HTML files begin the same way—only the titles are different. What you've typed so far should look like this:

```
<HTML>
<HEAD>
<TITLE>Your Title: Describe Your Title</TITLE>
</HEAD>
<BODY>
</BODY>
</HTML>
```

Saving a Starting Template

If you want, you can save what you've done so far as a starting template for starting HTML files in the future. Save it as C:\HTML\START.HTM, for instance. After you save the file as START.HTM, save it again as C:\HTML\SCRATCH.HTM (or whatever working title you want to give it) so you won't accidentally save over your starting template later.

NOTE I'm sure you've noticed on the Web that Web pages can have either an .HTM or an .HTML extension. The .HTML extension is the conventional extension for HTML files on a Unix Web server. The .HTM extension is also allowed on almost all Unix Web servers. Windows 3.1 only recognizes a three-letter file extension. Because this book is written with both Windows 3.1 and Windows 95/98 users in mind, I've stuck to using .HTM as the extension for any HTML files created in this book.

If you were now to hop over to your browser and load this file, it would display nothing but the title in the title bar, as shown in Figure 2.1.

NOTE In Netscape Navigator, the Reload button loads the updated version of your HTML file, and *reload* is the term used in this book to describe the reload operation. Internet Explorer, however, uses the Refresh button. In both Navigator and Internet Explorer, you can also press Ctrl+R to do the same thing.

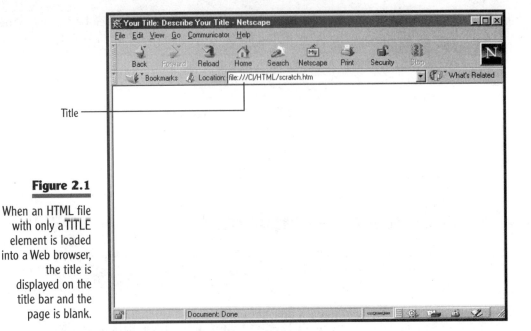

Title

Figure 2.1

When an HTML file
with only a TITLE
element is loaded
into a Web browser,
the title is
displayed on the
title bar and the
page is blank.

DYNAMICALLY UPDATING YOUR WORK

As you work through the Basic HTML Tutorial this morning, you'll
want to *dynamically* update items as you go, switching back and forth
between your text editor and your Web browser to see your results.

Only by being able to make on-the-fly changes to your HTML file can
you tell exactly how your page is going to look in a browser while
you're still in the process of creating it. Doing this is the key to success for rapidly learning HTML, as well as for quickly creating your
own Web pages.

If you're using a word processor such as Word, WordPad, or Windows
Write, you won't be able to hop back and forth between it and your
browser to dynamically update your work as you go, because you
can't keep the same file open in both your word processor and your
Web browser. That's why I recommend sticking with a text editor

such as Windows Notepad, because you can have the same file open at the same time in both your text editor and your Web browser.

To dynamically update changes to your HTML files, you must switch back and forth between your text editor and your Web browser. (See the "Windows Navigation Tips" sidebar if you don't know how to switch between applications in Windows.) To make this hop, follow these steps:

1. Run Notepad (or whatever text editor you're using). Load an HTML file and edit it. Save those changes but don't exit or clear the window.

2. In Windows 3.1, switch to the Program Manager. In Windows 95, minimize the current window to reveal the desktop.

3. Run your browser, preferably in offline mode, and open the HTML file you just edited in Notepad (in Navigator 4.0+ use File, Open Page, Choose File; in Internet Explorer 4.0+ use File, Open, Browse). It will be displayed in your browser, showing the changes you just made. Now switch back to your text editor.

4. In your text editor, make more changes to your HTML file and save those changes. Now switch back to your browser.

5. Click the Reload or Refresh button to display your HTML file again. This will show the changes you just made.

Using Heading Level Tags

You use headings to organize your Web page into hierarchical levels. The top-level heading (denoted by the H1 tag) is the title that will be displayed at the top of your Web page. (Don't confuse this with the title that appears in the browser's title bar, which you just set up using the TITLE tag.) Because the H1 tag functions as the title for a Web page, each Web page should have only one H1 tag. (This is the conventional use for this tag. Otherwise, nothing positively forbids including multiple H1 tags in a Web page.)

WINDOWS NAVIGATION TIPS

In this book, the words *switch* or *hop* refer to switching between open applications.

You can switch among the open applications in several ways—the best way mainly boils down to your individual preference. You can choose the method that works best for you:

- ✪ Alt+Tab. **Hold down the Alt key while tapping the Tab key to cycle through all currently open applications. This works in both Windows 3.1 and Windows 95/98. When you see the application you want, release the Tab key to bring that application to the foreground.**

- ✪ Alt+Esc. **This is similar to Alt+Tab. It toggles among the open windows, one by one. Hold down the Alt key and tap the Esc key until the window you want comes to the foreground.**

- ✪ Ctrl+Esc. **In Windows 3.1, doing this brings up the Task List window, which allows you to select from a list of currently open applications. In Windows 95/98, Ctrl+Esc displays the taskbar at the bottom of the screen—the one that shows buttons for all your open applications—and opens the Start menu.**

- ✪ Control Menu. **In Windows 3.1, you can select Switch To from the Control menu of any windowed application currently in the foreground. Just click the button in the upper-left corner of the window and select Switch To. This is actually the same as simply pressing Ctrl+Esc, so it can only be recommended to the dedicated keyboard-a-phobe. In Windows 95/98, the Switch To option is no longer included in the Control menu, so this feature is only relevant to Windows 3.1.**

As you work through the HTML tutorials today, the figures show you what each tag looks like in a browser. These figures might not exactly match what you see in the particular browser you're using; therefore, you should use them as cues to hop over to your browser to have a look. Also, you can only debug your HTML file for errors by hopping over to your browser and previewing the HTML file you are actually creating.

You use a second-level heading (denoted by the H2 tag) to define a major division in your page, and you use a third-level heading (using the H3 tag) to define a sublevel division within a major division. Most browsers support up to six different heading levels. Within the BODY element you typed earlier, type six heading level tags, like this:

```
<BODY>
<H1>This is a top-level heading</H1>
<H2>This is a second-level heading</H2>
<H3>This is a third-level heading</H3>
<H4>This is a fourth-level heading</H4>
<H5>This is a fifth-level heading</H5>
<H6>This is a sixth-level heading</H6>
</BODY>
```

As a practical matter, you'll probably seldom use more than four heading levels. When displayed in a browser, different level headings appear as different size fonts, from large to small (although each browser decides which fonts to use). Figure 2.2 shows how a Web browser displays different heading levels.

Just because a tag displays similarly or identically in Navigator and Internet Explorer doesn't mean this will be the case in other Web browsers, such as NCSA Mosaic, Sun HotJava, and so on. NCSA Mosaic 2.0, for instance, displays H1 through H6 in a normal, nonboldfaced font while using different

Figure 2.2

Web browsers display heading levels in different font sizes.

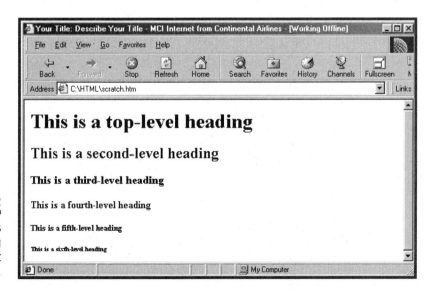

size fonts than Navigator and Internet Explorer. The only way to be sure how a particular tag is going to make text look in a particular browser is to check it out in that browser.

NOTE   Don't forget to periodically save your HTML file in Notepad and then hop over to your browser to see the results of your work. You only need to load your HTML file the first time you hop over to your browser—after that, just press Ctrl+R to reload the page. If you're in doubt about how to do this, see the sidebars, "Dynamically Updating Your Work" and "Windows Navigation Tips."

Creating Paragraphs and Line Breaks

The P (Paragraph) and BR (Line Break) tags let you insert paragraphs and lines of text on your page.

The P (Paragraph) Tag

You can't just type text into an HTML document. Always tag any plain text (text not included in some other element, such as a heading, list, block quote, and so on) that you want to include with the P tag. You shouldn't have any untagged text in an HTML document.

The P tag is a container element that has an implied ending. You don't have to include the </P> end tag. The end of the tag is implied by any following start tag that defines a new block element (a heading, a list, another paragraph, and so on). Therefore, when you use the P tag, just insert the <P> start tag at the beginning of a paragraph but leave off the </P> end tag at the end. Any paragraph that you tag with the P tag should show up in a browser with at least one blank line after it.

Enter the following paragraph using just the P start tag (<P>):

```
<P>This is paragraph text. This is paragraph text. This is paragraph
text. This is paragraph text. This is paragraph text. This is para-
graph text.
```

The problem is that even though this is spelled out in specifications for HTML 2.0, some browsers still won't interpret a paragraph properly in every case without the </P> at the end. A list following a paragraph, for instance, should be separated by extra space. An earlier version of Internet Explorer (version 2.0), however, doesn't insert the extra space unless you include the </P> end tag at the end of a paragraph preceding a list. Other earlier browser versions may also have the same problem, but current Web browsers should be able to handle this properly.

Part of the confusion surrounding how to use this tag element properly goes back to HTML 1.0, where the P tag was defined as a standalone element functioning as a separator. HTML 2.0, however, specifically defined this element as a container, but with an implied ending. HTML 3.2 and 4.0 reconfirm the HTML 2.0 definition.

If that isn't confusing enough, the new XML (Extensible Markup Language) standard requires the </P> end tag be added at the end of every paragraph.

So, what should you do? Put them in or leave them out? The safest course is to always add a </P> end tag at the end of a paragraph. On the other hand, the point of leaving off the </P> end tag is simply that it's a timesaver.

In general, you should feel free to leave off the </P> end tag. Browsers that don't handle this right clearly deserve to be spanked. I'll try to keep you clued in as to the rare cases where you might run into problems. If you want to be conservative, however, feel free to include the </P> end tag at the end of your paragraphs.

Figure 2.3 shows how a Web browser ought to display a paragraph without the end tag when the next element is a list.

TIP A Web browser automatically wraps text in an HTML file to fit inside its window. Therefore, you don't have to insert returns at the ends of your lines to get them to fit inside a browser window. This wouldn't work anyway, because Web browsers completely ignore hard returns. Let Notepad wrap your text (make sure Word Wrap is turned on). This is purely for your convenience while working in Notepad. It has no effect on where the text will break in your Web browser.

Figure 2.3

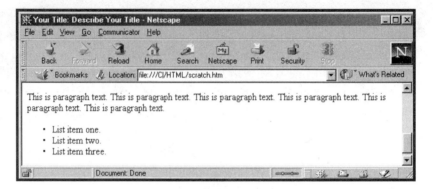

Figure 2.3

A browser should insert extra space between a paragraph and a following block element, such as a list, even if the </P> end tag is left off.

Nesting Paragraphs

Generally, your paragraphs are nested in the BODY tag. You also can nest paragraphs in block quotes (BLOCKQUOTE), glossary definitions (DD), list items (LI), and address blocks (ADDRESS). A paragraph can contain plain text, highlighting (B, I, EM, STRONG, and so on), special characters (such as accented letters or the copyright symbol), line breaks (BR), hypertext links (A), and inline images (IMG). You'll learn about these codes later in this session.

Avoid Using Multiple P Tags to Add Blank Lines

Generally, a P tag that contains no text has no effect. None of the major browsers let you add blank lines by simply adding P tags, although some browsers might. To illustrate this point, type three <P> tags following the text paragraph you just typed (leave off the </P> end tags), followed by another paragraph of text:

```
<P>This is paragraph text. This is paragraph text. This is paragraph
➥text. This is paragraph text. This is paragraph text. This is
➥paragraph text.
<P>
<P>
<P>
<P>This is paragraph text.
```

Go ahead and hop over to your Web browser to see what this looks like. Multiple P tags, with or without their end tags, should have no effect. Most

Figure 2.4

The multiple P tags
inserted between
two paragraphs
should be
completely ignored
by a Web browser.

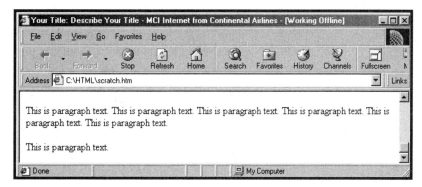

browsers completely ignore them, as shown in Figure 2.4. Even if a browser
does display them, you wouldn't want to write exclusively for it anyway.

The BR (Line Break) Tag

The BR (Line Break) tag is an empty, or *standalone*, tag that simply inserts a
line break. Type three text lines separated by BR tags:

```
<P>These lines are separated by BR (Line Break) tags.<BR>
These lines are separated by BR (Line Break) tags.<BR>
These lines are separated by BR (Line Break) tags.
```

As Figure 2.5 shows, only a single line break separates these lines when a
browser displays them. (Paragraphs, you may remember, are separated by a
line break and an extra blank line.)

Figure 2.5

Use the BR tag to
insert a line break
at the end of a line.

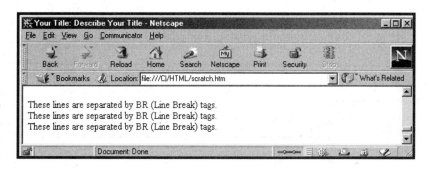

You can use the BR tag almost anywhere you have text, not just inside P tags. For example, you can put them inside an H1 or H2 tag to force a heading to show up on two lines.

Using Multiple BR Tags to Add Blank Lines

You might think you could use multiple BR tags to add blank lines to your page. To see what happens when you try this, type a line of text followed by four BR tags:

```
<P>Four BR (Line Break) tags follow this line.<BR>
<BR>
<BR>
<BR>
Four BR (Line Break) tags precede this line.
```

You're not supposed to get away with such a maneuver (according to the official HTML specs, that is). Netscape Navigator, however, has always let you get away with it, and the latest versions of Internet Explorer also let you get away with it, as shown in Figure 2.6.

Both Navigator and Internet Explorer treat multiple BR tags in a *nonstandard* fashion. To quote from the draft specification for HTML 4.0, "a sequence of contiguous white space characters, such as spaces, horizontal tabs, form feeds, and line breaks, should be replaced by a single word space."

Figure 2.6

Both Navigator and Internet Explorer will display multiple BR tags, but in contravention of the standards for HTML.

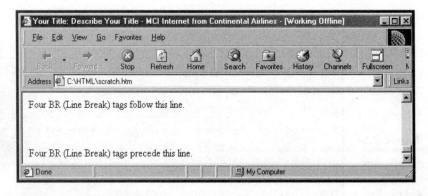

So, should you or shouldn't you use BR tags for blank lines? Even though Netscape Navigator, Internet Explorer (versions 3.0 and 4.0), and any number of other Web browsers let you use multiple BR tags, it still doesn't constitute standard HTML. Your best bet is to avoid nonstandard HTML, even if your favorite Web browser allows you to get away with using it (and even if that Web browser happens to be Navigator). Besides, you can get the same result in a perfectly legal way.

TIP

■ ■

This trick for inserting blank lines into a Web page works for all browsers (even text-based browsers such as Lynx). To insert blank lines into your HTML file, enclose regular hard returns inside the PRE (Preformatted Text) tags:

```
<P>Inserting a PRE tag containing hard returns will add extra space
➥between paragraphs.
<PRE>


</PRE>
<P>This line should be three lines down.
```

For more information on the PRE tag, see the section "Using Preformatted Text," later in this chapter.

■ ■

Spacing, Tabs, and Returns: For Your Eyes Only

In HTML, the tags themselves do all your page's formatting. A browser ignores more than one space inserted into text (two, five, or ten spaces all appear as if they are a single space), as well as all tabs and hard returns (unless they're inside a PRE tag). Any formatting of your HTML file using extra spaces or tabs and returns is "for your eyes only." Feel free to use all the extra spaces, tabs, and returns you want to make your raw HTML files more readable as you work on them.

TIP   ██

Other than inserting a totally transparent image, the only way to insert multiple horizontal spaces in your HTML file is to use nonbreakable space characters. You insert these into an HTML file as either   or . To simulate a paragraph tab, for example, you would insert   three times at the start of a paragraph:

This will work in virtually all Web browsers, although a couple X-Windows Web browsers won't display nonbreakable spaces at all (instead displaying them as zero-width characters). Still, if you want horizontal space in a line of text, other than using tables, this is the only way to do it.

██

Adding Comments

You can also add comments to annotate your HTML files. The *comment tag* is a standalone tag that enables you to include a messages that will not be displayed in a Web browser while your HTML file is being read. Comments are useful for future reference. What's a little confusing about this tag, however, is that no "name" is included in the tag. Instead, a comment always begins with

```
<!--
```

and ends with

```
-->
```

Any text inserted between these tags is comment text, which a browser completely ignores. Here's an example of the form in which you would enter a comment into an HTML file:

```
<!--Put your comment here-->
```

Now, go ahead and type a comment between two lines of text, like this:

```
<P>This line is followed by a comment.
<!--Comments are not displayed by a browser.-->
<P>This line follows a comment.
```

These two paragraph lines appear in a Web browser without any additional vertical space between them. The browser ignores any text inside the comment tag.

Highlighting Your Text

Just as in a normal book or report, an HTML document can use highlighting to clarify the text's meaning. For instance, you can easily make text in an HTML file boldfaced or italicized.

Using Italic and Bold Highlighting

HTML has two ways to include italic or bold text on your Web page. The first way involves using "literal" tags: the I (Italic) and B (Bold) tags. The second way is to use "logical" tags: the EM (Emphasis) and STRONG (Strong Emphasis) tags. Most browsers should display the I (Italic) and EM (Emphasis) tags identically, just as they should display the B (Bold) and STRONG (Strong Emphasis) tags identically.

So what's the difference? The basic philosophy behind HTML is to logically represent the elements of a page rather than literally describe them. The browser can freely interpret the logical elements of an HTML page and display them as it sees fit. Therefore, the philosophically correct method is to always use logical tags and to avoid using literal tags. On the other hand, however, the B and I tags are quicker. So if you want to be more true to the basic spirit of HTML, use the EM (Emphasis) tag rather than the I (Italic) tag and the STRONG (Strong Emphasis) tag rather than the B (Bold) tag. Or you can also do it the other way around, because you get the same result (and save some keystrokes).

As an example of using the I, B, EM, and STRONG tags for text highlighting, type the following lines of text:

```
<P><I>This is italic text.</I>
<P><B>This is bold text.</B>
<P><B><I>This is bold italic text.</I></B>
<P><EM>This is emphasized text.</EM>
<P><STRONG>This is strongly emphasized text</STRONG>.
```

Figure 2.7 shows how these tags appear in Netscape Navigator.

The previous example nests the I tag inside the B tag to get text that is bold and italic. You could also do it the other way around, nesting the B tag inside the I tag. (You just don't want to overlap them.) Although not shown in the previous example, you could also nest the EM tag inside of the STRONG

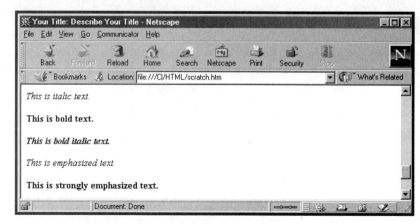

Figure 2.7

You can use literal
tags (I and B) or
logical tags (EM
and STRONG)
to italicize or
bold text.

tag, or vice versa, to get the same result. (You can also nest the STRONG tag inside of the I tag here.)

You can use two other tags, CITE (Citation) and VAR (Variable), to highlight text—but because Web browsers interpret them exactly like the I (Italic) and EM (Emphasis) tags, there's not much reason to bother using them.

Embedding Monospace Text

You may want to embed monospace text within a paragraph to request keyboard input or represent screen output. A *monospace font,* also called a *fixed-pitch font,* is a font in which all the characters occupy the same amount of space on a line (in a *proportional font,* on the other hand, each character occupies a unique amount of space on a line). For example, the following line uses a monospace font:

```
This line uses a monospace font.
```

The most widely used tag for embedding monospace text is the TT (Teletype) tag. It appears as a monospace font in all Web browsers. You can think of it as a general-purpose monospace text tag that you can use whenever you want to embed monospace text within a paragraph. Two other tags, the CODE and SAMP tags, produce the same results as the TT tag.

The TT tag is sometimes also called the "Typewriter" or "Typewriter Text" tag, probably because most people under the age of 35 or so don't have the

foggiest notion what a "teletype" is. (*Hint:* Bill Gates and Paul Allen first learned how to program on a teletype at Lakeside High School in Seattle, way back when.)

The only other possibly useful monospace tag is the KBD (Keyboard) tag. Unfortunately, how a Web browser displays this tag is rather unpredictable. Navigator displays it the same as the TT tag. Earlier versions of Internet Explorer display it in a boldface monospace font, although the latest versions of Internet Explorer follow Navigator's example. NCSA Mosaic, following the beat of a different drummer, displays this tag as an italicized proportional font.

Type the following text as an example of using the TT and KBD tags:

```
<P>This is regular text. <TT>This is an example of the TT (Teletype
or Typewriter Text) tag.</TT> This is regular text. <KBD>This is an
example of the KBD (Keyboard) tag.</KBD>
```

The KBD tag might be useful because it would allow you to distinguish between screen output (the TT tag) and keyboard input (the KBD tag). Because both Navigator and Internet Explorer treat these tags identically, as shown in Figure 2.8, you should probably just stick to using the TT tag and ignore the KBD tag.

TIP By using styles, you can apply different display characteristics to the TT and KBD tags, allowing you to distinguish between output and input, for instance. See the Intermediate HTML and Tables Tutorials, scheduled for this afternoon and evening, for some examples of using styles.

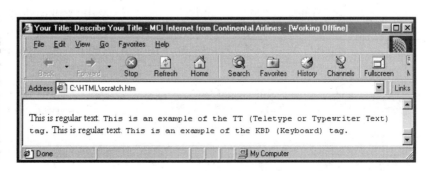

Figure 2.8

The tendency among current Web browsers is to display text marked with the TT and KBD tags identically

To insert monospace text as a separate text block rather than embedding it inside a paragraph, see "The PRE (Preformatted Text) Tag" section, later in this session.

Inserting Reserved and Special Characters

You may need to enter a special code for a character into your HTML file under two different circumstances: If you want to insert a reserved character that's used to parse (interpret and display) an HTML file, and if you want to enter a special or extended character that isn't part of the regular keyboard character set.

You insert both of these characters into an HTML file in the form of a numerical entity code or a named entity code. Numerical entity codes are inserted in the following form, where *number* is a three-digit decimal number between 000 and 255:

`&#number;`

Named entity codes are inserted in the following form, where *name* is the name of a character as listed in the HTML specs:

`&name;`

Reserved Characters

HTML uses the <, >, &, and " characters to parse or interpret an HTML document for display. Except for angle brackets, you rarely need to automatically replace these characters with their entity codes:

- ✪ Angle brackets (< and >) should always be replaced by their corresponding entity codes if you want them to display properly in an HTML file. Use them only to signal the beginning or the end of an HTML tag.

- ✪ Double quotes (") only need to be replaced if they're part of an HTML tag that you want to appear "as is" rather than as interpreted by a browser.

❂ An ampersand (&) signals the beginning of an entity code. It only needs to be replaced if it's part of an HTML entity code that you want to appear "as is" rather than as interpreted by a browser. You never need to replace standalone ampersands.

CAUTION

◆ ◆

If you use a word processor to create HTML files, be sure to turn off the "smart quotes" feature. When creating HTML files, you always want to use regular "keyboard" quotes. In other words, each quotation mark should be straight up and down, not curled to the left or right.

◆ ◆

You can use character entities exclusively to insert any of these characters into an HTML file when you want an HTML tag to appear on your Web page "as is" rather than as interpreted by the browser. To have a browser show "<EM>" onscreen instead of interpreting it as a formatting code, you would enter it like this:

`&lt;EM&gt;`

All Web browsers recognize the named entity codes for these characters, so you don't have to use the numerical entity codes here. For an easy reference, Table 2.1 shows the named entity codes for inserting HTML reserved characters.

TABLE 2.1 HTML RESERVED CHARACTER ENTITY CODES		
Character	**Entity**	**Code**
Less than	<	`&lt;`
Greater than	>	`&gt;`
Ampersand	&	`&amp;`
Double quote	"	`&quot;`

Special Characters

Suppose you want to post a page devoted to an article you've written, and you want to protect it by showing your copyright. Because the copyright symbol (©) isn't available on the keyboard, you can't just type it into your HTML document as you would a normal keyboard character. Instead, you must use a special code that tells the browser to insert the character where you want it.

In HTML, you can enter such characters in two ways: as numerical entity codes or as named entity codes. You can insert the copyright symbol, for example, by using its numerical entity code (©) or its named entity code (©).

HTML uses the ISO 8859-1 character set, which is an 8-bit character set that provides 256 positions (000 to 255). Of these, however, 000 through 032 and 127 correspond to control characters, and 128 through 159 are designated as not displayable. Therefore, only the last 95 codes (160 through 255) represent all the special characters that, according to the ISO 8859-1 standard, should be legally used on a Web page. These include many special symbols (cent, copyright, degree, and so on), plus many accented characters (such as a capital A with an acute accent) that are commonly used in many foreign languages.

 NOTE

• •

One possible exception exists to the general rule that codes outside of 160 through 255 should not be used: the trademark symbol. The numerical code (™) will display the trademark symbol on Windows, Macintosh, and Unix computers, which is pretty darn close to universal support—but that's only because the native character sets of all these platforms include it. You can't rely on its availability on every single computer platform. Therefore, whether you should use it or not is really a toss-up. You should, however, avoid using the named entity code (™), because, even though Internet Explorer, NCSA Mosaic, and many other Web browsers will recognize it, Navigator won't. One workaround is to insert (TM) inside SMALL and SUP (Superscript) tags (see "HTML 3.2 Text Highlighting Tags" in the Intermediate HTML Tutorial for how to use these tags).

• •

Numerical character entities use the actual decimal numeration of the character in the ISO-8859-1 character set. For instance, you could insert a copyright symbol into a Web page by using its numerical character entity, like this:

©

Named entity codes have been designated to correspond to many of these special characters. To insert a copyright symbol using its named character entity, you would type this:

©

Whether a Web browser will display a named character entity is another matter. Other than the uppercase and lowercase accented characters (A-grave, a-acute, and so on) that many foreign languages require, only the copyright and registration symbols have anything close to universal support. Certain Web browsers can interpret and display almost all these named entities, but other than those just mentioned, Netscape Navigator won't. Feel free to use the named entity codes for the copyright and registration symbols as well as for any of the accented characters; otherwise, stick to the numerical character entities.

◆ ◆

Although the ISO-8859-1 character set is used to designate special characters to insert in a Web page, it's not the universal native character set for all computer operating systems. That is, it's the native character set for both Unix and Windows, but not for the Macintosh or DOS. On a Macintosh, certain characters in the ISO-8859-1 character set aren't available, so if you try to display one of these characters in a Web page on a Macintosh, you'll see a different character than the one that you intended. The solution is to avoid using these characters on a Web page. Table 2.2 shows these characters as well as what you want to appear onscreen versus what the Macintosh substitutes.

◆ ◆

TABLE 2.2 CHARACTERS THAT WON'T DISPLAY ON A MACINTOSH

Numerical Entity	Named Entity	Character	Macintosh Displays
&#166;	&brvbar;	¦ (Broken Bar)	|
&#178;	&sup2;	² (Superscript 2)	2
&#179;	&sup3;	³ (Superscript 3)	3
&#185;	&sup1;	¹ (Superscript 1)	1
&#188;	&frac14;	¼ (One Quarter)	π
&#189;	&frac12;	½ (One Half)	Π
&#190;	&frac34;	¾ (Three Quarters)	≤
&#215;	&times;	× (Multiply)	x
&#221;	&Yacute;	Ý (Y-acute)	Y
&#253;	&yacute;	ý (y-acute)	y

Of these, you might possibly use only the broken bar (¦) and the multiplication sign (×), because Macintosh substitutes a straight vertical bar (|) for the broken bar and a lowercase x for the multiplication sign. For the others, you can see that Macintosh uses entirely different characters.

Table 2.3 shows some of the most commonly used special characters, their numerical and named entity codes, and support by browsers (universal support for named entities cannot be guaranteed).

Table 2.3 is just a partial list of special characters you can insert into an HTML file. For a full listing of all the special characters you can use, see Appendix B, "Special Characters."

TABLE 2.3 SPECIAL CHARACTERS

Character	Number	Name	Name Support
™	™	™	Not Navigator (all versions)
¢	¢	¢	Only latest 4.0+ browsers*
©	©	©	All browsers
®	®	®	All browsers
×	×	×	Only latest 4.0+ browsers*
÷	÷	÷	Only latest 4.0+ browsers*

CAUTION Named entity codes such as **©** and ® are case sensitive. You should type them exactly as they are listed. **À** and **à**, for instance, stand for two separate accented characters: an uppercase *A* with a grave accent and a lowercase *a* with a grave accent, respectively.

Go ahead and enter the following example of using the numerical entity code for the copyright symbol and the named entity code for the registered symbol:

```
<H2>&#169; Copyright 1998.</H2>
<H2>Crumbies&reg;</H2>
```

See Figure 2.9 for how these display in a Web browser.

Using Block Quotes

The BLOCKQUOTE (Block Quote) tag double-indents a block of text from both margins. You generally use it to display quotations, as the name

Figure 2.9

You can insert
special characters
such as the
copyright and
registered symbols
using numerical
and named
entity codes.

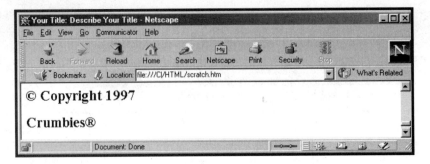

of the tag implies. You can use it to double-indent any block of text—you aren't limited to using it on just quotations. According to the specification for the tag, you aren't supposed to put raw text inside a block quote—you're only supposed to put other text elements, such as paragraphs (P tag elements), inside a block quote and then put the text in those other elements. No harm is done, however, in any browser I know of, if you put untagged text inside a block quote.

Type a paragraph of text, followed by a paragraph of text inside a BLOCK-QUOTE tag:

```
<P>In <EM>Notes From Underground</EM> Dostoevsky plumbs the
➥depths of human psychology, revealing the complexity and
➥contradictions underlying even the most normal and decent of
➥human beings:
<BLOCKQUOTE>
<P>Every man has some reminiscences which he would not tell to
➥everyone, but only to his friends. He has others which he
➥would not reveal even to his friends, but only to himself, and
➥that in secret. But finally there are still others which a man
➥is even afraid to tell himself, and every decent man has a
➥considerable number of such things in his mind.
</BLOCKQUOTE>
```

The BLOCKQUOTE tag displays text indented from both margins in a regular proportional font. (See Figure 2.10.)

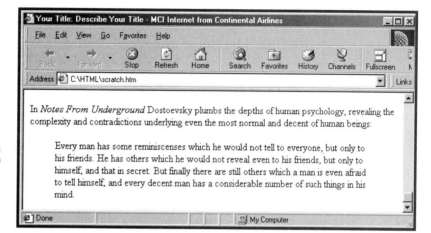

Figure 2.10

The BLOCKQUOTE
tag is used to
double-indent text
from the margins.

It has become fairly common to see the BLOCKQUOTE tag used in HTML pages as a formatting device, causing a block of text to be double-indented from the margins (even if it isn't a "block quote" per se). You can even increase the amount of the indent by nesting BLOCKQUOTE tags inside each other. With all the current browsers I know of, this is not a problem. You should be aware, however, that some earlier browsers, such as Internet Explorer 2.0 and NCSA Mosaic 2.0, treat this tag a bit differently. Internet Explorer 2.0 displays it in a bold italic font. NCSA Mosaic 2.0 displays it in a bold font. Because of how earlier browsers might display this tag, you may want to consider sticking to using it just for displaying block quotes, as it was originally intended to do, rather than as a formatting device for other blocks of text. If you want to double-indent text, you should consider using a table (see "Saturday Evening: The Tables Tutorial").

TIP

Nesting the P tags inside a BLOCKQUOTE tag enables you to include multiple paragraphs within a block quote. Besides paragraphs, you can also nest headings, lists, definition list tags, preformatted text, inline images, and even other block quotes inside a block quote. Everything will be double-indented until it reaches the </BLOCKQUOTE> end tag. (I cover using lists, definition lists, preformatted text, and inline images later in this tutorial.)

Using BR (Line Break) Tags in a Block Quote

You can use BR (Line Break) tags in a block quote to display stanzas of poetry, the verses of a song, or other indented text for which you don't want the lines to wrap. Type a paragraph of text, followed by a paragraph of text using BR tags inserted inside a BLOCKQUOTE tag.

```
<P>In <EM>Porgy and Bess</EM>, in the song "Summertime," George
➥Gershwin evokes the hazy, lazy days of a Southern summer:
<BLOCKQUOTE>
<P>Summertime and the living is easy,<BR>
Fish are jumping and the cotton is high.<BR>
Oh your Daddy's rich and your Ma is good looking,<BR>
So hush little baby, don't you cry.
</BLOCKQUOTE>
```

Figure 2.11 shows how a block quote using BR tags appears in a Web browser.

NOTE HTML 4.0 specifies a new attribute, CITE, that can be included in the BLOCKQUOTE tag. You would use it to specify the URL where the source for a quote can be found (`CITE="http://www.dummy.com/source.html"`, for instance). So far, however, I'm not aware of any browsers that support it. That shouldn't stop you, of course, from using it just to keep track of your online sources for quotes. Eventually, supporting browsers should display the source when the mouse is passed over the block quote.

Figure 2.11

By combining BR tags with the BLOCKQUOTE tag, you can create indented stanzas for a poem or song.

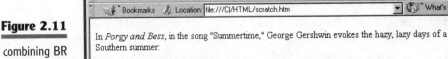

Using Preformatted Text

The PRE (Preformatted Text) tag is used to display text in a monospace (fixed-pitch) font. As its name implies, the PRE tag displays text "as is," including all spaces and hard returns. The primary use for this tag is to display text in a tabular or columnar format in which you want to make sure that columns are properly aligned.

TIP

Always use spaces, not tabs, to align columns when using the PRE tag, because different browsers might display tabs in PRE-tagged text differently.

Actually, the PRE tag is the original "tables" tag for HTML. Unlike the TABLE tag (part of HTML 3.2, but not HTML 2.0), all Web browsers support it, which is a real advantage. It can be particularly handy for displaying worksheets or reports. Another common usage is for displaying program code or output.

CAUTION

When typing tabular or columnar text with a PRE tag, make sure you have a fixed-pitch font such as Courier turned on in your editor or word processor. Notepad automatically displays all text in a monospace font. Word processors, however, normally use a proportional font as the default. Most, although by no means all, HTML editors also display PRE-tagged text in a monospace font.

For an example of using the PRE tag, type a table using rows and columns:

```
<PRE>
          Sales Figures for First Quarter of 1996
-----------------------------------------------------------

             January     February      March       Totals
Anderson    $ 10,200    $  20,015    $  14,685    $  44,900
Baker         30,500       25,885       50,225      106,610
Peterson      15,900       20,115       18,890       54,905
Wilson        40,100       35,000       29,000      104,100

             ---------    ---------    ---------    ---------
Totals      $ 96,700    $ 101,015    $ 112,800    $ 310,515
</PRE>
```

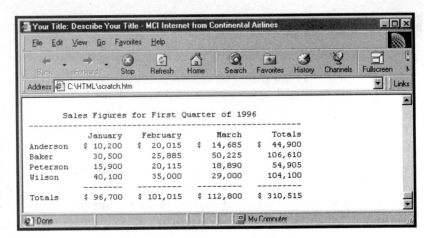

Figure 2.12

The PRE tag
displays text blocks
in a monospace
font, preserving all
spaces and line
breaks in columnar
and tabular text.

Figure 2.12 shows this table as it appears in a Web browser.

One way to double-indent preformatted text in both Netscape Navigator and NCSA Mosaic is to put it inside a BLOCKQUOTE tag. Enclose the PRE tag text you just typed inside a BLOCKQUOTE tag, as follows:

```
<PRE>
<BLOCKQUOTE>
        Sales Figures for First Quarter of 1996
- - - - - - - - - - - - - - - - - - - - - - - - - - - - - - - - - -

          January     February       March       Totals
Anderson  $ 10,200   $   20,015   $   14,685   $   44,900
Baker       30,500       25,885       50,225      106,610
Peterson    15,900       20,115       18,890       54,905
Wilson      40,100       35,000       29,000      104,100
          - - - - -    - - - - -    - - - - -    - - - - -
Totals    $ 96,700   $  101,015   $  112,800   $  310,515
</BLOCKQUOTE>
</PRE>
```

This doesn't work in Internet Explorer version 2.0, which will still display the table flushed left. Also, you might think that you could reverse the nesting order here, placing the PRE tags inside the BLOCKQUOTE tags, but a bug in Internet Explorer 4.0 will still cause it to be displayed flush to the left margin. This has been fixed in versions 4.01 and later of Internet Explorer, but plenty of people are still using version 4.0, so you should just stick to putting the BLOCKQUOTE tags inside the PRE tags.

Take a Break

This seems like a good place to take a break. Get up and stretch those arms and legs. Pour another cup of coffee or take the dog for a walk. I'll see you back in five or ten minutes for the remainder of this session.

Creating Lists

Only headings and paragraph text elements are used more commonly than lists. Many Web pages are nothing but lists of hypertext links. You, like anyone else surfing the Web, have been on that merry-go-round a few times—going from one page of lists to another page of lists to another. If you're going to create Web pages, you need to know how to make lists! HTML uses two types of lists: ordered and unordered. An ordered list is simply a numbered list, and an unordered list is a bulleted list.

TIP You don't have to physically type the numbers for the items in an ordered list or insert bullet characters for an unordered list. A Web browser automatically numbers any list items included in an OL (Ordered List) tag. When a Web browser encounters the UL (Unordered List) tag, it inserts the bullet characters for you.

The OL (Ordered List) Tag

The OL (Ordered List) tag defines a sequentially numbered list of items. Therefore, the OL tag must surround the entire list. The LI (List Item) tag is nested inside the OL tag and defines each individual item within the list.

Create an ordered list to see how these tags work together:

```
<P>When visiting Florence, one should be sure to visit:
<OL>
<LI>The Church of Santa Maria Novella
<LI>The Medici Chapels
<LI>The Church of San Lorenzo
<LI>The Baptistry of St. John
</OL>
```

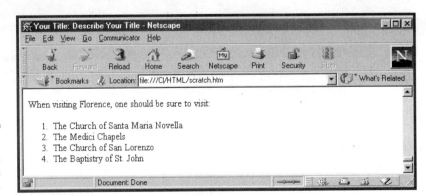

Figure 2.13

The OL (Ordered List) tag is used to create a numbered list.

NOTE

The LI tags do not have end tags in this example because the end tag (</LI>), like the end tag for the P tag, is implied. It's another case of a container tag masquerading as an empty tag. You should be aware, however, that HTML 4.0 treats this a bit differently than earlier versions of HTML, specifying that extra space should be added between list items if the end tag (</LI>) is present. I'm not aware of any browsers that support this yet, however.

Figure 2.13 shows how an ordered (or *numbered*) list is displayed in a Web browser.

The UL (Unordered List) Tag

The UL (Unordered List) tag defines a bulleted list of items. Once again, the LI (List Item) tag is nested inside the UL tag and defines each item within the list.

Create a bulleted list:

```
<P>In this course we will be studying the philosophical thought of
➡the Milesians:
<UL>
<LI>Thales
<LI>Anaximander
<LI>Anaximenes
</UL>
```

Figure 2.14 shows how an unordered (or *bulleted*) list is displayed in a Web browser.

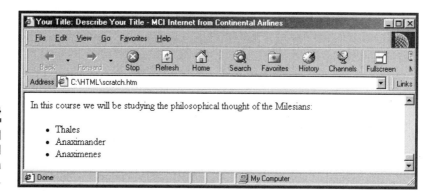

Figure 2.14

The UL (Unordered
List) tag is used
to create a
bulleted list.

 NOTE

So how do you create all those fancy 3-D bullets you see all over the Web? Well, first of all, you don't use OL or UL tags. Those fancy bullets are actually inline graphic images that the Web author has inserted into the page. The separate lines are simply paragraphs broken up by line breaks (BR tags). I cover how to insert inline images using the IMG tag later in this tutorial. In the Intermediate HTML Tutorial, scheduled for this afternoon, I'll show you how to create link lists with fancy 3-D bullet icons that will indent the following text, just like with a regular list. I'll also show you an even fancier way to do this using tables in the Tables Tutorial that's scheduled for this evening.

Nesting Lists

You can nest a list inside another list. The browser automatically indents nested list levels. You can also nest the same or different kinds of lists.

The following list uses spaces to indent the different nested levels. You could also use tabs. The only purpose of this spacing is to make the raw text here more readable during editing (the Web browser will completely ignore this spacing). Feel free to insert tabs or spaces to approximate the layout shown here:

```
<UL>
<LI>Some Pre-Socratic Philosophers
    <UL>
    <LI>The Milesians
        <UL>
        <LI>Thales
```

```
        <LI>Anaximander
        <LI>Anaximenes
        </UL>
    <LI>The Eleatics
        <UL>
        <LI>Parmenides
        <LI>Anaxagoras
        </UL>
    </UL>
</UL>
```

Web browsers can vary quite a bit in how they display bullets in an unordered list. Figures 2.15 and 2.16 show how different level bullets in a nested unordered list are displayed in Navigator and Internet Explorer, respectively.

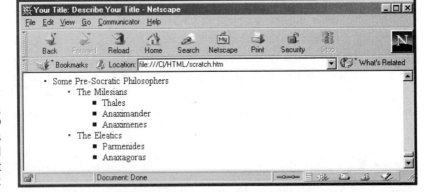

Figure 2.15

Navigator displays a multilevel bulleted list like this.

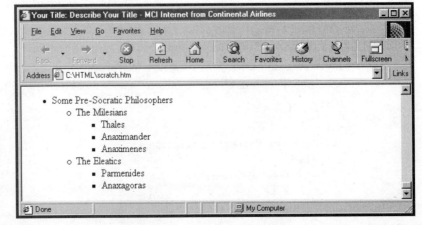

Figure 2.16

Internet Explorer displays a multilevel bulleted list like this.

Mixing Lists

You can nest an ordered list within an unordered list (or the other way around):

```
<UL>
<LI>King-Side Openings
    <OL>
    <LI>Ruy Lopez
    <LI>King Bishop's Opening
    <LI>King's Gambit
    </OL>
<LI>Queen-Side Openings
    <OL>
    <LI>Queen's Gambit Declined
    <LI>Queen's Gambit Accepted
    <LI>English Opening
    </OL>
</UL>
```

Figure 2.17 shows ordered (numbered) lists nested inside an unordered (bulleted) list.

HTML includes two other list tags: the DIR and MENU tags. The DIR tag was intended for displaying multicolumn directory lists (such as a file directory, for instance), whereas the MENU tag was intended for displaying single-column menu lists. In practice, all versions of Navigator and Internet Explorer display these tags exactly the same as the UL (Unordered List) tag. The only browser I know of that displays these tags any differently than the

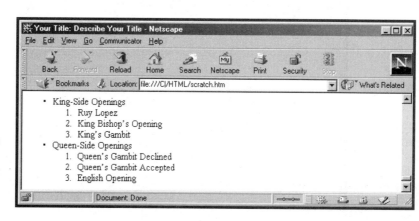

Figure 2.17

You can nest a numbered list inside a bulleted list, and vice versa.

UL tag is NCSA Mosaic 2.0. The HTML 4.0 specification also recommends that the UL tag be used instead of the DIR and MENU tags.

Creating Definition Lists

The DL (Definition List) tag allows you to create glossaries, or lists of terms and definitions. A glossary actually consists of three tag elements that all work together: the DL (Definition List) tag to define the list, the DT (Definition Term) tag to define the terms, and the DD (Definition Data) tag to define the definitions. Set up a short glossary now:

```
<DL>
<DT>Appeal
<DD>A proceeding by which the decision of a lower court may be
➥appealed to a higher court.
<DT>Arrest
<DD>The legal apprehension and restraint of someone charged with a
➥crime so that they might be brought before a court to stand trial.
<DT>Bail
<DD>A security offered to a court in exchange for a person's release
➥and as assurance of their appearance in court when required.
</DL>
```

Figure 2.18 shows the preceding glossary list code as it appears in a Web browser.

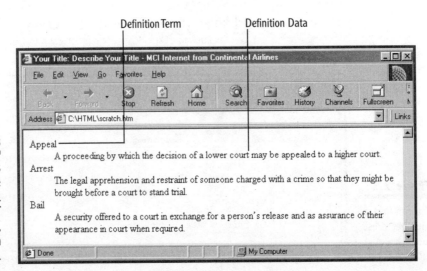

Figure 2.18

A glossary is created using three tags: the DL (Definition List), DT (Definition Term), and DD (Definition Data) tags.

As you've probably noticed, the end tags for the DT (Definition Term) and DD (Definition Data) tags are implied, as is the LI (List Item) tag in a regular list. The only difference is that a glossary or definition list has a two-part item (both a term and a definition), rather than a one-part item. As long as you keep this in mind, you should have no trouble creating glossaries.

By itself, a glossary list is a bit bland. You can dress it up by adding emphasis or tagging the definition terms with a heading tag. Here's an example of adding bold italic emphasis to a definition term:

```
<DT><I><B>Appeal</B></I>
```

Here's an example of tagging a definition term using an H3 heading tag:

```
<DT><H3>Appeal</H3>
```

TIP You can include multiple DD (Definition Data) elements following a DT (Definition Term) element. If you want space to be inserted between multiple DD elements, however, you should insert a P tag following the second and any following DD tags: `<DD><P>`*Your definition item text*, for instance.

Creating Hypertext Links

One of the main reasons to create a Web page is to create links to other pages, right? To do that, you need to know how to use the A (Anchor) tag.

If you've surfed the Web at all, you should be quite familiar with hypertext links. You've probably used hypertext links not only to jump to and view another Web page, or jump to a specific place in either the same or another Web page, but to read a Gopher file, display an image, download a program, send an e-mail message, play an audio or video clip, run a script, access a database, telnet to a server, and so on. You can use hypertext links to jump to anything that has an address on the Internet (not just on the Web), as long as you don't need a password. Of course, what happens after you make the jump depends on where you go.

In a sense, the Web is a kind of giant "What's behind door #3?" game, although this perhaps helps explain much of its basic appeal. It's all quite easy and transparent: just click and go. However, explaining how to make this happen on your Web page isn't nearly as easy or transparent. This section will make the A (Anchor) tag as clear as possible. Here are the three basic kinds of hypertext links:

○ **Links to other HTML documents or data objects.** These are by far the most commonly used links on the Web. They allow you to jump from one Web page to another, as well as to anything else that has an address on the Net (not just the Web), such as Gopher files, FTP archives, images, and so on.

○ **Links to other places in the same HTML document.** These links allow you to jump from one place in a Web page to another point on the same Web page. Many Web pages have directories or "tables of contents" at the beginning of the page, allowing you to decide which part of the page you want to view. You simply click the link to jump to that section of the page or document.

○ **Links to places in other HTML documents.** These links are quite similar to links to places in the same document, except you can jump to certain sections on other pages. If you've clicked a hypertext link and then jumped to some point halfway down another Web page, you've used this type of link.

You use the A (Anchor) tag to anchor one or both ends of a hypertext link. The first kind of link, where you link to another Web page or data object, requires only one anchor. The second and third kinds of links, where you link to another place in the same or another Web page, require both ends of the link—that is, both a launch pad and a landing spot. This other end of a hypertext link, where you link a specific place in the same or another Web page, is often called a *target anchor*.

NOTE You can include a target anchor inside a Gopher text file, which is just a plain text file, and then have a hypertext link jump to that specific place in the file, even though it isn't an HTML file. You don't see this often, but you can do it.

Anatomy of the A (Anchor) Tag

Think of a hypertext link as being composed of the following three elements:

- Start and end tags that enclose the whole link
- The link target
- The link text

Figure 2.19 illustrates the three parts of a hypertext link.

In Figure 2.19, the HREF (Hypertext Reference) attribute specifies the URL or address of the object of the link, which here is simply another Web page. Note that the full address (URL) is not given, just the file name. This means that the object of the link, most commonly another Web page, is located in the same folder as the Web page from which the link is being made. If you want to make a link with a Web page somewhere else on the Web, you have to include the full URL: for example, **http://www.somewhere.com/some-page.html**, or something like that, rather than just the file name (SOMEPAGE.HTML).

When using the A (Anchor) tag, you must include either an HREF attribute or a NAME attribute. If you're linking to another Web page or some other data object, you only need to use *one* anchor tag with an HREF attribute. If you're linking to a location in the same or another Web page, you need to use *two* anchor tags: the first with an HREF attribute defining the take-off location, and the second with the NAME attribute defining the target location.

If you find this a bit confusing, don't worry—it is confusing! The following sections provide some hands-on examples of creating the three kinds of links as well as using both the HREF and NAME attributes. Learning by doing should go a long way toward dissipating your confusion.

Figure 2.19

A hypertext link has three parts: the start and end tags, the link target, and the link text.

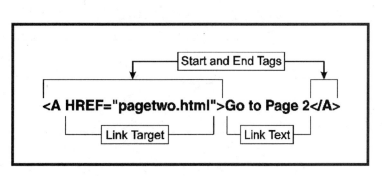

Linking to a File or Data Object

You can form an HTML link to anything on the Web that has an address. To create a hypertext link that jumps to a file that's somewhere on the Web (as opposed to a folder on your own server), include the whole URL of the file to which you want to jump. Here's an example:

```
<P>Click here to jump to <A HREF="http://www.
somewhere.com/else.html">somewhere else</A>.
```

TIP Notice that the A tag falls inside a P tag. You should always nest the A tag inside a document element, not simply within the BODY tag. You can nest an A tag inside a P tag, a heading (such as H1 or H2), or an ADDRESS, PRE, LI, DT, or DD tag.

If "www.somewhere.com" actually existed with a file in its root directory named "ELSE.HTML," you could link to it by putting this A tag in your own HTML file. Substitute an actual URL for the dummy URL when you want to link to a real site. Do that now by creating a hypertext link that jumps to a real document on an actual Web site:

```
<P>You can find out more about the WWW at the home page of the <A
HREF="http://www.w3.org/">W3 Consortium</A>.
```

Figure 2.20 shows how this appears in a Web browser.

When you click the hypertext link shown in Figure 2.20, a hypertext "jump" takes you to the target address, displaying the page shown in Figure 2.21. (You must actually go online if you want to check this out on your browser.)

Figure 2.20

The underlining indicates a hypertext link to the home page of the W3 Consortium.

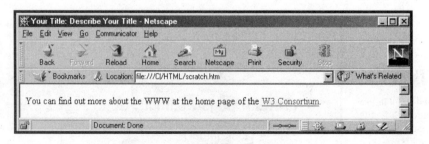

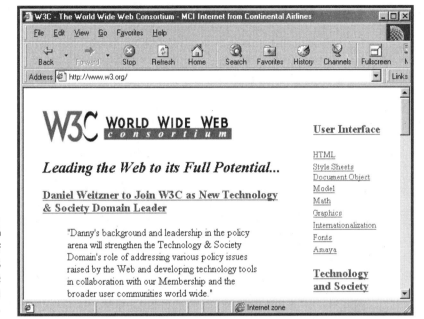

Figure 2.21

The home page of the W3C appears when you click the link shown in Figure 2.20.

 NOTE Netscape Navigator and Internet Explorer display a hypertext link in a blue, underlined font. NCSA Mosaic displays a hypertext link in a blue font without the underlining. Your browser may display links that you've already visited in a different color. Also, Web page authors can specify the color in which a regular link, a previously visited link, and an active link will be displayed—I'll show you how to do that in this afternoon's Intermediate HTML Tutorial. Style sheets can also now be used to exert even further control over how a hypertext link will appear on a Web page.

Linking to Non-WWW Files

Your browser should be able to directly display any text file or GIF or JPEG graphic on a Web, FTP, or Gopher server. Other kinds of files may require viewers or players, such as sound, animation, and video files. RealAudio and Shockwave allow audio and animation clips to be streamed (played while being downloaded) rather than downloaded first and then played.

Linking to a Place in the Same HTML File

Linking to another place in the same HTML file requires both an HREF anchor and a NAME anchor. An HREF anchor that links to a NAME anchor has a special form:

```
<A HREF="#anchorname">anchortext</A>
```

Notice the # sign. In an HREF anchor, the # sign is the only thing that identifies the HREF attribute as the name of a NAME anchor rather than an address or file name. (The # sign combined with the following anchor name is sometimes called a *fragment identifier*.)

Here are some of the more common uses for linking HREF and NAME anchors on the same page:

- ✪ Creating a directory or table of contents that links to the major headings of a page
- ✪ Making cross-references between different points in the same Web page
- ✪ Forming links to footnotes or endnotes

The following is an example of creating a menu or table of contents for the top of a Web page to link to subheading sections located lower on the same Web page (feel free to cut and paste to create the filler text for the paragraphs):

```
<H2>Table of Contents</H2>
<P><A HREF="#one">Section One</A><BR>
<A HREF="#two">Section Two</A><BR>
<A HREF="#three">Section Three</A>

<H2><A NAME="one">Section One</A></H2>
<P>This is the text following the first subheading. This is the text
following the first subheading. This is the text following the first
subheading. This is the text following the first subheading. This is
the text following the first subheading. This is the text following
the first subheading.

<H2><A NAME="two">Section Two</A></H2>
<P>This is the text following the second subheading. This is the
text following the second subheading. This is the text following the
```

```
second subheading. This is the text following the second subheading.
This is the text following the second subheading. This is the text
following the second subheading.

<H2><A NAME="three">Section Three</A></H2>
<P>This is the text following the third subheading. This is the text
following the third subheading. This is the text following the third
subheading. This is the text following the third subheading. This is
the text following the third subheading. This is the text following
the third subheading.
```

Figure 2.22 shows how this looks in a Web browser.

Only the first two subsections of the example are shown in the figure. Be sure to hop over to your browser and check out how the links in the table of contents work. (Don't, however, lengthen your browser window to contain all three subheadings—if you do that, you won't be able to see how the "hop" works from the link in the table of contents to the third subheading.)

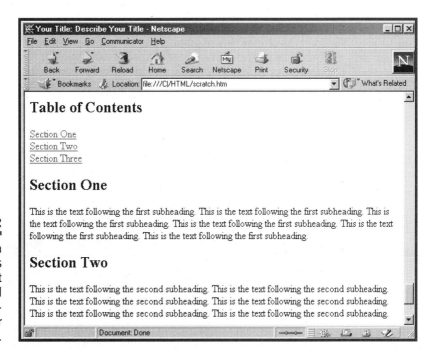

Figure 2.22

You can create a table of contents using hypertext links that will jump to subheadings within your document.

Linking to a Place in Another HTML File

Just as you can create a hypertext link to a place in the same HTML file, you can also make a link to a place in another HTML file. Both work the same way, except in the second instance, the NAME anchor (your landing spot) is placed in an entirely different file from the one where the link is being made. Here's the form for an HREF anchor that links to a place in another HTML file:

```
<A HREF="address#anchorname">anchortext</A>
```

This actually combines the forms for linking to another page and linking to a place on a page. The first part of the A tag (#*address*) links to another Web page, whereas the second part (#*anchorname*) links to a place in that page marked by the specified anchor name.

As an example, create a hypertext link that jumps to a place in another HTML file:

```
<P>Go to <A HREF="links.htm#parttwo">Part Two</A> of the <A
HREF="links.htm">How to Use Links</A> web page.
```

Figure 2.23 shows how these two links look in a Web browser.

I've created a LINKS.HTM file that's included with the example files you copied this morning. If you click the "Part Two" link shown in Figure 2.23, you'll hop to the corresponding section of the LINKS.HTM file. (Just click the Back button to return to your scratch-pad file, SCRATCH.HTM.)

The preceding example includes links to "Part Two" of the "How to Use Links" Web page as well as to the whole "How to Use Links" Web page. The only difference between linking to a location in a Web page and simply linking

Figure 2.23

The first link jumps to a place in the "How to Use Links" Web page, and the second link jumps to the Web page itself.

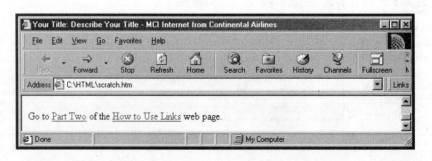

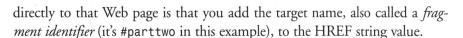

directly to that Web page is that you add the target name, also called a *fragment identifier* (it's #parttwo in this example), to the HREF string value.

Also, don't forget that in order to hop to a location in another page, the location you're hopping to has to be marked with an A tag using a NAME attribute that matches the fragment identifier (or anchor name) in the link you're jumping from. For instance, the following is the target anchor that you jumped to in LINKS.HTM:

```
<H2><A NAME="parttwo">Part Two</A></H2>
```

Creating Link Lists

So far, the discussion has focused on creating lists and creating links, but it hasn't explained creating link lists. A *link list* is a list of hypertext links, usually bulleted but sometimes numbered. Because link lists are so ubiquitous, everybody should know how to create them. To create a link list, all you need to do is combine an unordered list and some hypertext links.

Creating a Simple Link List

Type the following to create a simple link list:

```
<H2>Yo Yo Links</H2>
<UL>
<LI><A HREF="http://www.li.net/~autorent/yo-yo.htm">Jon's Yo-Yo
➥Kingdom</A>
<LI><A HREF="http://pages.nyu.edu/~tqm3413/yoyo/index.htm">
Tomer's Page of Exotic Yo-Yo</A>
<LI><A HREF="http://www.socool.com/socool/yo-yo.html">Just Say
➥YO!</A>
<LI><A HREF="http://www.pd.net/yoyo/">American Yo-Yo Association</A>
<LI><A HREF="http://www.socool.com/socool/yo_hist.html">The History
➥of the Yo-Yo</A>
</UL>
```

CAUTION When you enter Web addresses (URLs), you should always type them exactly as they appear. Unix commands are case sensitive and most Web servers still run Unix.

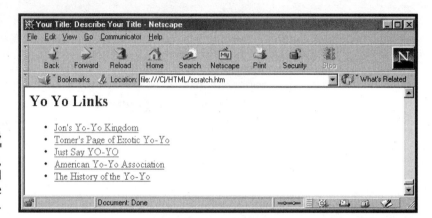

Figure 2.24

In a simple link list,
the link text and
the link items are
the same.

Figure 2.24 shows how the preceding link list example appears in a Web browser.

The hypertext links included in the previous example are, at the time of this writing anyway, all good. You'll have to connect to the Internet, however, if you want to check them out. (Don't go get lost out in Yo-Yo land though— you've still got lots to do!)

Creating a Link List with Descriptions

A simple list of links can prove somewhat empty. A nice touch is to add more information so visitors have a clearer idea of what awaits at the other end of the link. One option is to edit the link text to include more information than the title affords. However, you should to try to keep the actual link text as concise and succinct as possible so that a visitor can scan it at a glance. The solution is to add explanatory text following the hypertext link. In the list of links you just typed, add some explanatory text for each link:

```
<H2>Yo Yo Links</H2>
<UL>
<LI><A HREF="http://www.li.net/~autorent/yo-yo.htm">Jon's Yo-Yo
➥Kingdom</A> Claims to have the largest Yo-Yo link list on the Web.
<LI><A HREF="http://pages.nyu.edu/~tqm3413/yoyo/index.htm">Tomer's
➥Page of Exotic Yo-Yo</A> Dedicated to the "little-known, original,
➥unusual, difficult, or otherwise interesting tricks."
```

```
<LI><A HREF="http://www.socool.com/socool/yo-yo.html">Just Say
➥YO!</A> Features the Web's first Yo-Yo animation.
<LI><A HREF="http://www.pd.net/yoyo/">American Yo-Yo Association</A>
➥Read past issues of the AYYA Newsletter.
<LI><A HREF="http://www.socool.com/socool/yo_hist.html">The History
➥of the Yo-Yo</A> All you want to know about Yo-Yo history.
</UL>
```

Figure 2.25 shows the newly expanded list.

Other Ways to Create Link Lists

The preceding examples illustrate the most simple and direct ways to create link lists. A variation you might want to try is using a definition list in which the hypertext links are inserted in the DT tags, with the descriptions inserted in the DD tags. You could also tag the definition terms with a heading tag to display the links more prominently. Using a definition list for a list of links can be particularly handy if you want to provide more than just a sentence or two of explanatory or descriptive text. Later today, in the Intermediate HTML Tutorial and the Tables Tutorial, if you have time to get around to them, I'll show you how to create indented link lists using fancy 3-D bullet icons.

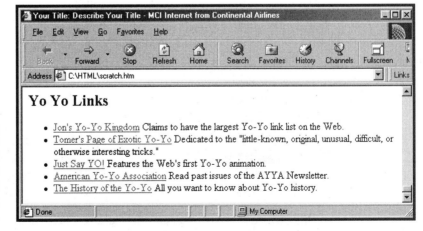

Figure 2.25

Sometimes a short list of links with explanations is better than a long one without.

Using Inline Images

The IMG (Image) tag allows you to display inline images on your Web page. The term *inline* here means that an image is inserted at a particular location in a line within a Web page.

The most commonly used formats for inline images are GIF and JPG. All current graphic Web browsers can display GIF and JPG files as inline images. These two graphic formats tend to serve different purposes. GIF images are limited to 256 colors but can have a color set to transparent. GIF images can also be interlaced, thus allowing the image to be progressively displayed while its file is still being downloaded to the browser. GIF images can also be animated. JPG images can select from a palette of up to 16.7 million colors, but they can't be transparent or animated. A rule of thumb is to use JPG images when you want to include a photographic image, or a graphic using a gradient fill effect, where reducing the number of colors to 256 or less will negatively affect image quality (for example, by producing a banding effect). When you want to include a nonphotographic image, in most cases you should stick to using GIFs, because they're much less likely to require more than 256 colors to display effectively. GIF files also tend to be a bit sharper than JPG files because of the compression method used for JPG files.

A relatively new image format that's rapidly gaining support on the Web is the PNG graphic format. Like GIF images, PNG images can have a color set to transparent and be progressively displayed while still being downloaded. Additionally, the PNG format supports up to 48-bit true color images (the JPG format supports up to 24-bit true color images). PNG, at first glance, offers the best of both GIF and JPG. Both the latest versions of Navigator and Internet Explorer support PNG graphics. Paint Shop Pro, available on the CD-ROM included with this book, can open, edit, and save PNG images. The only holdup is that a lot of older browsers are still in use. The best advice, unless you want to create a Web site aimed only at the latest browsers, is to stick for now with GIF and JPG. In a couple of years, however, the advice might be different.

The IMG (Image) tag is an empty, or standalone, element. Here's its form:

```
<IMG SRC="imagefile">
```

The SRC (Source) attribute is a required attribute. It identifies the address of the image to be displayed, which can be its full or partial Web address (URL) or just its file name (that is, if it's saved in the same folder as the HTML file in which it is to be displayed).

Now, insert an inline image, SAMPLE.GIF, into your HTML file:

```
<P>The inline graphic, SAMPLE.GIF, is displayed here:</P>
<P><IMG SRC="sample.gif">
```

Notice that the IMG tag follows a P (Paragraph) tag. That's because the IMG tag inserts an *inline* image—therefore, if you want an image to be displayed on its own line, you need to precede it by a P or other block element tag.

Figure 2.26 shows SAMPLE.GIF as an inline image in a Web browser.

You *can* link to a graphics file anywhere on the Web and display it on your own Web page by using the IMG (Image) tag. For instance, you might do something like this:

```
<IMG SRC="http://www.anywhere.com/some.gif">
```

Doing so, however, generally is frowned upon on the Web. Not only might you be violating somebody's copyright, you most certainly would be generating traffic on that person's server simply so you can display a particular inline image on your Web page. Also, this can be traced back to you. This practice may not be against the law, but a complaint could be sent to whoever is running your server, which might get you kicked off your server. The bottom line is this: linking to someone else's graphics file is not the way to make friends on the Web.

Figure 2.26

All graphical Web browsers can display inline graphic images.

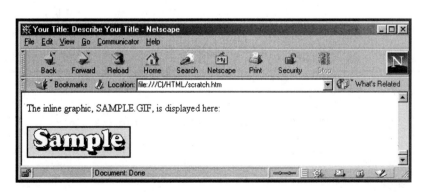

However, linking to others' Web pages is perfectly fine. At least in my opinion, anyway. That's how you make friends on the Web. Just don't claim their Web stuff as your own. If they give you permission to use any of their graphics, you can download them to your server and include them on your own Web page. Also, don't just go around downloading and using other people's graphics and WAV files. Plenty of repositories of public domain graphics exist on the Web.

Some users still believe that you should ask permission before linking to another's Web page. That's a bit old hat, I think—it dates back to when traffic allowances on the Web were a good deal skimpier than they are now. Of course, if someone should request that you remove a link to one of his pages, by all means, do.

Using the ALT Attribute

The ALT attribute can be included in the IMG tag to help identify an image. In the newer browsers, for instance, if you pass the cursor over an image, the contents of any included ALT attribute will be displayed. Also, because surfing the Web can often be more like wading through hip-deep molasses, a lot of people surf the Web with the display of images turned off in order to help speed things up. What's more, many people still use text-based browsers, such as Lynx, that don't display images at all. Using the ALT attribute will cue these surfers in on what an image contains.

Here's an example of how to use the ALT attribute with your IMG tags:

```
<IMG SRC="sample.gif" ALT="">
```

This example viewed in Lynx would show nothing. On a Web browser that has image loading turned off, the ALT="" attribute value has no effect.

To have a message replace the image in Lynx or display along with the dummy graphic in a graphical browser with the graphics turned off, enter the following:

```
<IMG SRC="sample.gif" ALT="A sample graphic">
```

Figure 2.27

SAMPLE.GIF is shown here, first without the ALT attribute and then with the ALT attribute, as displayed in Navigator with the display of images turned off.

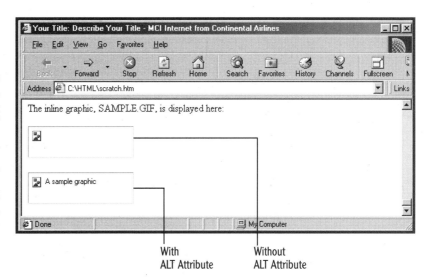

With
ALT Attribute

Without
ALT Attribute

This example, when viewed in Lynx, displays the message "A sample graphic" rather than just "[Image]." For a graphical Web browser with image-loading turned off, the message "A sample graphic" would appear alongside the dummy graphic, as shown in Figure 2.27.

NOTE

If an image is decorative and serves no informational purpose, use the ALT attribute with a blank attribute value (ALT=""). That way, you don't clutter up a Web page in a text-only browser with [Image] references. If your graphic has informational import, you should always include an ALT attribute text string: for example, **ALT="Georgy-Porgy's Home Page"** or **ALT="Diagram of the X-27P Circuit Board"** (or something like that). This is especially important where an image is being used by itself to perform a function, such as displaying the title of a Web page in a banner graphic (where no corresponding H1 element is included), or functioning as a navigational icon or image link where no text is included on the Web page to describe what the link is. Including an ALT attribute will allow somebody using a text-only browser or a graphical Web browser with graphics turned off (or a visually-impaired person using a Braille browser) to still see what's going on.

Using the ALIGN Attribute in Inline Graphics

The ALIGN attribute allows you to position an inline image relative to the line of text it's on. All current graphical Web browsers should recognize the values "top," "middle," and "bottom."

Insert an inline graphic using the "top" ALIGN value:

```
<P>The image on this line <IMG ALIGN="top" SRC="top.gif"> is
top-aligned.
```

Here's an example of the "middle" ALIGN value:

```
<P>The image on this line <IMG ALIGN="middle" SRC="middle.gif"> is
middle-aligned.
```

Insert an inline graphic using the "bottom" ALIGN value:

```
<P>The image on this line <IMG ALIGN="bottom" SRC="bottom.gif"> is
bottom-aligned.
```

Figure 2.28 shows these examples as they appear in a Web browser.

Two additional ALIGN attributes can be included in the IMG tag: "left" and "right." I show you how to use these in this afternoon's Intermediate HTML Tutorial. These are HTML 3.2 attributes used to wrap text around an image, rather than to merely align an image horizontally on a page. To simply

Figure 2.28

Inline images can be aligned relative to the baseline of the line on which they appear.

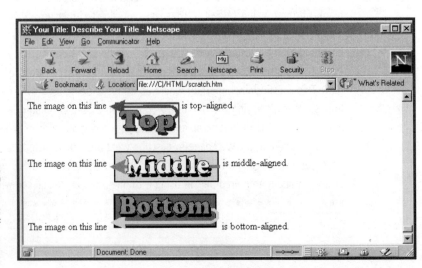

center-align or right-align an image on a page, you need to use another method, which I also tell you about in this afternoon's tutorial.

Using Relative URLs

When creating a hypertext link or inserting an inline image, you don't always need to specify a full, or *absolute*, URL or Web address. If a Web page or other file to which you are linking, or a graphic file you're inserting into your Web page, is in the same folder, in the same folder structure, or on the same server (in the same domain), you can leave off those parts of the URL that are common to both. A URL that provides only those parts of a Web address that are not common to both the linking and the linked file is often called a *partial URL*. One of the advantages of using this type of URL, apart from being shorter, is that you can move a Web page and its locally linked files from one directory to another, and even from one server to another, without having to redo the links.

NOTE You've already used some partial (or *relative*) URLs. For instance, **<IMG SRC="sample.gif">** uses a partial URL. The full (or *absolute*) URL would be **file:///C|/html/sample.gif**, which is what the full URL for a local file on your own hard drive looks like. If you used the full URL here, you wouldn't be able to put your Web page, along with any included inline images, on the Web without having to redo all your links. You want to create and test your Web pages on your computer and then FTP them up to your Web site (when you get one) on your server without having to redo any of the links.

Linking to a File in a Subdirectory of the Linking Page's Directory

If C:\HTML is the directory where you currently store your HTML files, you might want to store your graphic files in C:\HTML\IMAGES. You could then use a relative or partial URL (rather than an absolute or full URL) to display the graphic, like this:

```
<IMG SRC="images/sample.gif">
```

If you plan to create a Web site that uses multiple subpages, you might want to store your subpages in a separate directory from your home page. For example, if your home page is in the \HTML directory and the subpage (SUBPAGE.HTM) to which you want to link is in the \PAGE\SUBPAGES directory, a hypertext link between the two might look like this:

```
<A HREF="subpages/subpage.htm">
```

The two previous examples would indicate a directory structure something like this:

```
\HTML - | - \IMAGES
        |
        | - \SUBPAGES
```

Linking to a File in a Subdirectory of a Directory in Which Your HTML File Is a Subdirectory

Suppose your HTML files are stored in /PUB/HTML, but your graphic files are stored in /PUB/IMAGES. To display the inline image FLOWER.GIF, stored in /PUB/IMAGES, you would use this partial URL in your Web page:

```
<IMG SRC="../images/sample.gif">
```

Or, suppose you want to insert a hypertext link in the same Web page mentioned earlier (/PUB/HTML) to another Web page, PRICES.HTM, stored in a parallel directory, /PUB/SALES. To do so, the hypertext link between the two would look like this:

```
<A HREF="../sales/prices.htm">
```

The two previous examples would then indicate a directory structure like this:

```
\PUB - | - \HTML
       |
       | - \IMAGES
       |
       | - \SALES
```

Using Horizontal Rules

The HR (Horizontal Rule) tag is a standalone (or *empty*) document element that allows you to add horizontal rules to your Web pages. Set up a text paragraph followed by an HR tag:

```
<P>A horizontal rule is displayed below this line.
<HR>
```

Figure 2.29 shows a horizontal rule displayed in a Web browser.

I'll show you some more things you can do with horizontal rules in this afternoon's Intermediate HTML Tutorial, including setting the width and height, changing the shading, and even adding color. I'll also show you how to use graphical rules, which can allow you to add multicolored, and even animated, rules to your Web page.

Signing Your Work

You generally use the ADDRESS tag to define a signature block for your Web page. It might contain your name, title, organizational or business affiliation, and information on how to contact you. A horizontal rule usually separates an address from the rest of a Web page.

Following the HR tag you created in the last example, type some address text separated into individual lines by BR tags (type your name, company name, and phone number where indicated):

```
<HR>
<ADDRESS>
Type your name here<BR>
```

Figure 2.29

Horizontal rules are often used in Web pages as separators.

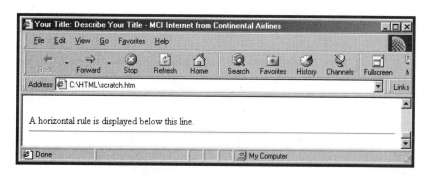

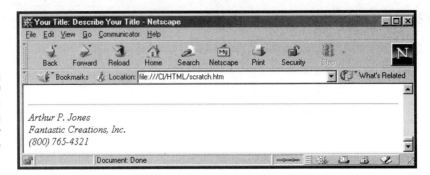

Figure 2.30

The address section
of a Web page is
used to tell your
visitors how they
can contact you.

```
Type your company name here<BR>
Type your area code and phone number here
</ADDRESS>
</HTML>
```

For instance, your address section might look in a browser like what is shown in Figure 2.30.

Adding a Mailto Link to Your Address

You'll probably want to put more than just your phone number in the address section. For instance, you can add your e-mail address. (It's the Web after all.) To add your e-mail address, you use a special form of hypertext link, called a *Mailto link*. When a user clicks a Mailto link, the browser pops up a form that allows the reader to send a message to the e-mail address in the link.

To add your e-mail address to your address section, add the following:

```
<HR>
<ADDRESS>
Your name<BR>
Your company name<BR>
Your phone number<BR>
E-Mail: <A HREF="mailto:type your e-mail address">type your e-mail
↪address</A>
</ADDRESS>
```

Note that you have to insert your e-mail address twice—once as the link and then again as the link text.

Not all browsers support Mailto links. Internet Explorer 3.0 requires that Internet Mail be installed. Internet Explorer 4.0 requires that you have Outlook Express installed. What's more, even if your browser supports Mailto links, it still has to be configured properly. Therefore, no matter which way you cut it, you're going to have viewers who can't use your Mailto link.

Does that mean you should avoid Mailto links? Absolutely not! The solution is to make sure that your full e-mail address is the link text for your Mailto link. This means you need to enter your e-mail address twice for a Mailto link, as shown in the previous example. That way, if someone can't use your Mailto link, that person can always click and drag to copy your e-mail address or just write it down and then send you a message using his or her regular e-mail client.

In a browser that supports Mailto links, when someone clicks a Mailto link to your e-mail address, a message composition window will pop up with your e-mail address already filled in as the recipient of the message. The user just has to type a message and click the Send button. Figure 2.31 shows what Navigator's message composition window looks like.

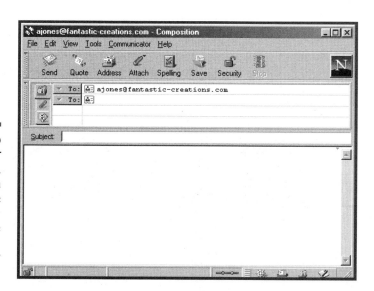

Figure 2.31

Clicking a Mailto link, in a browser that supports it, brings up a message composition window with the recipient's e-mail address already filled in.

Adding Your URL to Your Address

Once you get your Web pages up on the Web, you should include your URL (the Web address of your home page) in your address section (although your may want to skip this on your actual home page). To do this, just include a hypertext link to your home page. Because you probably don't have a home page yet, just enter the following URL:

```
<HR>
<ADDRESS>
Your name<BR>
Your company name<BR>
Your phone number<BR>
E-Mail: <A HREF="mailto:type your e-mail address">type your e-mail
➥address</A><BR>
URL: <A HREF="http://www.fantastic-creations.com">http://www.fantas
➥tic-creations.com</A>
</ADDRESS>
```

Figure 2.32 shows how the final address section appears in a Web browser.

Saving Your Work

Save the HTML file you just created. You can use it later as a reference. When you first saved it, you named it SCRATCH.HTM. If other users are going to be doing this tutorial and you want to make sure this file doesn't get overwritten, you might want to give it a new name. For instance, you could

Figure 2.32

An address section might contain your name, company name, street address, phone numbers, as well as a Mailto link to your e-mail address and a hypertext link to your home page.

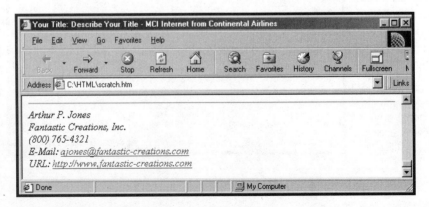

use your first initial and last name for the file name (JMILLER.HTM, for example, if your name is John Miller).

What's Next?

If you've completed the Basic HTML Tutorial, you should now be able to say, "I know HTML!" The HTML covered in the Basic HTML Tutorial detailed everything you need to know to start creating your own Web pages. Everything else is frosting on the cake.

Don't worry if you don't remember or fully understand absolutely everything that you've done in this tutorial. The best way to learn is simply by doing. The more HTML you do, the more comfortable you'll get. You've also saved your scratch-pad file, either as SCRATCH.HTM or with another name you've given it, so you can use it as a reference later. Feel free to load it into your text editor and view it in your Web browser to familiarize yourself with how a particular tag works.

If doing the Basic HTML Tutorial has taken you most or all of the day, or you just think you've reached the point of "information overload," feel free to call it a day (or a night). Even if you've taken all weekend to do just this one tutorial, that's okay.

All the other tutorials in this book are optional. I recommend, however, that you do the Intermediate HTML Tutorial (scheduled for Saturday Afternoon) before trying to do any of the other tutorials.

So, if you still have time and energy left over after doing the Basic HTML Tutorial and are ready for more, take a break, stand up and stretch those muscles, and get a bite to eat. I'll see you back in a bit for the Intermediate HTML Tutorial.

The Intermediate HTML Tutorial

- ⚙ Superscripts, subscripts, underlining, and strikethrough
- ⚙ Horizontally aligning paragraphs, headings, and divisions
- ⚙ Wrapping text around images
- ⚙ Fancy 3-D icon link lists
- ⚙ Font sizes, colors, and faces
- ⚙ Background colors and images

Hey, it's Saturday afternoon! That is, at least if you're managing to keep up with our schedule. If not, don't worry. You can do the Intermediate HTML Tutorial any time you choose, even on Sunday afternoon. Just make sure you do it before attempting any of the following tutorials.

By now, you should have finished the Basic HTML Tutorial scheduled for Saturday morning. If you haven't completed it, you should do so before continuing with this session.

The Intermediate HTML Tutorial covers the following items:

- Some HTML 2.0 features not covered in the Basic HTML Tutorial, including creating banner graphics and image links
- Most of HTML 3.2, including wrapping text around images, creating indented icon link lists, and making font size, color, and face changes
- A few of the new HTML 4.0 features, including marking insertions and deletions, and applying styles to a span of text

This tutorial does not cover the more advanced features of HTML, such as forms, scripts, applets, embedded objects, frames, and image maps. The tables feature, although not covered in this tutorial, is covered in a separate bonus tutorial that you can do this evening if you have the time and energy. You'll find software tutorials scheduled for Sunday that will show you how to apply shareware and freeware software tools to add frames, forms, and image maps to your Web pages. Appendix A, "HTML Quick Reference," additionally describes all the HTML 4.0 tags and attributes.

 NOTE   You should have already installed the example files for this tutorial at the start of the Basic HTML Tutorial. If you haven't installed these files, return to "Installing the Example Files" in the Saturday Morning session before doing this tutorial.

Running Your Web Browser

Run your Web browser, preferably offline, so you'll be able to check the results of your work in your browser while doing this tutorial. You can easily hop back and forth between Notepad and your Web browser, dynamically updating your work as you go. After doing the Basic HTML Tutorial, you should be quite familiar with doing this.

To deal with this tutorial, you need a Web browser that is HTML 3.2–compliant. At minimum, you should use Netscape Navigator 2.0 or greater or Microsoft Internet Explorer 3.0 or greater to do this tutorial. In case you don't currently have either of these browsers installed, I've included Opera 3.21, an excellent HTML 3.2–compliant Web browser, on the CD-ROM. Other *current* graphical browsers may also possibly be used, but because I haven't tested them out, I can't guarantee how HTML 3.2–compliant they are.

If you want to be able to do the HTML 4.0 sections of this tutorial, you should use the latest version of Netscape Navigator or Microsoft Internet Explorer. I've tested this tutorial with the beta version of Navigator 4.5 and the release version of Internet Explorer 4.01 that's included with Windows 98. If you're using an earlier browser than these, feel free to skip the few HTML 4.0 sections I've included—you can do them later after you've downloaded one of these latest versions.

Running Your Text Editor

Run the text editor you want to use to edit HTML files. As mentioned earlier, I highly recommend using Notepad until you master the fundamentals of HTML. In Windows 3.1, you can usually find Notepad in the Accessories window in Program Manager. In Windows 95/98, you can find it on the Start Menu, under Programs and Accessories.

 TIP If you're using Notepad in Windows 3.1 or Windows 95, don't forget to turn Word Wrap on. Just select Edit, Word Wrap. If you're using Notepad in Windows 98, Word Wrap should still be on from your last session.

Loading Your Starting Template

Load the starting template you saved this morning:

1. In Notepad, select File, Open and then go to the C:\HTML folder.
2. Select "All Files (*.*)" as the file type (in the Files of Type box).
3. Double-click *start.htm.*

Your template should look like the following listing (if you didn't save the template, just retype it now):

```
<HTML>
<HEAD>
<TITLE>Your Title: Describe Your Title</TITLE>
</HEAD>
<BODY>
</BODY>
</HTML>
```

 NOTE If you substituted a title of your own for "Your Title: Describe Your Title," don't worry if your version of START.HTM differs in this regard. Otherwise, your START.HTM should look like the example.

Saving Your Scratch Pad File

Save your "scratch pad" file that you'll be using in this afternoon's tutorial. In Notepad, follow these steps:

1. Select File, Save As.
2. Change the folder to C:\HTML and then save your file as SCRATCH2.HTM.

Working with Text

This section covers some additional things you can do when working with text that weren't covered in the Basic HTML Tutorial, including using additional HTML 3.2 text highlighting tags and some new HTML 4.0 text highlighting tags, as well as right-aligning and center-aligning paragraphs, headings, and other document sections.

HTML 3.2 Text Highlighting Tags

HTML 3.2 recognizes a number of character rendering tags, including the SUP (Superscript), SUB (Subscript), U (Underline), and STRIKE (Strikethrough) tags.

SUP, SUB, and U were all proposed HTML 3.0 tags that have been implemented widely in current browsers. The STRIKE tag was a proposed HTML 2.0 tag that never made it to the final cut, but it nonetheless gained wide acceptance from browsers anyway. An S tag for strikethrough was proposed for HTML 3.0 but was dropped in favor of STRIKE in HTML 3.2. (The S tag has since been added back into HTML 4.0 and is covered in the "HTML 4.0 Text Highlighting Tags" section that follows.)

The SUP and SUB tags are highly useful tags that you should use wherever you need superscripts or subscripts. The STRIKE command comes in handy mainly when you're using the Web in workgroup document preparation processes, rather than for displaying final renditions. Most current Web browsers support these tags.

The U tag was not initially supported by Netscape Navigator 2.0 but has since been supported by Navigator 3.0 and later versions. Internet Explorer has always supported the U tag, as have a number of other browsers, including NCSA Mosaic. Because quite a few people are still using Navigator 2.0 (and even Navigator 1.0), you should avoid the U tag. Quite frankly, adding underlining in HTML files doesn't make much sense—underlining is merely a convention from the old typewriter days when it was used to emphasize text. If you want to emphasize text, use the I or EM tags instead.

If you want to check out how these tags look in your browser, enter the following code:

```
<P>This is regular text. <SUP>Use SUP for superscripts.</SUP> This is
regular text. <SUB>Use SUB for subscripts.</SUB> This is regular
text. <U>Use U for underlining.</U> This is regular text. <STRIKE>Use
STRIKE for strikethrough.</STRIKE>
```

Figure 3.1 shows how this appears in an HTML 3.2–compliant Web browser.

TIP

■ ■

Browser's that aren't HTML 3.2–compliant generally won't display superscripts or subscripts. To account for these browsers, enclose superscripts or subscripts within parentheses to set them apart from preceding or following text. For instance, to include a superscripted trademark symbol, you might type:

```
Xerox<SUP>(TM)</SUP>
```

That way, it appears in Lynx as "Xerox(TM)" rather than as "XeroxTM." The tradeoff here, of course, is that in a browser that does support superscripting, you're stuck with the parentheses—but, oh well, who ever said it was a perfect world?

■ ■

Figure 3.1

In HTML 3.2, you can add superscripting, subscripting, underlining, and strikethrough to text.

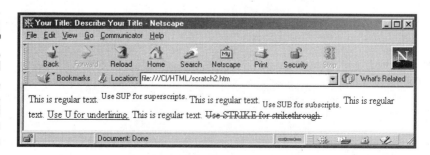

HTML 4.0 Text Highlighting Tags

A number of new text highlighting tags have been incorporated in HTML 4.0. These include the DEL (Delete), INS (Insert), S (Strikethrough), Q (Quote), and SPAN tags. So far, the DEL and INS tags are only supported by the 4.0 version of Internet Explorer. The 4.0 version of Navigator does not support either of these tags. Neither browser yet supports the Q tag, but both support the S tag. The SPAN tag is supported by the 4.0 versions of both Navigator and Internet Explorer.

The DEL (Delete) and INS (Insert) Tags

The DEL and INS tags allow you to mark deletions and insertions in an HTML file. Enter the following code for an example of using these tags:

```
<P><DEL>This text is marked for deletion.</DEL> This is regular text.
<INS>This text is marked for insertion.</INS>
```

Figure 3.2 shows how this appears in Internet Explorer 4.01.

NOTE   Two attributes, CITE and DATETIME, can be used with the DEL and INS tags. Neither of these attributes, however, are supported by current browsers. They might be utilized, at some point, by third-party software tools that automate workgroup HTML document revision, in which case I can only assume these attributes would automatically be inserted for you. If you're into hand-coding your HTML, don't bother. To find out more about these attributes, see Appendix A, "Quick HTML Reference."

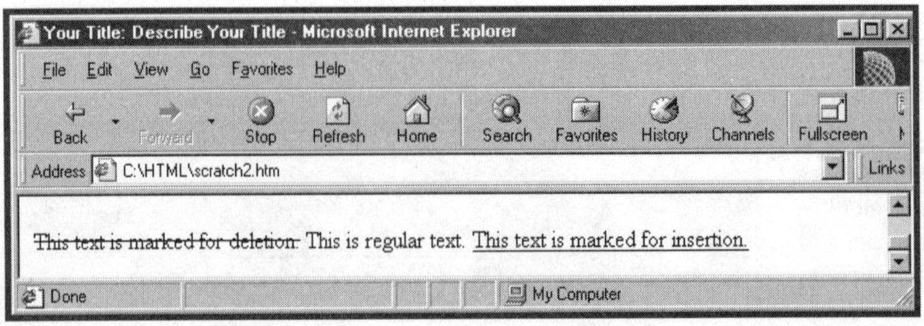

Figure 3.2

In HTML 4.0, you can mark deletions and insertions, but so far this only works in the latest version of Internet Explorer.

Your Title: Describe Your Title - Microsoft Internet Explorer
File   Edit   View   Go   Favorites   Help
Back   Forward   Stop   Refresh   Home   Search   Favorites   History   Channels   Fullscreen
Address C:\HTML\scratch2.htm   Links
~~This text is marked for deletion.~~ This is regular text. <u>This text is marked for insertion.</u>
Done   My Computer

The S (Strikethrough) Tag

The S (Strikethrough) tag should be displayed in a browser that supports it exactly the same as the STRIKE or DEL tags. The STRIKE tag was covered this morning in the Basic HTML Tutorial. Even though the S tag is supported by the latest versions of both Navigator and Internet Explorer, it's hardly worth bothering with because earlier versions of Navigator don't support it. STRIKE is the better choice for rendering strikethrough text in that it's more likely to be supported by both older and newer browsers.

TIP

Nothing stops you from using a scattergun approach to snag as many browsers as possible. For instance, `<DEL><STRIKE><S>strikeout text</S></STRIKE></DEL>` will render strikeout text in any browser that supports any of these tags.

The Q (Quote) Tag

The Q (Quote) tag, on the other hand, could potentially be quite useful. It's supposed to be a "smart" container tag that will automatically detect whether quotation marks are already present and, if absent, add the quotes that are appropriate to the language type that has been specified for the page. I also assume that a browser would display text marked with this tag in "curly" quotes, which would be pretty neat. Unfortunately, no browser currently supports this tag.

The SPAN Tag

The SPAN tag is a kind of general-purpose text highlighting element. By itself, SPAN does absolutely nothing, but in a style sheet, it comes to life. For an example of how the SPAN tag works with a style sheet, enter the following code:

```
<P>Regular text. <SPAN>Spanned text.</SPAN> Regular text
```

Next, nest the following code inside the HEAD element, right after the TITLE element:

```
<TITLE>Your Title: Describe Your Title</TITLE>
<STYLE type="text/css">
```

```
<!--
SPAN {font-family: sans-serif; font-style: italic; font-size: 125%;
➥color: #FF8000}
-->
</STYLE>
</HEAD>
```

NOTE

Notice the "comment" tags (`<!--` and `-->`) in the previous example. The STYLE tag can actually be placed anywhere in an HTML file, not just in the HEAD element. A Web browser that's savvy to styles will simply ignore the comment tags, whereas one that isn't will read the contents of the STYLE tag as a comment and not display any of it. So, why use the comment tags in the HEAD element? Because if you don't include the comment tags, search engine robots are liable to index and display your STYLE tag rather than the first sentences or paragraph of your page.

Figure 3.3 shows how this appears in a Web browser that supports using Cascading Style Sheets.

This is just a small sample of what can be done with style sheets. I'll show you more examples of using style in the Table Tutorial scheduled for this evening. I've also included with the example files an example HTML file, STYLE.HTM, which includes a sample style sheet. For links to where you can find out more about using cascading style sheets, see Web Links at the Web site for this book.

ON THE

CD

A shareware software program, CoffeeCup StyleSheet Maker++, is included on the CD-ROM that can help you automate creating HTML style sheets for your Web pages.

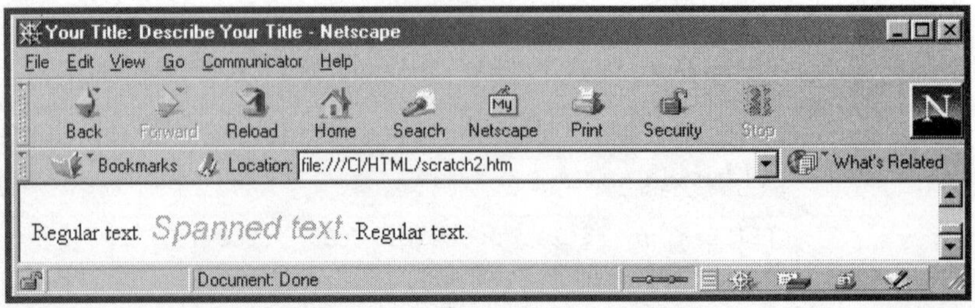

Figure 3.3

In HTML 4.0, you can use the SPAN tag to apply a style to a "span" of text.

Your Title: Describe Your Title - Netscape

File Edit View Go Communicator Help

Back Forward Reload Home Search Netscape Print Security Stop

Bookmarks Location: file:///C|/HTML/scratch2.htm   What's Related

Regular text. *Spanned text.* Regular text.

Document: Done

Aligning Headings, Paragraphs, and Divisions

You can align paragraphs, headings, and other document divisions in a number of ways in HTML 3.2. You can use the ALIGN attribute with paragraphs and headings to center-align, right-align, or left-align these elements. A new HTML 3.2 element, the DIV tag, can also be used with the ALIGN attribute. Additionally, you can use the CENTER tag to center-align any of the divisions noted here, plus many other document elements. The following sections look at each of these individually.

Aligning Headings and Paragraphs

In HTML 3.2, you can use the ALIGN attribute to center-align or right-align headings and paragraphs by using an attribute value of either "center" or "right" ("left" is the default). For instance, to center-align a level-two heading, you would tag your heading like this:

```
<H2 ALIGN="center">Your Heading Here</H2>
```

You would right-align a level-two heading, like this:

```
<H2 ALIGN="right">Your Heading Here</H2>
```

You would center-align or right-align paragraph text in exactly the same way as headings. For instance, to center-align a text paragraph, you would tag your paragraph like this:

```
<P ALIGN="center">Your paragraph text here.
```

You would right-align a text paragraph like this:

```
<P ALIGN="right">Your paragraph text here.
```

To see what this looks like in your browser, enter the following code, save your file, and hop over to your browser to check it out:

```
<H3 ALIGN="right">This is a Right-Aligned Level-Three Heading</H3>
<P ALIGN="right">This is a right-aligned text paragraph. This is a
right-aligned text paragraph. This is a right-aligned text paragraph.
This is a right-aligned text paragraph.
<H3 ALIGN="center">This is a Center-Aligned Level-Three Heading</H3>
```

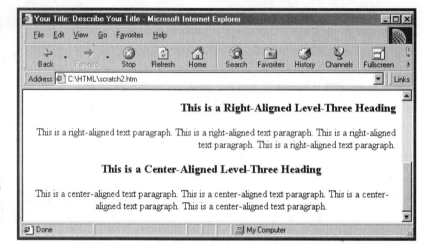

Figure 3.4

You can right-align or center headings and paragraphs.

```
<P ALIGN="center">This is a center-aligned text paragraph. This is a
center-aligned text paragraph. This is a center-aligned text para-
graph. This is a center-aligned text paragraph.
```

Figure 3.4 shows how this appears in a Web browser that supports horizontal alignment of headings and paragraphs.

Aligning Document Divisions

The DIV (Division) tag defines a division within a document. Within it, you can nest and align headings, paragraphs, unordered and ordered lists, definition lists, preformatted text, address blocks, tables, and even images.

The DIV tag is an HTML 3.2 element that was previously an HTML 3.0 proposed tag. It allows you, for instance, to block tag a whole section (a division) of a document as right-aligned or centered. It is also a very handy tag to use in conjunction with a style sheet.

Enter the following code for an example of using the DIV tag to apply center alignment to a document division that includes a level-two heading, a paragraph, and a bullet list:

```
<DIV ALIGN="center">
<H2>Level-Two Heading</H2>
<P>This paragraph, and the level-two heading above it, is centered
```

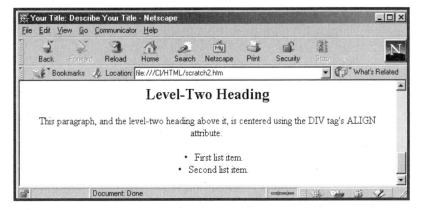

Figure 3.5

You can center (or right-align) a document division (here including the heading), paragraph text, and a bullet list using the DIV tag.

```
using the DIV tag's ALIGN attribute.
<UL>
<LI>First list item.
<LI>Second list item.
</UL>
</DIV>
```

Figure 3.5 shows how this appears in a Web browser.

The DIV tag also works well for aligning images. For an example of using the DIV tag to align inline images, see "Working with Images," later in this session.

Style sheets, which are part of HTML 4.0, make this tag even more useful, allowing you to apply different formatting or display characteristics to different sections of a document, such as a table of contents, an index, or a glossary. To find out more about using style sheets in your Web pages, go to this book's Web site and click the Web Links button.

Using the CENTER Tag

The CENTER tag is a Netscape extension that has been included in HTML 3.2, where it now officially represents a shortcut for `<DIV ALIGN="center">`. Anything that can be nested inside a DIV element can also be nested in a CENTER element. All current browsers support the use of the CENTER tag.

For an example of using the CENTER element to center-align text and other document elements, copy and paste the text you just entered for the DIV tag. Edit it, replacing `<DIV ALIGN="center">` and `</DIV>` with `<CENTER>` and `</CENTER>`, so it looks like this:

```
<CENTER>
<H2>Level-Two Heading</H2>
<P>This paragraph, and the level-two heading above it, is centered-
➥aligned using the CENTER tag.
<UL>
<LI>First list item.
<LI>Second list item.
</UL>
</CENTER>
```

The end result in your browser should look the same as when you used the DIV tag with center alignment set, as shown previously in Figure 3.5.

 TIP   ■

Some older browsers, such as Navigator 2.0, support the CENTER tag but not the DIV tag. Some other browsers may support the DIV tag but ignore the CENTER tag. To cover all bases, just combine both at the same time, like this:

```
<CENTER><DIV ALIGN="center">The text to be centered.</DIV></CENTER>
```

■ ■

Working with Images

The Basic HTML Tutorial covered adding inline images to your Web page, as well as vertically aligning an inline image relative to the top, middle, and bottom of a line of text. It also covered using the ALT attribute with inline images to make life easier for users of text-only browsers or graphical browsers with display of graphics turned off. This section of the Intermediate HTML Tutorial covers several additional things you can do with inline images, such as using a banner graphic, right-aligning or center-aligning a graphic, wrapping text around a graphic, and creating image links.

Adding a Banner Graphic

A *banner graphic* is an inline image that runs along the top of your Web page. It might be your company name or logo, or perhaps a piece of art to add some graphic appeal and pizzazz to your page. You don't have to create a banner graphic right now—the following example uses a sample banner graphic I've created and included with the tutorial example files.

Of course, if you want to create your own banner graphic, go ahead. Just use a graphics editor such as Paint Shop Pro (included on the CD-ROM) to create a GIF or JPG file. You want to keep your graphic smaller than 600 pixels wide (my sample graphic is 595 by 134 pixels).

NOTE If you create a banner graphic that is wider than 600 pixels, it may be too wide to be completely displayed in a browser's maximized window running in 640 by 480 screen resolution. If the browser window is not maximized, it may allow even less space to display the banner.

To add the example banner graphic to your Web page, go to the top of your Web page and add the following code (if you've created a banner graphic of your own you'd like to use, just copy it to C:\HTML and substitute its file name for "banner.gif" below):

```
<BODY>
<P ALIGN="center"><IMG SRC="banner.gif">
<H1 ALIGN="center">The Intermediate HTML Tutorial</H1>
```

Even if your banner graphic takes up most or all of the screen, you should place it on a center-aligned paragraph. That way, it will always be centered, regardless of the screen resolution. I also include a centered level-one heading, because it's fairly common for a banner graphic to be followed by the main heading for the page.

Also, in this example, the SRC attribute uses a relative URL, the file name of the banner graphic file. As long as an image is in the same folder as the Web page in which you want to display it, you only need to use the file name as the SRC attribute value. (For more information on absolute versus relative URLs, see the section "Using Relative URLs," in the Basic HTML Tutorial.)

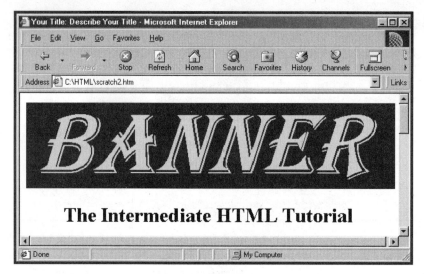

Figure 3.6

A banner graphic
runs across the top
of a Web page.

Figure 3.6 shows how your page should look after you add the banner graphic.

Reducing Image Sizes

Graphic images can take up a lot of bandwidth and are a major culprit behind slow-loading Web pages. Smart Web publishers do everything they can to reduce the size of the images they use on their Web pages.

One way to manipulate the size of an image is to change its format. Although all the example graphics used in this book are GIF format graphics, most current Web browsers now allow you to display both GIF and JPG graphics as inline images. GIF graphics are limited to 256 colors, whereas JPG graphics can have up to 16.7 million colors. JPG graphics also use a compression scheme that can make a continuous-tone color or grayscale photograph smaller than a corresponding GIF image. With images other than photos, a GIF file is almost always smaller than a JPG file. Therefore, if you want to include continuous-tone photographic images, JPG is the best format to use. For other images, stick to GIFs.

NOTE You need to look out for two things when it comes to using JPG files. First, JPG files use what is called *lossy compression*, which achieves file size reductions by selectively subtracting pixels from the image. If the compression ratio is set too high, it can have a deleterious effect on image quality. Finding the right compression ratio for a JPG image usually takes a bit of experimenting—you need to save an image (do it under another file name, so you can compare it against your original), check out the results, and then adjust the compression level up or down until you find the best mix of keeping your image sizes down (very important on the Web) while retaining satisfactory image quality.

Another way to reduce the size of a graphics file is to reduce its color depth. Many graphic editors and photo-paint programs, such as Paint Shop Pro, Adobe Photoshop, or even LView Pro, can do this.

You can also switch the color palette of the image to one that includes fewer colors (from 256 colors to 16 colors, for instance). However, although switching to a color palette that includes fewer or different colors than those in the original image will shrink the file size, it may also result in a significant loss of image quality. One solution is to create an *adaptive palette* that matches the actual colors in the graphic. For instance, you might have a palette of 16 colors but an image that has only eight colors in it—by creating an adaptive palette that has only those specific eight colors in it, you could significantly reduce the size of the file with no loss in image quality. The actual methods for doing this will vary according to the graphics program used.

Setting Image Height and Width

HTML 3.2 allows you to specify the height and width of an inline image. Normally, a Web browser has to download an image before allocating space for it on a Web page. This means that if you have a relatively large graphic, everything else has to wait until the image downloads. A banner graphic, usually the largest graphic on your page, can be especially guilty of this.

However, if you set the dimensions of the graphic using the HEIGHT and WIDTH attributes of the IMG tag, Netscape Navigator and Internet Explorer can allocate space for the graphic and then display the remainder of the page without waiting for the banner graphic to download completely. Therefore, if

you want to use a banner graphic, especially if it takes longer to load than it takes ice to melt, be gracious and set the height and width of the image. Here's how to add WIDTH and HEIGHT attributes to your banner graphic:

```
<P ALIGN="center"><IMG SRC="banner.gif" WIDTH="595" HEIGHT="134">
```

The dimensions set here are the actual dimensions of the graphic. Using dimensions other than the actual ones provides no immediate advantage in this case. True, you could increase the dimensions of a smaller graphic to fit, but image quality would probably suffer. Likewise, you could reduce the dimensions of a larger graphic to fit, but that would be a waste of band-width—better that you reduce it to fit in your graphic editor rather than on your Web page.

◄ ◄

Bandwidth is the transmission capacity of a network, but also the amount of capacity being consumed by a single connection. A Web page containing many graphics will consume more bandwidth than one containing only text.

◄ ◄

Many Web gurus will tell you to set the WIDTH and HEIGHT attributes for *all* images you want to include in a Web page. I, quite frankly, don't bother doing this for small graphics such as icon bullets, but I do include them in any other images. Also, note that I don't bother including these attributes in the other example images used in this tutorial, because the scratch pad file you're creating will only be viewed by you locally. If you were to put the tutorial up on the Web as a regular Web page, you would probably want to add WIDTH and HEIGHT attributes to any images other than really small ones.

Using Width Percentages

You can also specify a percentage for the WIDTH attribute in the IMG tag. For instance, to set a width of 75 percent, you would use a WIDTH attribute of 75%, like this:

```
<P ALIGN="center"><IMG SRC="banner.gif" WIDTH="75%">
```

This will automatically resize the graphic so it fills 75 percent of the width of the browser window, regardless of the screen resolution or the width of the browser window. The height of the graphic will be resized relative to the

width. Setting the HEIGHT attribute to a percentage should be avoided. Also, realize that older browsers that don't support WIDTH percentages will display the image at its actual size.

Using Interlaced and Transparent GIF Graphics

An interlaced GIF will load progressively over several passes, generating what has been called a *venetian blind effect*. It allows the reader to see what the image is going to be before it comes through. A transparent GIF is a GIF graphic that has one of its colors set to transparent, allowing any background color or background image to show through the graphic. This can be handy if you want your graphic to look like it's floating on top of the background.

I cover creating interlaced and transparent GIF graphics in the Graphics Tutorial that's scheduled as a bonus session for Sunday evening.

Horizontally Aligning Images

In the Basic HTML Tutorial, you used the ALIGN attribute to vertically align an image relative to a line of text. Contrary to what you might think, you can't use ALIGN attributes in the IMG tag to right-align or center an image.

Two additional ALIGN attribute values exist: `ALIGN="left"` and `ALIGN="right"`. However, these attribute values are not used to left- or right-align an image—they're used to wrap text or other elements around the right or left side of an image. For information on using these attribute values, see "Wrapping Text Around Images," later in this tutorial.

The best way to horizontally align an image on your Web page is to place it in a center- or right-aligned paragraph. (You could also place it in a center- or right-aligned DIV tag, or inside a CENTER tag.)

Right-Aligning an Image

Go to the end of your file, just above the </BODY> and </HTML> end tags, and enter the following line of code to right-align an image using paragraph alignment:

```
<P ALIGN="right"><IMG SRC="right.gif">
```

Figure 3.7

You can right-align an image in an HTML 3.2–compliant Web browser by placing it inside a right-aligned paragraph.

Figure 3.7

You can right-align an image in an HTML 3.2–compliant Web browser by placing it inside a right-aligned paragraph.

Figure 3.7 shows how a right-aligned graphic looks in a Web browser that supports paragraph alignment.

Centering an Image

To center an image using paragraph alignment, enter this:

```
<P ALIGN="center"><IMG SRC="center.gif">
```

Figure 3.8 shows how this appears in a Web browser that supports paragraph alignment.

Other Ways to Horizontally Align Images

You can also use the DIV or the CENTER tag to horizontally align an image. The CENTER tag is more widely supported, but the DIV tag allows

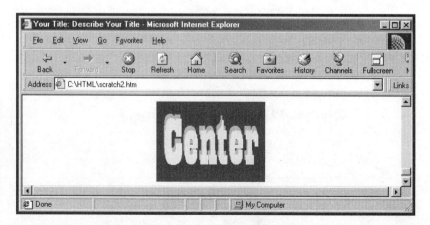

Figure 3.8

You can center an image in an HTML 3.2–compliant Web browser by placing it inside a center-aligned paragraph.

you to right-align an image as well. (Philosophically, however, the DIV tag is intended for displaying whole divisions within an HTML document, not just single elements.) Here are some examples of using these tags to right-align or center an image:

```
<DIV ALIGN="right"><IMG SRC="right.gif"></DIV>
<DIV ALIGN="center"><IMG SRC="center.gif"></DIV>
<CENTER><IMG SRC="center.gif"></CENTER>
```

Wrapping Text Around Images

In the Basic HTML Tutorial, you learned how to align an image relative to a line of text using the ALIGN attribute values of "top," "bottom," and "middle." In addition to these attribute values, HTML 3.2 allows you to set two additional ALIGN attribute values: "left" and "right." You might think that the purpose of these attributes is to align an image at either the left or right margin, but that's not so. Rather, these attributes are used to wrap text around the right side or left side of an image.

Wrapping Text Around a Left-Aligned Image

Enter the following code as an example of wrapping text around a left-aligned image:

```
<P><IMG ALIGN="left" SRC="left.gif">If you set left-alignment in an
inline image, the text will wrap around the right side of the graph-
ic. If you set left-alignment in an inline image, the text will wrap
around the right side of the graphic. If you set left-alignment in
an inline image, the text will wrap around the right side of the
graphic.<BR CLEAR="left">
```

NOTE You're probably wondering what the <BR CLEAR="left"> code is doing at the end of the paragraph. You'll notice similar BR tags using the CLEAR attribute in some of the following examples. Their purpose is to stop the text from wrapping—otherwise, the following image is liable to wrap as well. Later, in the "Clearing Images" section, I'll tell you more about using the CLEAR attribute.

Wrapping Text Around a Right-Aligned Image

Enter the following code as an example of wrapping text around a right-aligned image:

```
<P><IMG ALIGN="right" SRC="right.gif">If you set right-alignment in
an inline image, the text will wrap around the left side of the
graphic. If you set right-alignment in an inline image, the text
will wrap around the left side of the graphic. If you set right-
alignment in an inline image, the text will wrap around the left
side of the graphic.<BR CLEAR="right">
```

Figure 3.9 shows text wrapped around both a left-aligned and a right-aligned image in a Web browser.

You aren't limited to just wrapping text around an image. All other elements, including headings, lists, and other images, will wrap around an image with either left or right alignment set. (You don't have to do anything to make this happen, other than use a left- or right-aligned image. The trick is stopping it from happening. For that, see "Clearing Images," later in this tutorial.)

Adding Spacing Between an Image and Wrapping Text

When you hopped over to take a look at the last example in your browser, you may have noticed that text wrapping around an image, especially around

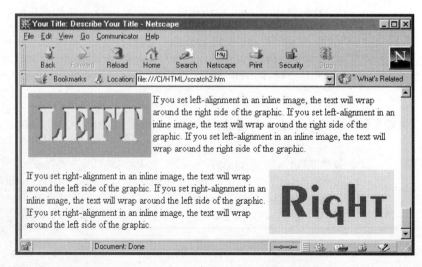

Figure 3.9

Using the IMG tag's ALIGN attribute, you can wrap text around the left or right side of an image.

a left-aligned image, is not separated from the image by much space. To add spacing between wrapping text and a left- or right-aligned image, you can insert an HSPACE (Horizontal Space) attribute in the IMG tag. Edit the example you created for wrapping text around a left-aligned image and add the following code to insert 10 pixels on either side of the image:

```
<P><IMG ALIGN="left" SRC="left.gif" HSPACE="10">If you set left-
alignment in an inline image, the text will wrap around the right
side of the graphic. If you set left-alignment in an inline image,
the text will wrap around the right side of the graphic. If you set
left-alignment in an inline image, the text will wrap around the
right side of the graphic.<BR CLEAR="left">
```

Figure 3.10 shows what this looks like in a Web browser.

Flowing Text Between Images

You not only can wrap text around the right or left side of an image, you can also flow text between two images. For example, enter the following code:

```
<P><IMG ALIGN="left" SRC="left.gif"><IMG ALIGN="right"
SRC="right.gif">Text will flow between a left-aligned and a right-
aligned image. Text will flow between a left-aligned and a right-
aligned image.<BR CLEAR="all">
```

Figure 3.11 shows what this looks like in a Web browser.

Figure 3.10

Using the IMG tag's HSPACE attribute, you can add space between an image and wrapping text.

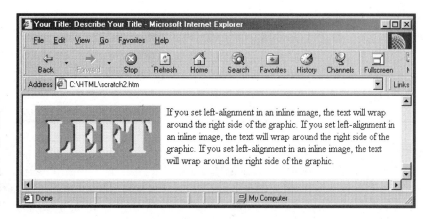

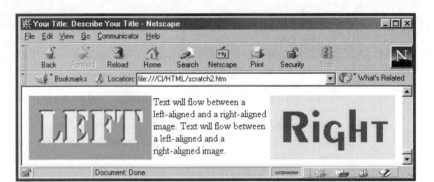

Figure 3.11

You can flow text
between a left-
aligned image and
a right-aligned
image in an HTML
3.2–compliant
Web browser.

Flowing an Image Between Two Other Images

You can even flow a center-aligned image between a left-aligned image and
a right-aligned image. This is a bit of a parlor trick, but both Navigator and
Internet Explorer handle it fine, as does Opera 3.21 (included on the CD-
ROM). I've seen some other supposedly HTML 3.2–compliant browsers
flub this though, usually by not aligning the middle image even with the
other images.

For an example of how to do this, enter the following code:

```
<P><IMG ALIGN="left" SRC="one.gif"><IMG ALIGN="right"
SRC="three.gif"><P ALIGN="center"><IMG SRC="two.gif"><BR CLEAR="all">
```

Notice that two P (Paragraph) tags are used. The first one is used to hold the
left- and right-aligned images (ONE.GIF and THREE.GIF), whereas the
second is used to center-align the image that flows between the two other
images.

See Figure 3.12 for what this *should* look like in an HTML 3.2–compliant
Web browser.

Clearing Images

The BR tag's CLEAR attribute, as its name indicates, is used to cause anything that follows to *clear* a horizontally aligned image. The CLEAR attribute
can take three values: "left," "right," and "all." `CLEAR="left"` moves down

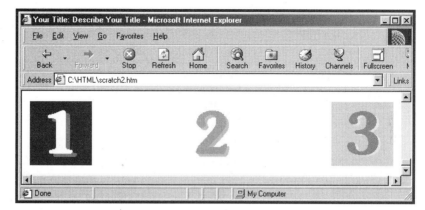

Figure 3.12

You can also flow an image between a left-aligned image and a right-aligned image.

following text or elements until the left margin is clear (unobstructed by a left-aligned image). CLEAR="right" moves down all following text or elements until the right margin is clear (unobstructed by a right-aligned image). CLEAR="all" moves down all following text or elements until both the right and left margins are clear (unobstructed by either a left-aligned or a right-aligned image).

Clearing a Left-Aligned Image

To see how this works with a left-aligned image, go back to the example you created earlier for wrapping text around a left-aligned image and then insert the following BR tag (or just retype the example shown here):

```
<P><IMG ALIGN="left" SRC="left.gif">If you set left-alignment in
➥an inline image, the text will wrap around the right side of the
➥graphic.
<BR CLEAR="left">
If you set left-alignment in an inline image, the text will wrap
➥around the right side of the graphic. If you set left-alignment in
➥an inline image, the text will wrap around the right side of the
➥graphic.<BR CLEAR="left">
```

As Figure 3.13 shows, CLEAR="left" has the effect of moving all following text past a left-aligned graphic to a position where the left margin is clear.

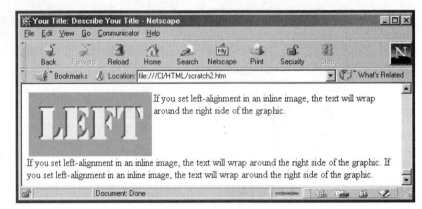

Clearing a Right-Aligned Image

To see how this works with a right-aligned graphic, in the example you created earlier for wrapping text around a right-aligned image, insert the following BR tag (or just retype the example shown here):

```
<P><IMG ALIGN="right" SRC="right.gif">If you set right-alignment in
➥an inline image, the text will wrap around the left side of the
➥graphic.
<BR CLEAR="right">
If you set right-alignment in an inline image, the text will wrap
➥around the left side of the graphic. If you set right-alignment in
➥an inline image, the text will wrap around the left side of the
➥graphic.<BR CLEAR="right">
```

As you can see in Figure 3.14, the CLEAR="right" attribute has the effect of
moving all following text past a right-aligned graphic to a position where the
right margin is clear.

Clearing Both Left-Aligned
and Right-Aligned Images

Finally, to see how this works when flowing text between both a left-aligned
and a right-aligned graphic, insert the following code into the example you

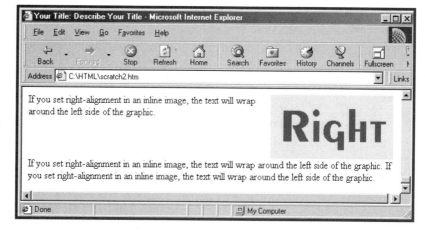

Figure 3.14

A BR tag with
`CLEAR="right"`
set will cause
following text to
break past a right-
aligned image.

created for flowing text between a left-aligned image and a right-aligned image (or just retype the example shown here):

```
<P><IMG ALIGN="left" SRC="left.gif"><IMG ALIGN="right"
➥SRC="right.gif">Text will flow between a left-aligned and a
➥right-aligned image.
<BR CLEAR="all">
Text will flow between a left-aligned and a right-aligned image.<BR
➥CLEAR="all">
```

As Figure 3.15 shows, the `CLEAR="all"` attribute has the effect of moving all following text past a left-aligned graphic and a right-aligned graphic to a position where both margins are clear.

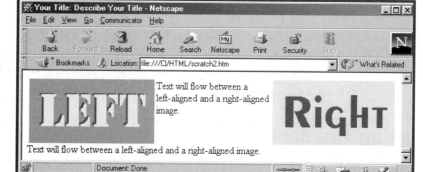

Figure 3.15

A BR tag with
`CLEAR="all"` set
will cause following
text to break past
both a left-aligned
image and a right-
aligned image.

Creating Image Links

In the Basic HTML Tutorial, you learned how to place inline images on your page, and you also learned how to create hypertext links. What you haven't learned yet, however, is how to create an inline image that functions as a hypertext link, where clicking on the image will activate the link. Hey, if you want to brag about knowing HTML, you've got to know how to create image links!

Including an Image in a Link

To activate an image as a hypertext link, all you have to do is nest it inside an A (Anchor) tag, like this:

```
<P><A HREF= "link.htm">
<IMG SRC= "link.gif">This is the text.</A>
```

You'll be using this same text, or close variants of it in several of the following examples. To save yourself some retyping, copy the example text you just created to the Clipboard (click and drag to highlight it with the mouse, then press Ctrl+C to copy it). Later, when needed, you can just paste it in from the Clipboard (Ctrl+V) rather than having to retype it.

I've included LINK.HTM with the example files you installed this morning so that if you click the image in your browser, you can see how the link works. Just click the Back button in your browser to return to SCRATCH2.HTM.

Figure 3.16 shows that when an image is placed inside a hypertext link, the image itself becomes a *hot link*.

NOTE   If you include ALIGN="right" in the IMG tag in the previous example, the image will be displayed flush to the right margin while still being included in the link.

Using an Image Link by Itself

In the previous example, the link included both the image and the text, meaning that clicking on either one activates the link. You can also specify the image, but not the text, as the link. Press Ctrl+V to paste in the example

Figure 3.16

The image,
displayed with a
blue border, and
the link text,
underlined with a
blue line, are both
part of the same
hypertext link.

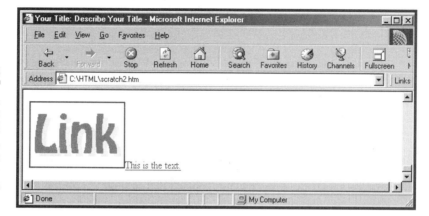

Figure 3.16

The image,
displayed with a
blue border, and
the link text,
underlined with a
blue line, are both
part of the same
hypertext link.

that you previously copied to the Clipboard, then move the </A> end tag so
only the image is enclosed within the A (Anchor) start and end tags, like this:

```
<P><A HREF="link.htm">
<IMG SRC="link.gif"></A>This is the text.
```

Figure 3.17 shows how this looks in a Web browser.

Using Navigational Icons

A navigational icon is often used when a picture, by itself, is enough to convey the action that will occur when the user activates the link. For instance,
a left-hand arrow at the top or bottom of a page indicates returning to the
previous page, a right-hand arrow indicates going to the next page, and a
house indicates returning to the home page. You create a navigational icon

Figure 3.17

An image, by itself,
can function as a
hypertext link when
placed inside an A
(Anchor) tag.

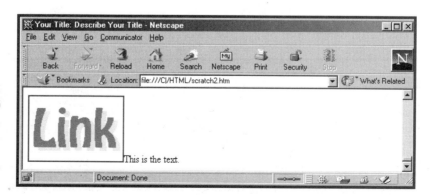

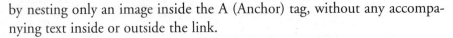

by nesting only an image inside the A (Anchor) tag, without any accompanying text inside or outside the link.

To take care of text-only browsers or graphical browsers with graphics turned off, you should always include ALT text in a navigational icon's IMG tag, indicating that it's a link and describing what it links to. Here's an example of including ALT text in an image link:

```
<P><A HREF="prev.htm">
<IMG SRC="back.gif" ALT="Go to Previous Page"></A>
```

Figure 3.18 shows the navigational icon as it appears in a Web browser with the display of graphics turned on. Figure 3.19 shows this same image with the display of graphics turned off.

You'll have to exit and rerun Navigator before turning the display of graphics off will take effect. If you're using Navigator, feel free to skip this right now if you wish. In Explorer, click the Refresh button after turning the graphics display off to cause the setting to take effect immediately. In case you want to try this, I've included the steps for Navigator 4.0 and Internet Explorer 4.0 to turn the display of images off.

Figure 3.18

Navigational icons are usually displayed by themselves, without any accompanying text.

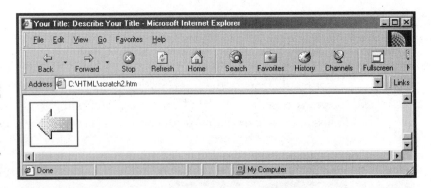

Figure 3.19

Including ALT text in the IMG tag for a navigation icon will clue in users who have turned the graphics display off or who use a text-only browser.

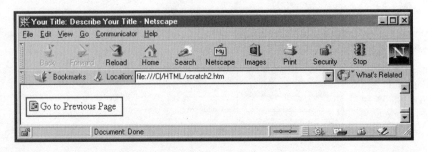

In Netscape Navigator 4.0 or greater, follow these steps:

1. Select Edit, Preferences; then select Advanced in the Categories menu.
2. Click the "Automatically load images" check box so that it's unchecked. Click OK.
3. Exit and then rerun Navigator. Open C:\HTML\SCRATCH2.HTM.
4. Follow the same steps to turn the display of images back on (you don't have to exit and rerun Navigator, however—just click the Reload button or press Ctrl+R).

In Internet Explorer 4.0 or greater, follow these steps:

1. Select View, Options (in Internet Explorer 4.0) or Internet Options (in Internet Explorer 4.01); then select the Advanced tab.
2. Under Multimedia, click the "Show pictures" check box so that it's unchecked. Click OK.
3. Click the Refresh button (or press Ctrl+R).
4. Follow the same steps to turn the display of images back on.

Controlling Image Link Borders

The IMG tag's BORDER attribute allows you to specify a custom width for the border that is displayed around an image link. The default border-width may vary from browser to browser (it's two pixels in Navigator). Press Ctrl+V to paste in the example that you previously copied to the Clipboard, then increase the width of the border around the image link to 10 pixels, like this:

```
<P><A HREF="link.htm">
<IMG SRC="link.gif" BORDER="10">This is the text.</A>
```

As shown in Figure 3.20, when you increase the border width to 10 pixels, you *really* increase it.

NOTE If you previously clicked the LINK.HTM link, the border around your image link will not be blue but rather whatever color is set for displaying visited links. To see what this will look like in blue, you'll need to clear your browser's History list. In Internet Explorer 4.01, select View, Internet Options, click the General tab, and then click the Clear History button. In Netscape Navigator 4.0, select Edit, Preferences and then click the Clear History button.

Figure 3.20

Using the BORDER attribute in the IMG tag, you can increase the width of the border around an image link.

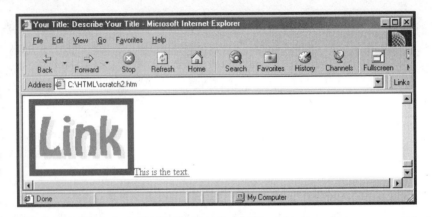

Turning the Image Link Border Off

Navigational icons often have their borders turned off. You may want to turn the border of an image link off in other situations. Press Ctrl+V to paste in the example that you previously copied to the Clipboard, then insert a BORDER attribute set to zero, like this, to turn off the image link border:

```
<P><A HREF="link.htm">
<IMG SRC="link.gif" BORDER="0">This is the text.</A>
```

Figure 3.21 shows how this should look in a Web browser.

Aligning Image Links and Text

You have many available ways to align image links relative to associated link text or descriptive text. The following are just some of the possibilities.

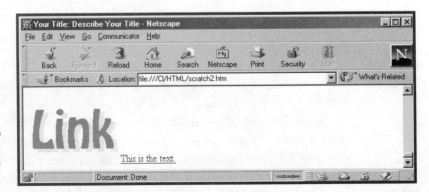

Figure 3.21

Even without a border, the image here is still a link.

Vertically Aligning the Link Text

You can use the "top" and "middle" ALIGN attribute values ("bottom" is the default) in the IMG tag to horizontally align link text with an adjacent image link. For this example, press Ctrl+V to paste in the example that you previously copied to the Clipboard, and then insert ALIGN="middle" in the IMG tag, like this:

```
<P><A HREF="link.htm">
<IMG SRC="link.gif" ALIGN="middle">This is the text.</A>
```

See Figure 3.22 for how this should look in a Web browser.

To align the link text with the top of the image link, you would just insert ALIGN="top" as the attribute value.

NOTE You can position only a single line of text relative to an image using ALIGN="top" or ALIGN="middle"—any additional lines will wrap below the image.

Horizontally Aligning the Image Link

You can also align an image link relative to the Web page by using an ALIGN attribute in the P (Paragraph) tag that contains the link. For example, to center the link text and image link relative to the page, add the following code:

```
<P ALIGN="center"><A HREF="link.htm">
<IMG SRC="link.gif" ALIGN="middle">This is the text.</A>
```

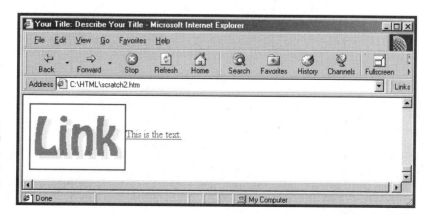

Figure 3.22

You can middle-align an image link relative to the link text.

Figure 3.23

You can center an
image link and link
text by placing
them in a center-
aligned paragraph.

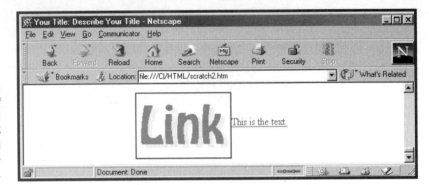

Figure 3.23 shows the centered image and text.

Using a right-aligned paragraph in the HTML code for Figure 3.23 rather
than a center-aligned one would cause the link text and image link to be
right aligned. Left alignment, on the other hand, is the default.

Displaying the Link Text under the Image Link

You can also center the link text under the image link by inserting a BR tag
in front of the link text, as shown here:

```
<P ALIGN="center"><A HREF="link.htm">
<IMG SRC="link.gif" ALIGN="middle"><BR>This is the text.</A>
```

Figure 3.24 shows how this looks in a Web browser.

Figure 3.24

By inserting a BR
tag, you can
position the link
text beneath an
image link.

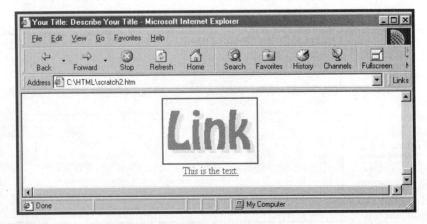

Reversing the Image Link and Link Text

You can reverse the relative position of an image link and its associated link text by placing the image link after the link text. As an example, enter the following code, with positions of the image link and link text reversed:

```
<P ALIGN="center"><A HREF="link.htm">This is the text.
<IMG SRC="link.gif"></A>
```

Figure 3.25 shows the positions of the link image and link text reversed.

Displaying the Link Text over the Image Link

You can also display link text above the image link if you've put the link text ahead of the image. All you need to do is put a BR tag at the end of the link text, as shown here:

```
<P ALIGN="center"><A HREF="link.htm">This is the text.<BR>
<IMG SRC="link.gif"></A>
```

In your browser, the link text is centered directly above the image link, as shown in Figure 3.26.

◆◆

CAUTION Whenever a center-aligned or right-aligned paragraph (using ALIGN="center" or ALIGN="right" is followed by an OL (Ordered List) or UL (Unordered List) block element, you should always add the </P> end tag at the end of the paragraph block. This is due to a rather egregious bug in Microsoft Internet Explorer 3.02—it doesn't recognize that a list should be a new block element following a paragraph and will also center- or right-align the list along with the paragraph if the </P> end tag does not precede the list.

◆◆

Figure 3.25

You can also put the link text to the left of the image link.

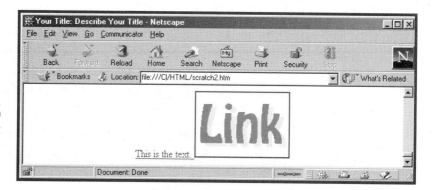

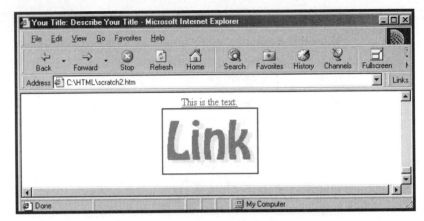

This is the text.

Link

Figure 3.26

You can center the link text directly above an image link.

Because the following examples deal with creating lists, add the </P> end tag at the end of the previous example, like this:

```
<P ALIGN="center"><A HREF="link.htm">This is the text.<BR><IMG
SRC="link.gif"></A></P>
```

Working with Lists

The Basic HTML Tutorial covered creating ordered (numbered) lists and unordered (bulleted) lists. It also covered nesting lists within each other and mixing and matching lists. This section of the Intermediate HTML Tutorial covers some additional ways you can control the display of ordered and unordered lists.

Specifying Number Types

Netscape provided the TYPE attribute as an extension to HTML 2.0 that allows you to specify the number type for an ordered (OL) list. This attribute value has been incorporated into HTML 3.2. Besides making it possible for you to specify a number type for a numbered list, this attribute also allows you to create multilevel outlines.

You can use the TYPE attribute to specify the number type for an ordered (OL) list. The values you can use with this attribute are "A" (uppercase letters), "a" (lowercase letters), "I" (uppercase roman numerals), "i" (lowercase

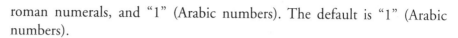

roman numerals, and "1" (Arabic numbers). The default is "1" (Arabic numbers).

Enter the following code for an example of specifying uppercase roman numerals for an ordered list:

```
<OL TYPE="I">
<LI>This is item one.
<LI>This is item two.
<LI>This is item three.
<LI>This is item four.
</OL>
```

Figure 3.27 shows how this looks in a Web browser that supports the TYPE attribute for ordered (numbered) lists.

Creating Multilevel Outlines

You might expect Web browsers to vary the number types of nested ordered lists automatically. After all, they usually automatically vary the bullet types of nested unordered (bulleted) lists, as you saw in the Basic HTML Tutorial this morning. However, no current Web browser automatically varies the number type in nested ordered lists. To vary the number types, you need to use the TYPE attribute to specify the number type for each level of the ordered list.

CAUTION You should realize, however, that a multilevel outline can look utterly awful in a Web browser that doesn't support the TYPE attribute for ordered lists; therefore, if you use this feature, you might want to label your page as "HTML 3.2 or greater only."

Figure 3.27

The TYPE="I" attribute causes an ordered list to be displayed with roman numerals.

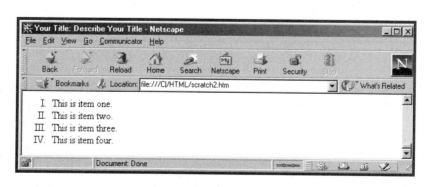

Enter the following code as an example of using TYPE attributes in the OL tag to create a multilevel outline:

> This example—and two of the next three examples—utilize spaces to indent the nested list levels and make it easier for you to visually recognize the different list levels. Feel free to tab or space to create the indents, but realize that this is for your eyes only—it will have no effect when displayed in a browser. Your browser will automatically indent nested ordered lists. Also, be careful that you "nest" instead of "overlap" the different nested list levels.

```
<OL TYPE="I">
<LI>Level-one outline level.
    <OL TYPE="A">
    <LI>Level-two outline level.
        <OL TYPE="1">
        <LI>Level-three outline level.
            <OL TYPE="a">
            <LI>Level-four outline level.
            <LI>Level-four outline level.
            </OL>
        <LI>Level-three outline level.
        </OL>
    <LI>Level-two outline level.
    </OL>
<LI>Level-one outline level.
</OL>
```

Figure 3.28 shows how this appears in an HTML 3.2–compliant Web browser. Remember, the indenting you see in the figure (or in your browser) comes from nesting the OL tags; it has nothing to do with any spaces or tabs you may have added here.

You can dress up your outline by bolding or italicizing different levels. You can also apply any of the heading-level tags to have your different outline levels appear in fonts of varying sizes. Later in this tutorial, you'll learn how to use the FONT tag to specify font sizes and colors, which you can also use to further emphasize your outline levels. When you use any of these tags to vary the size or color of an outline level, always nest the OL start and end tags inside the tags you want to use to visually differentiate your outline levels.

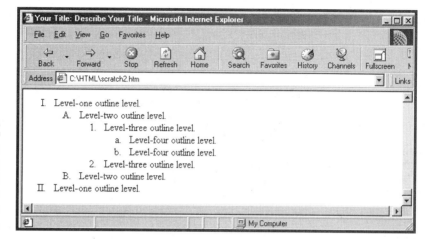

Figure 3.28

By using the TYPE attribute to assign different number types, you can create a multilevel outline.

Including Paragraphs in a Multilevel Outline

You can insert paragraphs inside a multilevel outline by inserting a paragraph following a list item. The paragraph will automatically line up vertically with the text of the preceding list item. For instance, insert the following code:

```
<OL TYPE="I">
<LI>Level-one outline level.
<P>Paragraph text following a list item will automatically be
➥indented flush with the list item text.</P>
    <OL TYPE="A">
    <LI>Level-two outline level.
    <P>Paragraph text following a list item will automatically be
    ➥indented flush with the list item text.</P>
        <OL TYPE="1">
        <LI>Level-three outline level.
        <P>Paragraph text following a list item will automatically
        ➥be indented flush with the list item text.</P>
            <OL TYPE="a">
            <LI>Level-four outline level.
            <LI>Level-four outline level
            </OL>
        <LI>Level-three outline level.
        </OL>
    <LI>Level-two outline level.
    </OL>
<LI>Level-one outline level.
</OL>
```

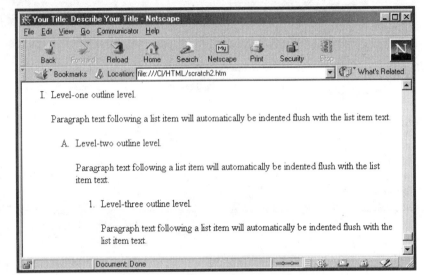

Figure 3.29

Paragraphs included in a multilevel outline automatically line up vertically with the preceding list item.

 NOTE

You'll notice in the previous example that the paragraph elements end with a </P> end tag. This is another case where you need to add the </P> end tag if you want a paragraph to be displayed properly—Navigator and Internet Explorer don't add extra space between the paragraph and the following list items without it.

Figure 3.29 shows how this looks in a Web browser.

Using START and VALUE Attributes

The START and VALUE attributes were Netscape extensions that were incorporated into HTML 3.2. You can use the START attribute in an OL start tag to start the numbering sequence at a particular number. You can use the VALUE attribute in an LI tag to restart the numbering sequence at a particular number. For an example of first starting the numbering sequence at 3 and then restarting it at 8, enter the following code:

```
<OL START="3">
<LI>This should be numbered as 3
```

```
<LI>This should be numbered as 4.
<LI VALUE="8">This should be numbered as 8.
<LI>This should be numbered as 9.
</OL>
```

Figure 3.30 shows how this appears in an HTML 3.2–compliant Web browser.

The numbering sequence will be started or restarted using the current TYPE attribute value. For instance, if TYPE="A" is used in the OL tag, then START="3" in an OL tag or VALUE="3" in an LI tag would start or restart the numbering at C.

Specifying Bullet Types

You can also use the TYPE attribute with unordered (bulleted) lists to specify the type of bullet to display. This was also originally a Netscape extension, but has since been included in HTML 3.2. Navigator 2.0 or greater and Internet Explorer 4.0 or greater support this attribute.

The values that you can use with the UL tag's TYPE attribute are "disc," "circle," and "square." Navigator and Internet Explorer (4.0 or greater) by default display nested bullet lists with the progression of a disc for the first level, a circle for the second level, and a square for the third level.

Figure 3.30

You can use the OL tag's START attribute and the LI tag's VALUE attribute to start or restart the numbering of an ordered list.

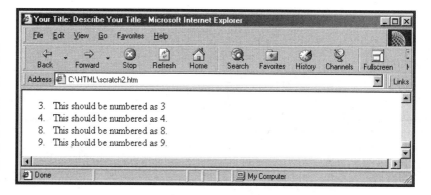

Enter the following code for an example of specifying a bullet-type sequence other than the default for a bullet list three levels deep:

```
<UL TYPE="square">
<LI>First-level bullet.
<LI>First-level bullet.
  <UL TYPE="disc">
  <LI>Second-level bullet.
  <LI>Second-level bullet.
     <UL TYPE="circle">
     <LI>Third-level bullet.
     <LI>Third-level bullet.
     </UL>
  </UL>
</UL>
```

Figure 3.31 shows how this looks in a Web browser that supports the UL tag's TYPE attribute.

TIP

■ ■

Just as you can include automatically indented paragraphs in an outline, you can do the same in a nested bulleted list. Just insert paragraphs following a list item but inside the list, and they will automatically line up to match the list item's indentation. Don't forget to include the </P> end tag at the end of the paragraphs.

■ ■

Figure 3.31

Using the TYPE attribute, you can specify the bullet types for different nested levels in a bullet list (or Unordered List).

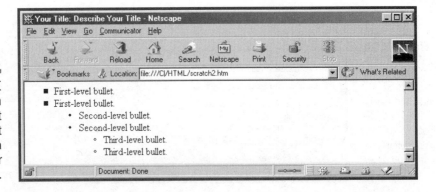

Take a Break

You've been going at this most of the day, so you're probably dying for a breather, right? Unglue your eyes from the screen and stare at the horizon (it'll help relax your eyes). Grab a snack or a soda. Give your dog or cat a good pet. I'll see you back in 5 to 10 minutes, when you'll learn all about creating fancy 3-D icon link lists.

Creating Icon Link Lists

An *icon link list* is a list of hypertext links that uses colorful 3-D graphical icon bullets (inline images) rather than plain, black-and-white bullets like those you get when you create an unordered list using the UL tag. This is a good way to add some pizzazz to your Web page.

Creating Left-Aligned Icon Link Lists

You can set up an icon link list in a number of ways. I'll show you one way of doing this in detail here, although I also describe some alternative methods you might want to try. Also, in the Tables Tutorial scheduled for this evening, I'll show you another way to create icon link lists.

This example uses the same links and descriptions you created in the Basic HTML Tutorial when learning to create hypertext link lists. To save yourself a little typing, you can open SCRATCH.HTM in another copy of Notepad and copy the following lines to the Clipboard, and then paste them here into SCRATCH2.HTM. Or you can just retype them, as shown here:

```
<A HREF="http://www.li.net/~autorent/yoyo.htm">Jon's YoYo Kingdom</A>
➥Claims to have the largest YoYo link list on the Web.
<A HREF="http://pages.nyu.edu/~tqm3413/yoyo/index.htm">Tomer's Page
➥of Exotic YoYo</A> Dedicated to the "little-known, original,
➥unusual, difficult, or otherwise interesting tricks."
```

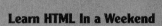

This method for creating an icon link list uses left-aligned bullet icons and BR tags. Edit the list of links, as shown here:

```
<P><IMG SRC="redball.gif" ALIGN="left" HSPACE="4" VSPACE="4">
<A HREF="http://www.li.net/~autorent/yoyo.htm">Jon's YoYo Kingdom</A>
➥Claims to have the largest YoYo link list on the Web.<BR
➥CLEAR="left">
<IMG SRC="redball.gif" ALIGN="left" HSPACE="4" VSPACE="4">
<A HREF="http://pages.nyu.edu/~tqm3413/yoyo/index.htm">Tomer's Page
➥of Exotic YoYo</A> Dedicated to the "little-known, original, unusual,
➥difficult, or otherwise interesting tricks."<BR CLEAR="left">
```

Figure 3.32 shows what this looks like in a Web browser that supports wrapping text around left-aligned images.

Notice that this is really one paragraph with a BR (Line Break) tag, with a CLEAR="left" attribute, used to separate the second icon link from the first. Create any additional icon links in the same way. If you want a blank line between your icon links, just use a P tag instead of the BR tag to separate the lines.

This method of creating an indented icon link list uses the ALIGN="left" attribute in the IMG tag to cause the following link and text to wrap around the bullet icon. The problem, however, is that the bullet icon is smaller than a single line of text, so the second line of text will wrap to the margin, rather than remaining indented flush with the first line of text. The trick is to use the VSPACE attribute in the IMG tag to add space above and below the bullet icon, causing the second line to be indented flush with the first. The limitation here is that you can only indent two lines of text—a third line will wrap to the margin. That's because the VSPACE attribute adds space both

Figure 3.32

An indented icon bullet list can be created by using left-aligned bullet images and BR tags with the CLEAR attribute.

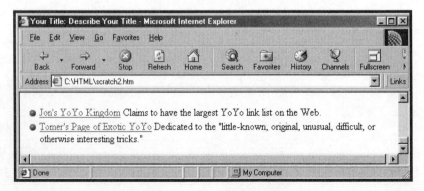

above and below the bullet icon, meaning that you can add only so much space and still have the bullet icon line up with the following link and text. In the previous example, a VSPACE value of 4 was used—you may need to adjust that number up or down, depending on the actual icon bullet image you're using.

The CLEAR attribute in the BR tags ensures that each icon bullet is flush to the left margin and isn't part of the previous bullet's wrap (in case you have a bullet item with only a single line of text).

■ ■

TIP Someone using a text-only browser or a graphical Web browser with graphics turned off might not realize that the graphics are icon bullets. To clue them in, you might want to edit the IMG tags for the previous icon bullets by adding ALT="*", so they look like this:

```
<IMG SRC="redball.gif" ALIGN="top" HSPACE="4" VSPACE="4" ALT="*">
```

■ ■

If you're wondering where to get more graphic icons to spice up your Web pages, you can find a collection of public domain graphic icons and other Web art on the CD-ROM. Also, at the Web site for this book, you can click the Web Links button to learn where you can find even more Web art that you can download and use.

Other Ways to Create Icon Link Lists

Another interesting alternative is to use a definition list, including the link with the bullet image in the DT (Definition Term) tag, while leaving any text describing or commenting on the link in the DD (Definition Data) tag. This can be a handy method if you don't want to be limited to just two lines.

In this evening's bonus session, if you have time to get to it, I'll show you how to create an indented icon link list using tables. The advantage of the tables method is that the number of indented lines is unlimited, unlike with the method shown in this tutorial. The disadvantage is that creating icon link lists using tables is a little more complicated than using left-aligned icon bullets. I use both methods frequently.

Finally, one more method can be used to create indented icon link lists. You can use a definition list with the COMPACT attribute set in the DL tag

(<DL COMPACT>). The trick is to include the IMG tag for the icon bullet in the DT tag, and the hypertext link and following descriptive text in the DD tag. In browsers that support it, the COMPACT attribute will cause the following DD element to line up horizontally on the same line with the DT element. (You may need to experiment with the VSPACE attribute in the IMG tag to get the bullet icons to line up with the following text. You can also experiment using the HSPACE attribute to indent the bullet icons in from the left margin). This should work in most HTML 3.2–compliant browsers, as well as in a few earlier browsers. The only problem with this method is that if a browser doesn't support it, unlike with the `ALIGN="left"` method shown previously, the results can be pretty horrendous (you'll have a stranded icon bullet on one line, and your hypertext link and descriptive text on another line). For that reason, you should probably skip this method, unless you only care about the very latest browsers.

Working with Rules

You learned how to use the HR (Horizontal Rule) tag in the Basic HTML Tutorial. In the following section, I'll show you how to create custom horizontal rules by changing their height, width, alignment, and shading. I'll also show you how to use inline images as graphic rules, which lets you include fancy and colorful horizontal rules in your Web pages.

The default horizontal rule looks rather bland. True, it does have some shading to give it a bit of a 3-D look—although it's entirely washed out in Internet Explorer if you've set your browser's background to white. This section covers some things you can do to dress up your horizontal rules, including changing their height, width, and alignment. You'll also learn how to use the 3-D graphic rules you may have seen on the Web.

The attributes used here in the HR tag were all originally Netscape Navigator extensions. HTML 3.2 includes them, so they can now qualify as "official HTML." Most current Web browsers support these attributes.

Setting the Height of a Horizontal Rule

To change the height of a horizontal rule, set the SIZE attribute value in the HR tag. The value you set is the rule's height, or *thickness*, in pixels. Enter the following code for an example of creating a horizontal rule that has a thickness of 10 pixels and another one that has a thickness of 15 pixels (along with a regular rule so you than can see the difference):

```
<P>This is the default horizontal rule:
<HR>
<P>This is a 10-pixel horizontal rule:
<HR SIZE="10">
<P>This is a 15-pixel horizontal rule:
<HR SIZE="15">
```

Figure 3.33 shows how this will look in Netscape Navigator.

Turning Shading Off

You can also turn a horizontal rule's shading off by including a NOSHADE attribute in the HR tag. The default setting for a horizontal rule is that it is shaded.

The "shading" is actually a thin drop shadow at the bottom and to the right of the horizontal rule and not, as you might think, the "shade" of the rule itself. In fact, when "shading" is turned off, most browsers will fill the horizontal rule with a gray or black shade.

To set an "unshaded" horizontal rule, just add the NOSHADE attribute to the HR tag, as shown here:

```
<P>This is an unshaded 15-pixel horizontal rule:
<HR SIZE="15" NOSHADE>
```

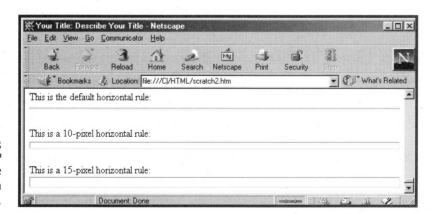

Figure 3.33

You can vary the thickness of a horizontal rule.

Figure 3.34

Internet Explorer
displays an
unshaded
horizontal rule with
square corners.

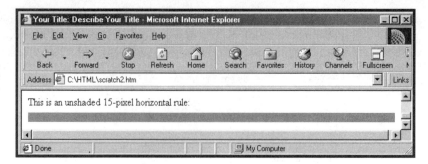

Figure 3.35

Navigator rounds
off the corners of
an unshaded
horizontal rule.

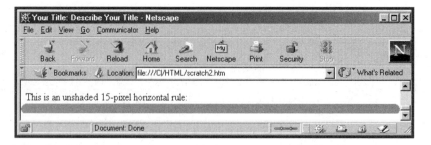

Figure 3.34 and Figure 3.35 show how this looks in Internet Explorer and Netscape Navigator, respectively, which take somewhat different approaches to displaying unshaded horizontal rules.

As you can see, Navigator fills an unshaded rule with a gray shade and rounds off its corners. Internet Explorer also fills an unshaded rule with a gray shade but displays it with square corners. Other browsers may display unshaded rules in still other ways—NCSA Mosaic 2.0, for instance, fills an unshaded rule with black and displays it with square corners.

Setting the Width of a Horizontal Rule

You also can change the width of a horizontal rule, either by setting the width in actual pixels or by specifying a percentage of the total width of the browser window. By default, horizontal rules are centered in the browser window. Enter the following code for an example of creating a 15-pixel horizontal rule with a width that's 75 percent of a browser's window:

```
<P>This is a 75% wide unshaded 15-pixel horizontal rule:
<HR WIDTH="75%" SIZE="15" NOSHADE>
```

Figure 3.36

You can alter the width and thickness of a rule, as well as turn shading off.

Figure 3.36 shows the resulting rule in Internet Explorer.

◆◆

CAUTION You might be tempted to stack up horizontal rules of different widths, to generate an effect similar to this:

Be advised that in a Web browser that doesn't support setting the WIDTH attribute for the HR tag, your effect will turn out to look something like this:

This is a good example of a situation in which both Navigator and Internet Explorer support a certain feature that you should still probably avoid using. The general rule is not to do tricks specific to only a few browsers if they're going to mess up other browsers. One way around this is to provide alternative pages, or at least label your page as "Netscape Navigator Only," "Microsoft Internet Explorer Only," or "HTML 3.2 Only."

◆◆

Aligning Horizontal Rules

HTML 3.2 allows the use of the ALIGN attribute in the HR tag to left-align or right-align a horizontal rule (center alignment is the default). Both

Figure 3.37

You can left- or right-align a horizontal rule that has been set to a width less than the width of the browser window.

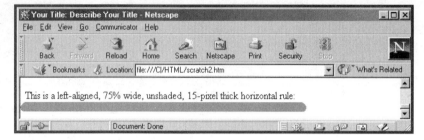

Netscape Navigator and Internet Explorer support left- or right-aligning a horizontal rule. Enter the following code for an example of doing this:

```
<P>This is a left-aligned, 75% wide unshaded 15-pixel horizontal
➥rule:
<HR ALIGN="left" WIDTH="75%" SIZE="15" NOSHADE>
```

Figure 3.37 shows how this looks in a Web browser.

Using Graphic Rules

Instead of using the HR tag, you can use a graphic rule, which is simply a graphic of a rule that you can insert on your page as an inline image. Enter the following code as an example of inserting a graphic rule on your Web page:

```
<P>This is a graphic rule:
<P><IMG SRC="rain_lin.gif">
```

Figure 3.38 shows what this looks like in any graphical Web browser.

Figure 3.38

Instead of a plain ordinary horizontal rule, you can use a fancy graphical horizontal rule.

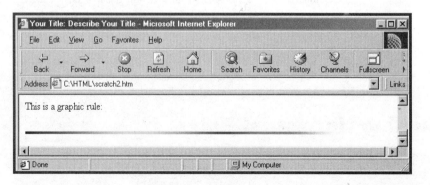

Centering a Graphic Rule

You can center a graphic rule like any inline image simply by placing it in a center-aligned paragraph. Edit the example you just created to center it, like this:

```
<P ALIGN="center"><IMG SRC="rain_lin.gif">
```

Now, as shown in Figure 3.39, the graphic rule appears centered in a Web browser.

Setting the Width and Height of a Graphic Rule

You can also get your graphic rule to extend across more (or less) of the screen by setting the width of the image. Also, while you're at it, you may as well enhance your graphic rule by increasing its height. Reedit the example you just created so it looks like this:

```
<P ALIGN="center"><IMG SRC="rain_lin.gif" HEIGHT="10" WIDTH="595">
```

As Figure 3.40 shows, the graphic rule now extends across more of the screen. The impact has been further enhanced by increasing the graphic rule's height.

■ ■

The capability to set the width and height of an inline image allows for a neat trick for creating a graphic rule. It also lets you create graphic rules that are much smaller, in total bytes, than a normal graphic rule. To do this, in your graphics editor, create a small graphic (say 5 by 5 pixels, or even smaller), coloring it with the color of your choice; then save the graphic to C:\HTML as a GIF file. Next, insert the graphic into your Web page as an inline image and then set the height and width attributes to 10 pixels and 595 pixels. For instance:

```
<P ALIGN="center"><IMG SRC="yourfile.gif" WIDTH="10" HEIGHT="595">
```

If the color of your tiny graphic is red, then a red graphic rule, 10 pixels high and 595 pixels wide, would appear onscreen. Also, notice the use of a center-aligned paragraph—those browsers that don't support setting the height and width of an inline image will still center your resized graphic rule onscreen (if they support paragraph center alignment).

■ ■

Figure 3.39

You can center a graphic rule by placing it on a center-aligned paragraph.

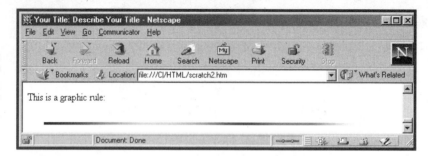

Figure 3.40

The width of the graphic rule has been increased to 595 pixels, and the height has been increased to 10 pixels.

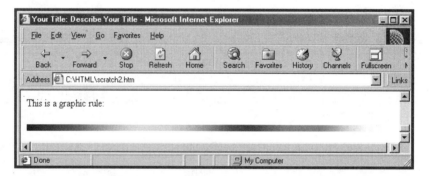

You also can set the width as a percentage of the total width of the browser window: just insert WIDTH="75%" in the IMG tag, for instance. However, don't set the height as a percentage (you can set the height in pixels, though).

Working with Fonts

The FONT tag allows you to change font sizes, colors, and faces. In the following sections, I'll show you how to apply the FONT tag's SIZE, COLOR, and FACE attributes.

NOTE   After having been recently included in HTML 3.2, the FONT tag has since been "deprecated" in HTML 4.0. Normally, deprecation of a tag in HTML should serve as a warning that the tag may be "obsoleted" (or disallowed entirely) in a future version of HTML. Deprecation, in this case, however, is meant to encourage use of style sheets to achieve the same results as the FONT tag. The FONT tag is much, much too useful to ever be obsoleted, in my opinion. It's much easier for a novice HTML user to learn and apply, for one thing. Also, so many

pages have already been created using this tag that future versions of HTML will have no choice but to continue to support it to maintain backward compatibility with those pages. So, feel free to continue to use the FONT tag to your heart's content! (So far, the only tags that have been obsoleted in HTML are tags that simply weren't being used, which is hardly the case with the FONT tag.)

● ●

Changing Font Sizes

The FONT tag allows you to specify the size and color of a section of text. The FONT tag uses the SIZE attribute to change the size of a font. You can set font sizes using absolute or relative size values.

You can set seven *absolute* (or fixed) sizes, numbered from 1 to 7, using the SIZE attribute of the FONT tag. The default is 3, which is the same as regular paragraph text; 1 is the smallest and 7 is the largest, which means you can set two absolute font sizes that are smaller than normal paragraph text and four sizes that are larger. Each Web browser determines the sizes of these fonts. To see what these different font sizes look like in your Web browser, enter the following code and then hop over to your browser:

```
<P><FONT SIZE="1">Font Size 1.</FONT><BR>
<FONT SIZE="2">Font Size 2.</FONT><BR>
<FONT SIZE="3">Font Size 3 (the default).</FONT><BR>
<FONT SIZE="4">Font Size 4.</FONT><BR>
<FONT SIZE="5">Font Size 5.</FONT><BR>
<FONT SIZE="6">Font Size 6.</FONT><BR>
<FONT SIZE="7">Font Size 7.</FONT>
```

As you can see in Figure 3.41 (or in your browser if you're using Netscape Navigator or Internet Explorer), the font sizes you can set range from very small to quite large.

■ ■

TIP

You can also nest font tags inside each other; therefore, you could do something like the following to switch back to the default font size in the middle of a larger set font size:

```
<FONT SIZE="4">This is Font Size 4. <FONT SIZE="3">This is the
default size font.</FONT> This is Font Size 4 again.</FONT>.
```

■ ■

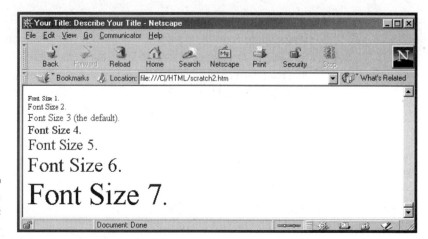

Figure 3.41

You can set seven
different absolute
font sizes.

Setting Relative Font Size Changes

You also can set relative font sizes. Relative font size changes are indicated by either a plus (+) or minus (–) sign preceding the font size number. For instance, FONT SIZE="+1" indicates a font size that's one size larger than the base font. Because the default base font is the same as a Size 3 absolute font size, a Size +1 relative font would be the same as a Size 4 absolute font (3 + 1 = 4). For instance, enter the following code for an example of using relative font size changes to indicate the seven possible font sizes:

```
<P><FONT SIZE="-2">Font Size -2.</FONT><BR>
<FONT SIZE="-1">Font Size -1.</FONT><BR>
Default Font Size.<BR>
<FONT SIZE="+1">Font Size +1.</FONT><BR>
<FONT SIZE="+2">Font Size +2.</FONT><BR>
<FONT SIZE="+3">Font Size +3.</FONT><BR>
<FONT SIZE="+4">Font Size +4.</FONT>
```

Figure 3.42 illustrates the seven font sizes, specified in relative terms.

You'll notice that a relative –2 is the same as an absolute 1, –1 is the same as 2, +1 is the same as 4, and so on. The default font size, which requires no font size change, is the same as 3.

Now, you may be asking, "If relative fonts are just another way to specify the same fonts as absolute fonts, why bother?" The next section, "Setting the Base Font Size," provides the answer to that question.

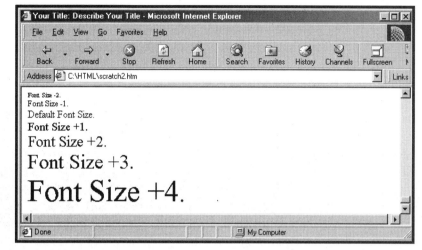

Figure 3.42

You can set seven different relative font sizes.

Setting the Base Font Size

The BASEFONT tag allows you to change the size of the *base font*—the font used in paragraph text. You can set it to any of the absolute font sizes, 1 through 7 (3 is the default). BASEFONT is a standalone (or *empty*) tag. You set the base font size the same way you set an absolute font size.

 NOTE The BASEFONT tag was a Netscape extension that never made it into HTML 3.2, but it was included in HTML 4.0—and then deprecated, along with the FONT tag. (It's the only tag to ever be approved and deprecated in one fell swoop.) However, the BASEFONT tag, like the FONT tag, is just too handy to ever be obsoleted. It's more limited than the FONT tag, only allowing you to change the size of the base font, but it's great for bumping the default base font size up a notch or two, for instance. Just too handy, in other words, to ever go away (and it's used on a gazillion Web pages, I'm sure). You may continue to use it in good conscience.

For instance, to increase the base font size one notch (3 is the default base font size), set the base font to an absolute font size of 4:

```
<BASEFONT SIZE="4">
```

When you change the base font size using the BASEFONT tag, all following relative font sizes will change relative to the new base font. For instance, if you change the base font size to 4 (as in the previous example), then a following relative font size of +1 would have the same effect as setting an absolute font size of 5 (4 + 1 = 5).

You can insert the BASEFONT tag at any point within a Web page to set the base font to any of the absolute font sizes. It stays in effect until another BASEFONT tag changes the base font size. It not only affects relative font sizes but also any SMALL and BIG font changes (described later in the session), as well as the size of all paragraph text, character rendering (italic, bold, and so on), list elements, definition lists, block quotes, predefined text, and address blocks that follow it. Headings and text set with absolute font size tags are not affected, however.

Other Ways to Change Font Sizes

The SMALL and BIG tags are Netscape extensions that were incorporated into HTML 3.2. They are container tags that specify a font size that's one size smaller and one size bigger than the current base font size. The tags can be nested to get even smaller and larger font sizes. These tags have been deprecated in HTML 4.0, and (unlike the other deprecated tags) they don't perform any function that cannot be done just as easily by other means—especially via the more versatile FONT tag. The BIG and SMALL tags have also been much less widely used than the FONT tag and are therefore much more likely to actually be obsoleted in a future version of HTML. Because these tags don't provide any functionality not offered by the FONT tag, I recommend that you avoid using them.

Changing Font Colors

The FONT tag uses the COLOR attribute to change the color of a font. To specify a font color, you can either use one of 16 color names that match the Windows 16-color palette, or you can use RGB hex codes—which is more difficult but gives you access to a much wider range of colors.

The 16 Windows color names are black, white, aqua, blue, fuchsia, gray, green, lime, maroon, navy, olive, purple, red, silver, teal, and yellow. Enter

the following code for an example of specifying font colors using color names (this example omits "black" and "white"):

```
<P><FONT SIZE=7>
<FONT COLOR="aqua">Aqua </FONT><FONT COLOR="blue">Blue </FONT>
<FONT COLOR="fuchsia">Fuchsia </FONT><FONT COLOR="gray">Gray </FONT>
<FONT COLOR="green">Green </FONT><FONT COLOR="lime">Lime </FONT>
<FONT COLOR="maroon">Maroon </FONT><FONT COLOR="navy">Navy </FONT>
<FONT COLOR="olive">Olive </FONT><FONT COLOR="purple">Purple </FONT>
<FONT COLOR="red">Red </FONT><FONT COLOR="silver">Silver </FONT>
<FONT COLOR="teal">Teal </FONT><FONT COLOR="yellow">Yellow </FONT>
</FONT>
```

The illustration in Figure 3.43, shown here in monochrome, gives only a rough idea of what this looks like in a browser. Be sure to hop over to your browser to see what the colors really look like.

Setting the font color using RGB hex codes is a much more difficult way to set font colors than using color names, but it gives you access to a very large range of colors. Essentially, it lets you specify values from 0 to 255 (00 to FF, in hexadecimal) for the red, green, and blue components of a color, providing you with a grand total of no less than 16.7 million different colors from which to choose.

Finding the perfect color when you use this method is somewhat akin to finding a needle in a haystack. Also, many of the possible color specifications

Figure 3.43

There are 16 color names, including black and white (not shown here), that you can use to set font colors.

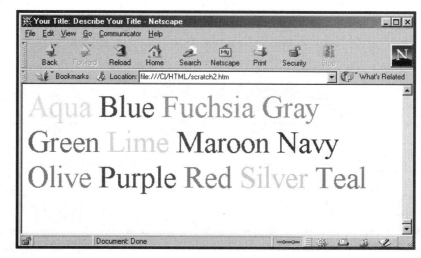

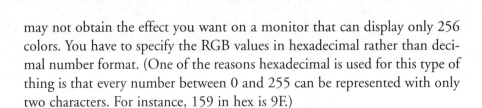

may not obtain the effect you want on a monitor that can display only 256 colors. You have to specify the RGB values in hexadecimal rather than decimal number format. (One of the reasons hexadecimal is used for this type of thing is that every number between 0 and 255 can be represented with only two characters. For instance, 159 in hex is 9F.)

You set the RGB hex code for a color in the FONT tag in this general form, where *rr* is the hex value for red, *gg* the hex value for green, and *bb* the hex value for blue:

```
<FONT COLOR="#rrggbb">This is the text to be colored.</FONT>
```

For instance, a red color here could be specified as FF0000, a green color as 00FF00, and a blue color as 0000FF. (FF is the highest hexadecimal number, equaling 255, whereas 00 is the lowest, equaling 0.) Enter the following code as an example of assigning font colors using RGB hex codes (the example also sets the font size so it will be more visible in your browser):

```
<P><FONT SIZE="6"><FONT COLOR="#FF0000">Red (FF0000) </FONT><FONT
COLOR="#00FF00">Green (00FF00) </FONT><FONT COLOR="#0000FF">Blue
(0000FF)</FONT></FONT>
```

Because this is shown in Figure 3.44 only in monochrome, you'll have to hop over to your browser if you want to check out what it really looks like.

Showing you how to count in hexadecimal or how an RGB color scheme works is beyond the scope of this book. Quite frankly, unless you already know hex and RGB color theory, the only practical way is to use some kind of color chart, wheel, or cube that allows you to select the color you want and get the corresponding hex code. Many charts, tables, and utilities are available

Figure 3.44

Here are just a few of the wide range of colors you can set using hex codes.

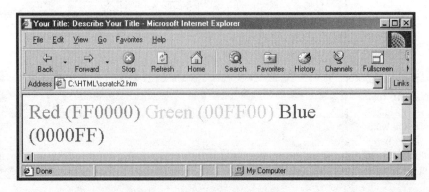

on the Web for getting the hex codes for colors. At this book's Web site, you can find where to locate many of these by clicking the Web Links button.

ON THE

CD

Many HTML editors have built-in color charts that allow you to choose a color and then insert the hex code into your Web page. This is a department in which an HTML editor can be far superior to a mere text editor such as Notepad. Figure 3.45 shows the built-in color picker that's in HTMLed32, one of the HTML editors included on the CD-ROM.

Paint Shop Pro 5, also included on the CD-ROM, shows you the hex code for any color you select in its window for selecting fill colors. For instructions for using Paint Shop Pro, see the Graphics Tutorial that is scheduled for the bonus Sunday Evening session.

Changing Font Faces

The FACE attribute for the FONT tag was a Microsoft extension, but it's now part of HTML 4.0. It allows you to specify a font, or a list of fonts, in which you would like to have text displayed. A browser that supports this attribute will check to see if any of the fonts specified are present on a local computer and then display the text in that font if it's available. If not, it will display the text in the default font.

One of the tricks to using this attribute is to specify a list of fonts that will snag as many computers as possible. You should realize that just because a font is available on your system doesn't mean it will be available on someone

Figure 3.45

Many HTML editors have built-in color pickers that make inserting the hex codes for colors a snap.

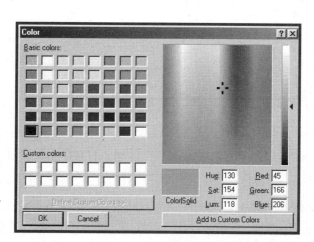

else's system. If most systems aren't liable to have a particular font, there really isn't much point in specifying it. For that reason, I don't think trying to specify one particular font is the way to go, and you certainly shouldn't base the design of your Web page on having any one particular font available. Even if you stick with fonts that are included with Windows 95 or Windows 3.1, you should realize that those fonts might not be available on a Macintosh or a Unix system.

A good way to use this attribute is to specify a list of fonts that fit into the same category, such as serif, sans serif, and monospaced fonts. For instance, to maximize the chances that the next example will be displayed in a sans serif font, enter the following code:

```
<P><FONT SIZE="6" COLOR="blue" FACE="Verdana, Arial, Helvetica">This
text will be in either Verdana, Arial, or Helvetica, depending on
which fonts are installed on a local system.</FONT>
```

Figure 3.46 shows what this looks like in a browser that supports the FONT tag's FACE attribute on a system that has the Verdana font available.

Alternatively, you could specify a monospaced font for a different effect:

```
<P><FONT SIZE="6" COLOR="blue" FACE="Courier New, Courier, Mono-
spaced, Memorandum,">This text will be in either Courier New, Couri-
er, Monospaced, or Memorandum, depending on which fonts are installed
on a local system.</FONT>
```

Figure 3.47 shows what this looks like in a browser that supports the FONT tag's FACE attribute on a system that has the Courier New font available.

Figure 3.46

The FONT tag's FACE attribute is an HTML 4.0 feature that can be used to display text in a font face (here, Verdana) that's different than the default font.

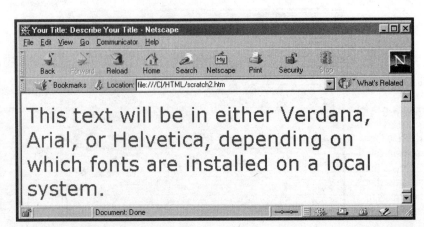

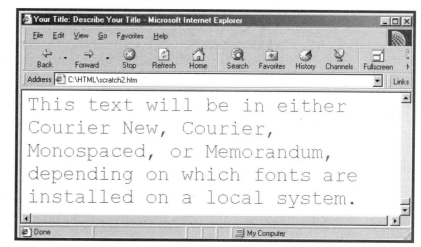

Figure 3.47

Here, the FACE attribute specifies a monospaced font face (Courier New).

 **CAUTION**

When using the FONT tag to assign sizes, colors, or faces, you should keep in mind some of the possibly deleterious effects that might result. You should keep in mind that not everyone can use a graphical browser (the visually disabled, for instance). Most important, you should avoid using the FONT tag as a substitute for any of the heading level tags (H1, H2, and so on). The reason for this is that text-based browsers and Braille browsers, for instance, rely on the heading level tags to convey the structure and order of precedence within a document. That doesn't mean, however, that you can't combine the two, either nesting a heading level tag inside a FONT tag, or vice versa (you'll get somewhat different results, one bold and the other not, depending on which way you do it).

Using Background Colors and Images

Using a background color or image is a great way to dress up the appearance of your Web page. In the following sections, I'll show you how to use a background color (as well as matching text and link colors) and how to use a background image with your Web page.

Using a Background Color

Using the right background color is a simple and easy way to make your Web page look really great (or really horrible, depending on the color you choose). In this section, I show you how to set a background color and matching text and link colors.

Background, text, and links colors for the entire page are set by including the following attributes in the BODY tag: BGCOLOR sets the background color, TEXT sets the text (or foreground) color, LINK sets the color of unvisited links, VLINK sets the color of visited links, and ALINK sets the color of activated links (where you hold down the mouse button on a link but haven't released it). These were originally Netscape extensions but have since been included in HTML 3.2. As with the FONT tag's COLOR attribute, you can set these attributes using any of the 16 color names (black, white, aqua, blue, fuchsia, gray, green, lime, maroon, navy, olive, purple, red, silver, teal, and yellow) or by using RGB hexadecimal codes.

The general form for entering these attributes as color names is shown here, where *colorname* refers to one of the 16 color names:

```
<BODY BGCOLOR="colorname" TEXT="colorname" LINK="colorname"
VLINK="colorname" ALINK="colorname">
```

The general form for entering these attributes as RGB hexadecimal codes is shown here, where *rrggbb* is three hexadecimal numbers forming the RGB code for setting the red, green, and blue components of an RGB color:

```
<BODY BGCOLOR="#rrggbb" TEXT="#rrggbb" LINK="#rrggbb" VLINK="#rrggbb"
ALINK="#rrggbb">
```

The following example sets the colors for the background, the text (or foreground), and the three varieties of links—regular links, visited links, and activated links. Go to the top of the Web page and then add the following code to the BODY tag as an example of setting these attributes:

```
<BODY BGCOLOR="#336699" TEXT="#FFFF00" LINK="#FFCC00" VLINK="#ff6666"
ALINK="#FF0000">
```

This sets the background color to slate blue, the text to yellow, the links to orange gold, visited links to a salmon peach (or something like that), and activated links to bright red.

 TIP

If you stick to hexadecimal codes 00, 33, 66, 99, CC, and FF when inserting RGB hex codes, you can reduce the total number of colors from which you must select to 216. The background, text, and link colors set in the example are all combinations of these codes. This will have the added benefit of making sure that your colors will display as anticipated on a 256-color system.

Because the illustrations in this book are not printed in color, Figure 3.48 can only show you the contrast and tone of the colors you set in the example. You need to hop over to your Web browser to see what it really looks like.

 **CAUTION**

If you decide to set colors (and nothing says you have to), you should try to avoid color combinations that render your text font less readable. The wrong color combination can render your Web page entirely unusable. The important thing is to develop and organize your content first, and then hone the appearance of your Web page. Setting the colors for a badly conceived and poorly organized Web page can only make it worse.

Figure 3.48

You can set a background color as well as matching text and link colors.

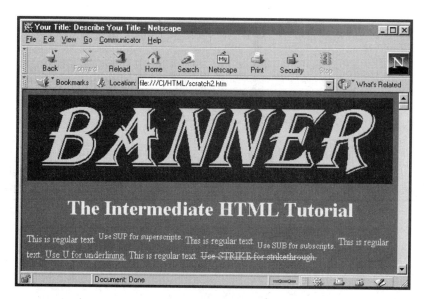

Using a Background Image

The BACKGROUND attribute of the BODY tag allows you to specify a background image. Originally a Netscape extension, it is now part of HTML 3.2. All current graphical Web browsers should support this attribute. The background image can be a GIF, JPG, or PNG file. The general format for entering this attribute is shown as follows, where *filename* is a graphic file that's in the same folder as the Web page, and *URL* is a relative or absolute address of a graphic file that's in a folder other than the Web page:

```
<BODY BACKGROUND="filename or URL">
```

A key consideration when using background images is to avoid busy or high-contrast images. If you're going to use a dark background image, you should set the color of your text and links to a lighter color. Go to the top of the Web page and then, as shown in the following example, comment out the previous BODY start tag. Next, add a new BODY start tag using the BACK-GROUND attribute to assign BACKGRND.GIF as the background image:

```
<!--<BODY BGCOLOR="#336699" TEXT="#66CC66" LINK="#FFCC00"
VLINK="#ff6666" ALINK="#FF0000">-->
<BODY BACKGROUND="backgrnd.gif">
```

Figure 3.49 shows a Web page that has BACKGRND.GIF tiled in the background. To see what this really looks like, you need to hop over to your browser.

Although the previous example doesn't include them, along with the BACK-GROUND attribute, you can use the TEXT, LINK, VLINK, ALINK, and BGCOLOR tags as well.

TIP

If you specify a dark background image (using the BACKGROUND attribute) in conjunction with light text and link colors, you should be aware that your text and links may not be readable in a browser that has the display of images turned off. To make sure that your page will be readable against the default white background in those browsers, use the BGCOLOR to set a background color against which the text will still be readable.

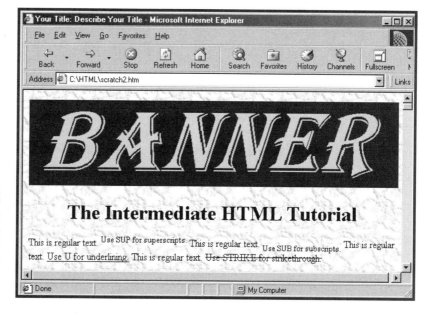

Figure 3.49

One of the more effective ways to add visual appeal to your Web page is to use a background image.

ON THE
CD

Lots and lots of background images are available on the Web that you can use to enhance the look of your Web pages. You'll also find many background images included in the Web art library that has been included on this book's CD-ROM.

Saving Your File

Save the HTML file you just created. You can use it later as a reference. When you first saved it, you named it SCRATCH2.HTM. If more than one person will be doing this tutorial and you want to make sure that this file doesn't get overwritten, you might want to give it a new name, such as using your first initial and last name for the file name (JMILLER2.HTM, for instance, if your name is John Miller).

What's Next?

If you've made it this far, you're doing excellent. You should now know plenty of HTML to be able to create a Web page that will amaze your family, friends, or associates. Don't be surprised if your work associates now start regarding you as their "HTML guru"! However, although you've come a long way, there's still lots more to learn.

None of the following tutorials are required for you to be able to create very effective and attractive Web pages. Literally, everything from this point on is frosting on the cake and can only enhance and build on what you already know.

If you're still following the schedule, the Tables Tutorial is lined up for you for tonight as a "bonus" session. However, if it's getting late, or you're just plain tuckered out, feel free to skip the Saturday evening session. You can always come back and complete it later.

If you've decided to skip the "bonus" session tonight, feel free to do the Tables Tutorial anytime tomorrow, if you want. The Tables Tutorial and the three software tutorials scheduled for Sunday are all optional. You may do them in whichever order you want.

The Tables Tutorial

(Bonus Session)

- ✿ Defining columns and rows
- ✿ Controlling borders and spacing
- ✿ Spanning columns and rows
- ✿ Using background colors and images
- ✿ Creating icon link lists using tables

One of the weaknesses of HTML 2.0 was its inability to display information or data in a tabular format, except by including it as raw text (spaces included) inside a PRE (Preformatted Text) element—a solution that, although highly practical, was rather bland, at best. Originally a proposed HTML 3.0 feature, tables have since been included in HTML 3.2. A few additional tags specifically designed for working with tables have also been included in HTML 4.0.

Just because tables were not included in the Intermediate HTML Tutorial, don't think they're an "advanced" HTML feature. Although you'll need to invest some time in learning how tables work and what they can do for you, it's nothing the average user can't master in a relatively short period of time.

This tutorial should take less time to complete than the Basic and Intermediate HTML Tutorials. You should be able to complete it in one to two hours. If you run short on time, feel free to leave any unfinished portion of the tutorial until another day.

 NOTE   If you've not yet completed the Intermediate HTML Tutorial scheduled for Saturday afternoon, you should finish it before attempting to do the Tables Tutorial.

This tutorial uses two example graphics files that have already been used in previous tutorials. No other example files are required. If the example graphics files have worked properly in the Basic and Intermediate HTML Tutorials, then you're all ready to use them in this tutorial.

If you haven't installed the example files, return to "Installing the Example Files" at the start of the Saturday Morning session and do so now before trying to do this tutorial.

In doing this tutorial, you'll be creating two tables. In the first table, you'll learn all the standard HTML 3.2 table tags, along with a couple of the new HTML 4.0 table tags. I'll even show you how to apply some styles to your table. With each new example, you'll just modify the same table you're creating—no need to create a separate table for each example. In the second table, you'll learn how to create a 3-D icon bullet list using tables so that you have no limit on the number of indented lines following the bullet.

Feel free to save your file after each example and hop over to your Web browser to see what it looks like.

■ ■

TIP   With the example files you copied from the CD-ROM, you'll find a file, TUTOR3A.HTM, that shows all the examples covered in this tutorial as separate tables. Don't bother to copy and paste each example as a separate table. Instead, make all the changes in a single table file and use TUTOR3A.HTM for future reference on how to implement each feature.

■ ■

Running Your Web Browser

Run your Web browser, preferably offline, so you'll be able to check the results of your work in your browser while doing this tutorial. You can easily hop back and forth between Notepad and your Web browser, dynamically updating your work as you go. After doing the Basic and Intermediate HTML Tutorials, you should be quite familiar with doing this.

An HTML 3.2–compliant Web browser is required to do this tutorial. If the browser you're using is Netscape Navigator 2.0 or greater or Microsoft Internet Explorer 3.0 or greater, you should be able to do all the HTML 3.2 sections in this tutorial.

In case you don't currently have an HTML 3.2–compliant Web browser installed, I've included Opera 3.21 on this book's CD-ROM. Opera is an excellent Web browser that can handle everything in this tutorial (except for the few HTML 4.0 features that are covered).

Other *current* graphical browsers may also be used, but because I haven't tested them out, I can't guarantee how HTML 3.2–compliant they are.

I've included a section in this tutorial on using the new HTML 4.0 TBODY, THEAD, and TFOOT tags. Currently, these tags are supported only by Microsoft Internet Explorer 4.0 or greater. If you're using a different browser, feel free to skip that section.

Also, I've tested out this tutorial with the beta version of Navigator 4.5 and the release version of Internet Explorer 4.01 that's included with Windows 98.

Running Your Text Editor

Run the text editor you want to use to edit HTML files. As mentioned earlier, I highly recommend using Notepad until you master the fundamentals of HTML. In Windows 3.1, you can usually find Notepad in the Accessories window in Program Manager. In Windows 95/98, you can find it on the Start Menu, under Programs and Accessories.

 TIP If you're using Notepad in Windows 3.1 or Windows 95, don't forget to turn Word Wrap on. Just select Edit, Word Wrap. If you're using Notepad in Windows 98, Word Wrap should still be on from your last session.

Loading Your Starting Template

Load the starting template you saved this morning:

1. In Notepad, select File, Open and then go to the C:\HTML folder.
2. Select "All Files (*.*)" as the file type in the Files of Type box.
3. Double-click *start.htm*.

The template should look like the following listing (if you didn't save the template, just retype it now):

```
<HTML>
<HEAD>
<TITLE>Your Title: Describe Your Title</TITLE>
```

```
</HEAD>
<BODY>
</BODY>
</HTML>
```

Saving Your Scratch Pad File

Save your "scratch pad" file that you'll be using in this tutorial. In Notepad, perform the following steps:

1. Select File, Save As.
2. Change the folder to C:\HTML and then save your file as SCRATCH3.HTM.

Starting Your Table

The TABLE tag needs to bracket your table. All other tags or text to be included in your table should be nested inside the TABLE tag. Enter the following HTML nested in the BODY tag:

```
<BODY>
<P><TABLE>
</TABLE>
</BODY>
```

 NOTE Because the TABLE element is not a block element but rather an inline element (like the IMG tag, for instance), you should place a P tag in front of the TABLE tag to make sure sufficient space is added above the table.

Defining Columns and Rows

You can use the TR (Table Row) and TD (Table Data) tags to create a grid of rows and columns. Here's an example:

```
<P><TABLE>
<TR><TD>1A</TD><TD>1b</TD><TD>1C</TD><TD>1D</TD></TR>
<TR><TD>2A</TD><TD>2B</TD><TD>2C</TD><TD>2D</TD></TR>
</TABLE>
```

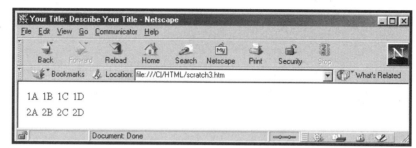

Figure 4.1

A table can
consist of columns
and rows.

Notice that the <TR> start tag and the </TR> end tag bracket each row. See Figure 4.1 for what this looks like in a Web browser.

Adding and Controlling Borders

A table hardly looks like a table without a border. Including a BORDER attribute inside the TABLE tag does the trick. Here's an example:

```
<P><TABLE BORDER="1">
<TR><TD>1A</TD><TD>1b</TD><TD>1C</TD><TD>1D</TD></TR>
```

See Figure 4.2 for what this change looks like in a Web browser.

HTML 3.2 also recognizes the BORDER attribute by itself, whereas HTML 4.0 recognizes the BORDER="border" attribute value. Both of these should have exactly the same result as BORDER="1". As long as a browser recognizes the BORDER attribute by itself, you could use BORDER="gumbie" and still get the same results.

Increasing the value of the BORDER attribute has a result you might not expect: It increases the thickness of the outer border of the table, displaying

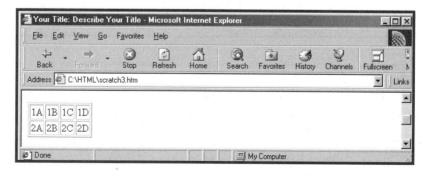

Figure 4.2

You can add
borders to a table.

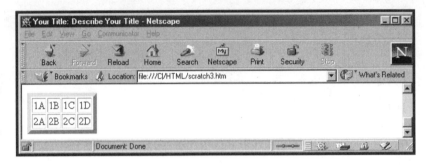

Figure 4.3

Table borders go
3-D when you
boost their
thickness.

it in 3-D relief. However, it doesn't affect the appearance of the interior lines
of the table. Increase the BORDER to six pixels:

```
<TABLE BORDER="6">
<TR><TD>1A</TD><TD>1b</TD><TD>1C</TD><TD>1D</TD></TR>
```

See Figure 4.3 for what this change looks like in a Web browser.

Setting Spacing and Padding

Your table looks a bit cramped, don't you think? The CELLSPACING
attribute adds space between cells, whereas the CELLPADDING attribute
adds space within each cell. Add six pixels of spacing and padding, like this:

```
<P><TABLE BORDER="6" CELLSPACING="6" CELLPADDING="6">
<TR><TH>A</TH><TH>B</TH><TH>C</TH><TH>D</TH></TR>
```

As shown in Figure 4.4, both the space between the cells and the padding
within the cells have been increased.

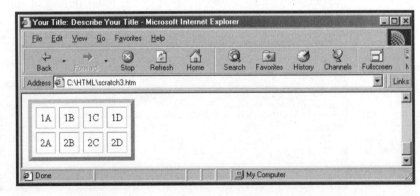

Figure 4.4

You can add
space between
cells and padding
within cells.

Defining Column Headings

What's a table without column headings, right? The TH (Table Heading) tag works just like the TD (Table Data) tag, except it defines a particular cell as a heading cell rather than as an ordinary data cell. To create a row of four column headings at the top of your table, use the TR tag to define a row; then, instead of using TD tags, insert TH tags to define the cells, like this:

```
<P><TABLE BORDER="6" CELLSPACING="6" CELLPADDING="6">
<TR><TH>A</TH><TH>B</TH><TH>C</TH><TH>D</TH></TR>
<TR><TD>1A</TD><TD>1b</TD><TD>1C</TD><TD>1D</TD></TR>
```

As Figure 4.5 shows, table headings automatically show up in centered bold-face type.

Adding a Caption

The CAPTION tag allows you to specify a caption for your table:

```
<P><TABLE BORDER="6" CELLSPACING="6" CELLPADDING="6">
<CAPTION>I. Table Example</CAPTION>
```

As you can see in Figure 4.6, a caption appears above the title, by default.

You can display the caption below the table by setting an ALIGN="bottom" attribute value in the CAPTION tag. The HTML 4.0 specifications state that you should also be able to use ALIGN="left" or ALIGN="right" to display the caption either to the left or right of the table. Navigator and Internet Explorer do not currently support this, however. (Internet Explorer

Figure 4.5

Table headings are automatically bolded and centered.

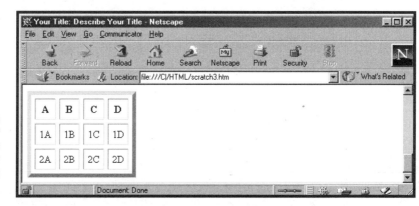

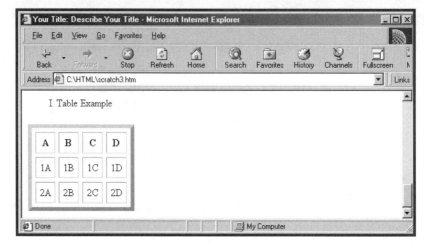

Figure 4.6

You can add a
caption to a table.

left- and right-flushes the caption in the caption cell, whereas Navigator
ignores these attributes entirely.)

Centering a Table

To center the table, just insert an ALIGN="center" attribute value in the
TABLE tag:

```
<P><TABLE ALIGN="center" BORDER="6" CELLSPACING="6" CELLPADDING="6">
<CAPTION>I. Table Example</CAPTION>
```

Figure 4.7 shows how this will look.

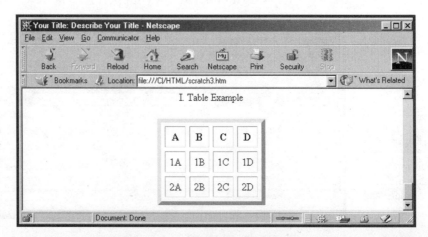

Figure 4.7

You can center
a table by
inserting the
ALIGN="center"
attribute value in
the TABLE tag.

Alternatively, you can get exactly the same result by putting your table inside a CENTER tag or by placing it in a center-aligned paragraph. To indent your table rather than center it, place it inside a BLOCKQUOTE tag.

TIP

■ ■

Tables are not block elements, as you might suspect, but rather inline elements that function on a Web page in a similar fashion to how inline images created with the IMG tag function. Just as with inline images, you can flow text around a table by inserting an ALIGN="left" or ALIGN="right" attribute value in the TABLE tag. (ALIGN="left" will flow text around the right side of a table, whereas ALIGN="right" will flow text around the left side of a table.) You can not only flow text around a table, but you can flow any other element as well, including even another table. Figure 4.8 shows two tables displayed side by side, with ALIGN="left" set in the first table and ALIGN="right" set in the second table. A BR tag with a CLEAR="all" attribute value set follows the second table.

You can also flow text around the left or right side of a table. Just make sure you insert a BR tag with the appropriate CLEAR attribute value ("left", "right", or "all") where you want the flowing to stop. Although Navigator recognizes the HSPACE attribute in the TABLE tag, Internet Explorer unfortunately doesn't, which renders doing this much less useful.

Unlike with inline images, however, you cannot flow text or other elements between two tables.

■ ■

Figure 4.8

You can display two tables side by side by using the ALIGN="left" and ALIGN="right" attribute values.

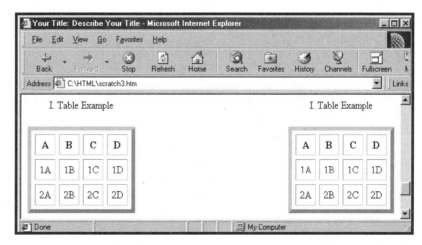

Setting Table Width and Height

You can include WIDTH and HEIGHT attributes to specify the size of your table. You can use either absolute values (number of pixels) or relative values (percentages). Go back to the original table you were working on (that is, don't use the side-by-side tables you pasted in for the example in the preceding tip) and specify a width of 75 percent, like this:

```
<P><TABLE ALIGN="center" BORDER="6" CELLSPACING="6" CELLPADDING="6"
➥WIDTH="75%">
<CAPTION>I. Table Example</CAPTION>
```

Figure 4.9 shows the table now occupying 75 percent of the browser window's width.

You can also set the HEIGHT attribute in the TABLE tag, although it's generally less useful than setting the WIDTH attribute. You can use this technique to increase the row heights in a table by setting an absolute value (number of pixels) for the height of the table that is greater than the normal height.

Adding Row Headings

Now you can add some row headings. To create a row heading, just add a TH cell (instead of a TD cell) at the start of a table row, like this:

```
<P><TABLE ALIGN="center" BORDER="6" CELLSPACING="6" CELLPADDING="6"
➥WIDTH="75%">
<CAPTION>I. Table Example</CAPTION>
<TR><TH></TH><TH>A</TH><TH>B</TH><TH>C</TH><TH>D</TH></TR>
<TR><TH>Row 1:</TH><TD>1A</TD><TD>1b</TD><TD>1C</TD><TD>1D</TD></TR>
<TR><TH>Row 2:</TH><TD>2A</TD><TD>2B</TD><TD>2C</TD><TD>2D</TD></TR>
</TABLE>
```

As Figure 4.10 shows, row headings are formatted just like column headings—centered and bolded.

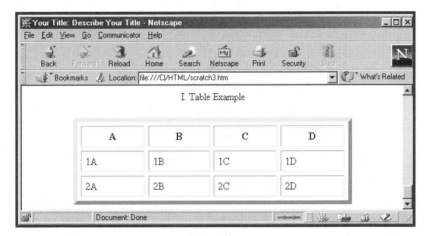

Figure 4.9

You can set the width of a table to a percentage (here, 75 percent) of a browser window.

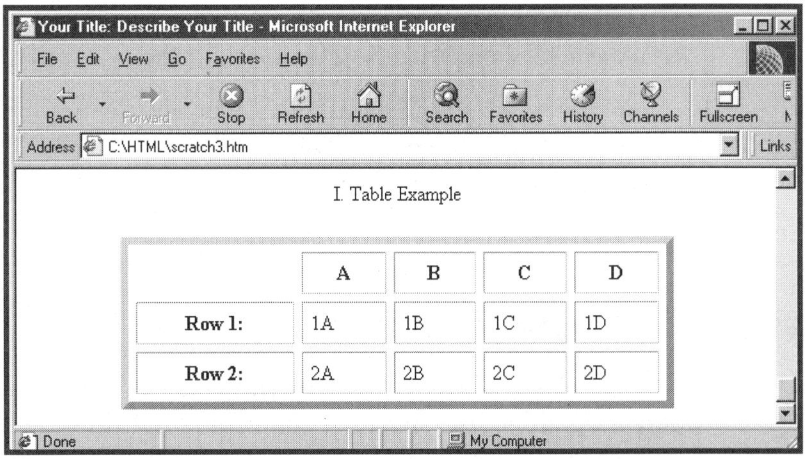

Figure 4.10

You can also add row headings to a table.

Horizontally Aligning Cell Contents

Right now, the text in the row headings and the data cells is left aligned. Use the ALIGN attribute to right-align the two rows of the table, like this:

```
<CAPTION>I. Table Example</CAPTION>
<TR><TH></TH><TH>A</TH><TH>B</TH><TH>C</TH><TH>D</TH></TR>
<TR ALIGN="right"><TH>Row
➡1:</TH><TD>1A</TD><TD>1b</TD><TD>1C</TD><TD>1D</TD></TR>
<TR ALIGN="right"><TH>Row
➡2:</TH><TD>2A</TD><TD>2B</TD><TD>2C</TD><TD>2D</TD></TR>
```

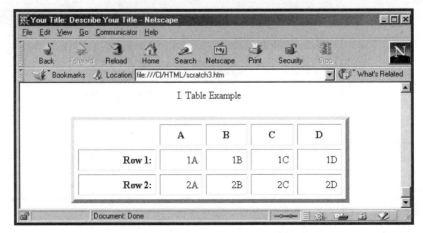

Figure 4.11

The two rows of
the table are now
right aligned.

Figure 4.11 shows the new alignment for the rows and their headings.

You can use the ALIGN attribute to horizontally align the contents of table rows (TR), table headings (TH), and table data cells (TD). Possible values are "left", "center", and "right". Center alignment is the default for TH cells and left alignment is the default for TD cells.

Setting Column Widths

By inserting a WIDTH attribute in the top cell of a column, you can specify the width of the entire column. Column widths can be set in either percentages or pixels.

The columns of your table are fairly equal in width. Only the first column, where the row header cells are, is somewhat wider than the other columns. A browser will expand or contract the columns depending on their contents (that's why the first column is wider, because its contents take up more horizontal space). In other words, you can't depend on any column remaining the same width once you've started to fill it in with real data.

Because the table has five columns, set each column to an equal width by inserting a WIDTH="20%" attribute in each of the TH tags in the top row of the table:

```
<CAPTION>I. Table Example</CAPTION>
<TR><TH WIDTH="20%"></TH><TH WIDTH="20%">A</TH><TH
➥WIDTH="20%">B</TH><TH WIDTH="20%">C</TH><TH WIDTH="20%">D</TH></TR>
```

The percentage for setting equal column widths will depend on the total number of columns. If your table has six columns, you would set each to "16%" (100 divided by 6).

Figure 4.12 shows what percentage-based column widths look like. (I'll spare you the pixel version.)

Column widths set in percentages will expand or contract depending on the width of the browser window. Column widths set in pixels will remain the same width, regardless of the browser window width. Nothing stops you from setting the first column of a table in pixels and the remaining columns in percentages, the other way around, or in any other combination you want. If you do set all the columns to a fixed width using pixels, you should not set a percentage width in the TABLE tag.

Figure 4.12

Each column of the table has been set to a width of 20 percent.

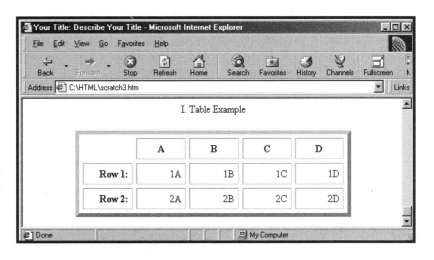

Inserting an Image

You can insert an image inside a table cell. The following HTML inserts a graphic, ONE.GIF, inside the upper-left corner cell (this graphic was used in the HTML tutorials, so it should already be available):

```
<CAPTION>I. Table Example</CAPTION>
<TR><TH WIDTH="20%"><IMG SRC="one.gif"></TH><TH WIDTH="20%">A</TH><TH
➥WIDTH="20%">B</TH><TH WIDTH="20%">C</TH><TH WIDTH="20%">D</TH></TR>
```

As Figure 4.13 shows, a graphic image of the number 1 has been inserted in the top-left cell.

Vertically Aligning Cell Contents

You can use the VALIGN attribute set to "top," "middle," or "bottom" to set the vertical alignment of a table row (TR), table heading (TH), or table data (TD) cell. Middle alignment is the default. Set the top row to bottom alignment:

```
<CAPTION>I. Table Example</CAPTION>
<TR VALIGN="bottom"><TH WIDTH="20%"><IMG SRC="one.gif"></TH><TH
➥WIDTH="20%">A</TH><TH WIDTH="20%">B</TH><TH WIDTH="20%">C</TH><TH
➥WIDTH="20%">D</TH></TR>
```

As Figure 4.14 shows, the top row of the table is bottom aligned.

Spanning Columns

The COLSPAN attribute lets you create cells that span across columns. Add a row to your table that includes two cells that span across two columns each, like this:

```
<TR><TH VALIGN="bottom" WIDTH="20%"><IMG SRC="one.gif"></TH><TH
➥WIDTH="20%">A</TH><TH WIDTH="20%">B</TH><TH WIDTH="20%">C</TH><TH
➥WIDTH="20%">D</TH></TR>
<TR><TH></TH><TH COLSPAN="2">A & B</TH><TH COLSPAN="2">C &
➥D</TH></TR>
<TR><TH ALIGN="right">Row 1:</TH><TD>1A</TD><TD>1b</TD>
➥<TD>1C</TD><TD>1D</TD></TR>
```

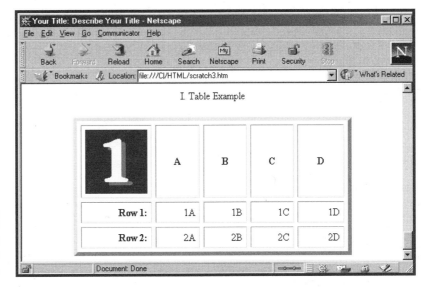

Figure 4.13

You can insert an inline image inside a table cell.

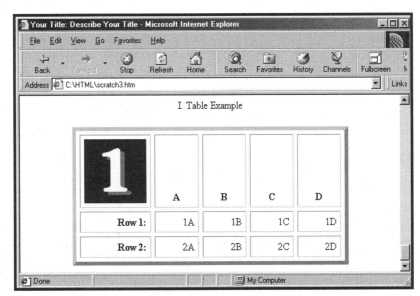

Figure 4.14

You can vertically align cell contents.

Figure 4.15 shows the result of inserting a new row that includes three cells: a blank cell in the first column and then two following cells spanning two columns each.

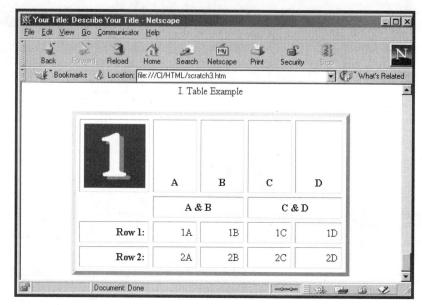

Figure 4.15

Table cells can span columns.

To span additional columns, specify the number with the COLSPAN attribute. Just make sure you don't exceed the total number of columns in the table. For instance, this example amounts to three cells spanning five columns (1 + 2 + 2 = 5).

Spanning Rows

You can also create cells that span rows. To create a cell that spans rows, use the ROWSPAN attribute to specify the number of rows to span. This gets a little tricky: The cells to be spanned need to be removed from any following rows. In the following example, the cell you need to delete has a line running through it:

```
<CAPTION>I. Table Example</CAPTION>
<TR VALIGN="bottom"><TH ROWSPAN="2" WIDTH="20%"><IMG
➥SRC="one.gif"></TH><TH WIDTH="20%">A</TH><TH WIDTH="20%">B</TH><TH
➥WIDTH="20%">C</TH><TH WIDTH="20%">D</TH></TR>
<TR><TH></TH><TH COLSPAN="2">A & B</TH><TH COLSPAN="2">C &
➥D</TH></TR>
```

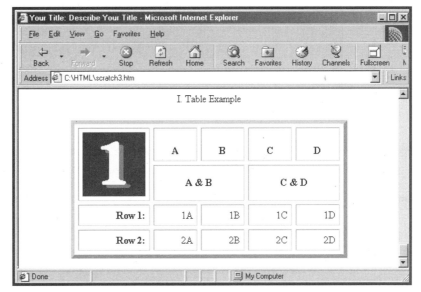

Figure 4.16

Table cells can
also span rows.

As Figure 4.16 shows, the cell with the graphic of the number 1 in it now
spans two rows.

Changing Font Sizes and Colors

You can change the font size and color of the contents of a table cell by
inserting a FONT tag bracketing the text you want to be affected. Set the
font size to "7" and the color to "blue" for one of the cells:

```
<CAPTION>I. Table Example</CAPTION>
<TR><TH ROWSPAN="2" WIDTH="20%"><IMG SRC="one.gif"></TH><TH
➥WIDTH="20%"><FONT SIZE="7" COLOR="blue">A</FONT></TH><TH
➥WIDTH="20%">B</TH><TH WIDTH="20%">C</TH><TH WIDTH="20%">D</TH></TR>
```

As Figure 4.17 shows, your first row heading has grown considerably and has
turned blue (you have to check out the color in your own browser, though).

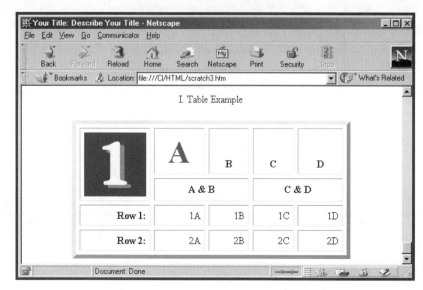

Figure 4.17

You can assign
different font sizes
and colors to text
inside a table cell.

Assigning Background Colors

You can assign a background color to an entire table, a row within a table,
or a single cell. A table can be made more readable by assigning different
background colors to row heading cells and row cells.

Assigning a Background Color in the TABLE Tag

Unfortunately, Navigator and Internet Explorer do not handle assigning a
background color to an entire table in the same fashion. In fact, the most
recent version of Internet Explorer doesn't even handle this the way earlier
versions of Internet Explorer did. Navigator displays the background color
only in the table's cells, not in the borders between the cells. Internet Explorer fills in the borders with the background color. Earlier versions of Internet
Explorer also fill in a table caption with the background color. In other
words, if you want to ensure your table is displayed at least similarly in both
of these browsers, you should probably avoid setting a background color in
the TABLE tag altogether. To see what it does, use the BGCOLOR attribute
to set a background color in the TABLE tag (you can delete it later):

```
<TABLE BGCOLOR="aqua" ALIGN="center" BORDER="6" CELLSPACING="6"
➥CELLPADDING="6" WIDTH="75%">
```

```
<CAPTION>I. Table Example</CAPTION>
```

Internet Explorer, as shown in Figure 4.18, displays a background color inserted in the TABLE tag behind the whole table.

Navigator, as shown in Figure 4.19, displays a background color inserted in the TABLE tag only inside the table's cells.

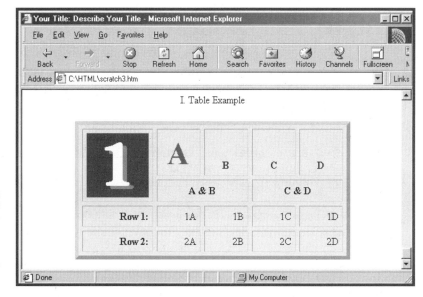

Figure 4.18

Internet Explorer displays a background color behind the whole table.

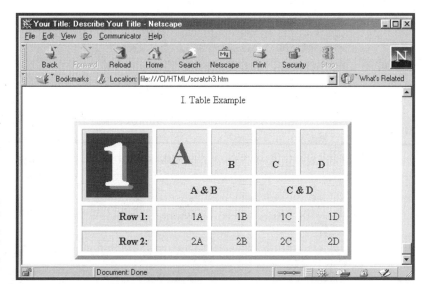

Figure 4.19

Navigator displays a background color only within the table's cells.

If you want to set the background color in the TABLE tag, that's okay. However, don't assume that because it looks one way in Internet Explorer, that it's going to look the same way in Navigator, or vice versa. If you want your table to look the same in both browsers, you should set background colors in the TR, TH, and TD tags, as shown next.

Assigning a Background Color in the TR, TH, and TD Tags

You can assign background colors to individual table rows (TR tags), as well as to individual table heading (TH) and table data (TD) cells. The following code will assign lime to the top row, red to the top-left TH cell (the one with the image in it), olive to the second row, and yellow to the bottom two rows (notice that BGCOLOR="aqua" should be deleted):

```
<P><TABLE BGCOLOR="aqua" ALIGN="center" BORDER="6" CELLSPACING="6"
➡CELLPADDING="6" WIDTH="75%">
<CAPTION>I. Table Example</CAPTION>

<TR BGCOLOR="lime"><TH BGCOLOR="red" WIDTH="20%" ROWSPAN="2"><IMG
➡SRC="one.gif"></TH><TH WIDTH="20%"><FONT SIZE="7"
➡COLOR="blue">A</FONT></TH><TH WIDTH="20%">B</TH><TH
➡WIDTH="20%">C</TH><TH WIDTH="20%">D</TH></TR>

<TR BGCOLOR="olive"><TH COLSPAN="2">A & B</TH><TH COLSPAN="2">C &
➡D</TH></TR>

<TR BGCOLOR="yellow"><TH ALIGN="right">Row
➡1:</TH><TD>1A</TD><TD>1b</TD><TD>1C</TD><TD>1D</TD></TR>

<TR BGCOLOR="yellow"><TH ALIGN="right">Row
➡2:</TH><TD>2A</TD><TD>2B</TD><TD>2C</TD><TD>2D</TD></TR>
```

As shown in Figure 4.20, different background colors appear behind one of the table cells, as well as the top, second, and last two table rows. You'll need to hop over to your Web browser, though, to really see what this looks like.

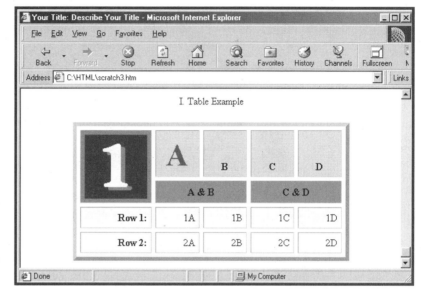

Figure 4.20

You can set different background colors for rows or individual cells.

Removing Borders and Cell Spacing

You might think that you can get rid of the spacing and borders just by removing the BORDER and CELLSPACING attributes in the TABLE tag. Not so. To get rid of them completely, you have to set the attribute values to zero, like this:

```
<P><TABLE ALIGN="center" BORDER="0" CELLSPACING="0" CELLPADDING="6"
➥WIDTH="75%">

<CAPTION>I. Table Example</CAPTION>
```

As shown in Figure 4.21, the borders and spacing between the table cells have now completely disappeared.

Using Background Images

You can also use background images in tables via the BACKGROUND attribute. However, this gets just a bit tricky because Navigator and Internet Explorer don't exactly work the same way:

✪   Just as was the case with a background color, Internet Explorer displays a background image set in the TABLE tag behind the entire

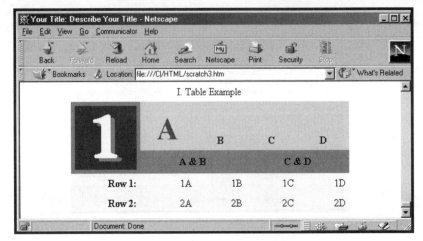

Figure 4.21

You have to set BORDER and CELLSPACING to zero to completely get rid of them.

table, including behind the cell spacing. Navigator puts it only behind the individual cells.

⚙ Internet Explorer does not recognize background images specified in the TR tag, but Navigator does. To specify a background image for a table row that will show up in both browsers, you need to specify it for each individual cell (TH or TD) in the row.

⚙ In Navigator, a background image specified in the TABLE tag takes precedence over any background colors set in the rows, heading cells, or data cells, but in Internet Explorer, it's the other way around. Therefore, if you want to specify a background image in the TABLE tag that will display identically in both browsers, get rid of any BGCOLOR attributes elsewhere in the table.

The BACKGROUND attribute for the table tags is actually not a standard HTML attribute (in either HTML 3.2 or 4.0), unlike the BGCOLOR attribute (most likely because of the wide variance between how the two main browsers interpret it). Still, background images in tables can give a very nice effect, so I wouldn't necessarily avoid using this attribute just because it hasn't got the official stamp of approval yet. Just be careful how you use it, as detailed above. To check out what a BACKGROUND attribute set in the TABLE tag looks like, specify a background image in the TABLE tag, reset the BORDER and CELLSPACING attributes as shown, and delete any BGCOLOR attributes, like this:

```
<P><TABLE BACKGROUND="backgrnd.gif" ALIGN="center" BORDER="6"
➡CELLSPACING="6" CELLPADDING="6" WIDTH="75%">
<CAPTION>I. Table Example</CAPTION>
<TR BGCOLOR="lime" VALIGN="bottom"><TH BGCOLOR="red" ROWSPAN="2"
➡WIDTH="20%"><IMG SRC="one.gif"></TH><TH WIDTH="20%"><FONT SIZE="7"
➡COLOR="blue">A</FONT></TH><TH WIDTH="20%">B</TH><TH
➡WIDTH="20%">C</TH><TH WIDTH="20%">D</TH></TR>
<TR BGCOLOR="olive"><TH COLSPAN="2">A & B</TH><TH COLSPAN="2">C &
➡D</TH></TR>
<TR BGCOLOR="yellow" ALIGN="right"><TH>Row
➡1:</TH><TD>1A</TD><TD>1b</TD><TD>1C</TD><TD>1D</TD></TR>
<TR BGCOLOR="yellow" ALIGN="right"><TH ALIGN="right">Row
➡2:</TH><TD>2A</TD><TD>2B</TD><TD>2C</TD><TD>2D</TD></TR>
</TABLE>
```

Figure 4.22 shows what this looks like in Internet Explorer.

Figure 4.23 shows what this looks like in Navigator.

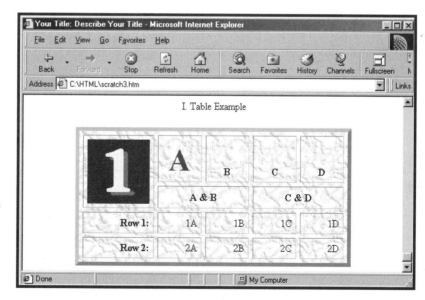

Figure 4.22

A background image in Internet Explorer is displayed behind the whole table.

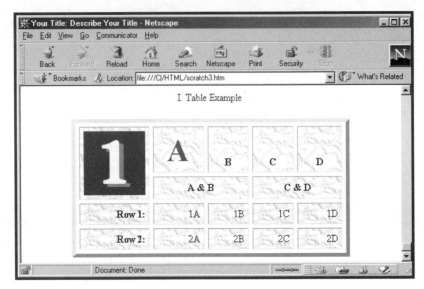

Figure 4.23

A background
image in Navigator
is displayed
only behind the
table cells.

Take a Break

Wow, if you've been at it all day long, you're definitely a long-distance run-
ner! Take a breather. Then, if you're not entirely out of breath, come back in
five or ten minutes for a little mini-tutorial I've added on creating fancy
3-D icon bullet link lists using tables. However, if your eyelids are drooping
and your fingers are cramping up, feel free to call it a night. I'll see you bright
and early tomorrow morning for the start of the Sunday Morning session,
"The Frames Tutorial." You can come back later to complete this tutorial.

Defining Table Head, Body, and Foot
Sections

The HTML 4.0 tags covered in this section are currently only supported in
Internet Explorer 4.0 or greater. If you're using Netscape Navigator as your
Web browser, feel free to skip ahead to the next section.

HTML 4.0 has three new table tags: THEAD, TBODY, and TFOOT. You
can use them to define different sets of rows as the head, body, and foot of
your table. Actually, by themselves, these tags do absolutely nothing. To get

them to strut their stuff, you've got to define a style sheet that will specify how the sections of the table nested in these tags are to be displayed.

NOTE THEAD, TBODY, and TFOOT are supported only by the latest version of Internet Explorer, version 4.01. No version of Netscape Navigator recognizes these tags.

Defining the Style Sheet

The following is just a sample style sheet meant to give you some idea of the possibilities. To find out where you can learn more about using style sheets, click the Web Links button at this book's Web site.

To create the style sheet, nest the following code in the HEAD element:

```
<HTML>
<HEAD>
<TITLE>The Table Tutorial</TITLE>
<STYLE type="text/css">
<!--
THEAD {font-family: sans-serif; font-style: bold; font-size: 200%;
➥color: maroon; background-color: yellow}
TBODY {font-family: monospace; font-style: bold; font-size: 125%;
➥color: navy; background-color: aqua}
TFOOT {font-family: sans-serif; font-style: italic; color: white;
➥background-color: #FF8000}
-->
</STYLE>
</HEAD>
```

TIP You can also include the style sheet codes in a linked style sheet. Just save the codes (from THEAD to TFOOT) as a text file, TABLE.CSS, in C:\HTML. Then replace the STYLE tag with this:

```
<LINK rel=stylesheet HREF="table.css" TYPE="text/css">
```

You should realize, however, that Netscape Navigator 4.0+ has a bug that causes it not to recognize a linked style sheet that is not in the same folder as the HTML that is linked to it.

Using TBODY as the Default

If no THEAD or TFOOT sections are included in a table, the TBODY start and end tags may be omitted. In this case, all you have to do is define TBODY in your style sheet to have its properties automatically applied to your table.

As shown in Figure 4.24, the TBODY properties defined in the style sheet (here a bold, monospace font set to navy and scaled up 125 percent in size) are applied to the entire table, even though the TBODY tag has been omitted.

Actually, this beats using the FONT tag to assign font colors within a table, which you have to set within *every* cell where you want it to take effect. A bit laborious, in other words, if all you want to do is reset the font size and color for all the cells. Now, if only Navigator would support the TBODY tag!

Figure 4.24

TBODY style properties will be applied to the whole table, even though THEAD, TFOOT, and TBODY are absent.

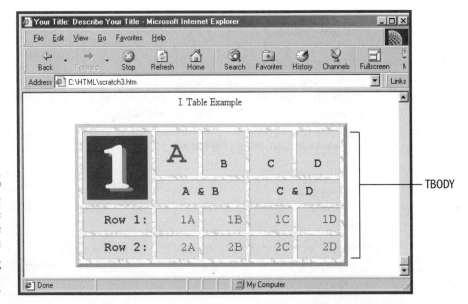

Using THEAD, TBODY, and TFOOT Together

To have one or more rows in your table show up with the properties defined
in the style sheet, just bracket them in the THEAD, TBODY, or TFOOT
tags. In the following example, apply the THEAD, TBODY, and TFOOT
tags to your table and add an additional table row (for the table foot):

```
<P><TABLE BACKGROUND="backgrnd.gif" ALIGN="center" BORDER="6"
➥CELLSPACING="6" CELLPADDING="6" WIDTH="75%">
<CAPTION>I. Table Example</CAPTION>
<THEAD>
<TR VALIGN="bottom"><TH ROWSPAN="2" WIDTH="20%"><IMG
➥SRC="one.gif"></TH><TH WIDTH="20%"><FONT SIZE="7"
➥COLOR="blue">A</FONT></TH><TH WIDTH="20%">B</TH><TH
➥WIDTH="20%">C</TH><TH WIDTH="20%">D</TH></TR>
<TR><TH COLSPAN="2">A & B</TH><TH COLSPAN="2">C & D</TH></TR>
</THEAD>
<TBODY>
<TR ALIGN="right"><TH>Row
➥1:</TH><TD>1A</TD><TD>1b</TD><TD>1C</TD><TD>1D</TD></TR>
<TR ALIGN="right"><TH ALIGN="right">Row
➥2:</TH><TD>2A</TD><TD>2B</TD><TD>2C</TD><TD>2D</TD></TR>
</TBODY>
<TFOOT>
<TR><TD COLSPAN="5" ALIGN="center">This is the table foot.</TD></TR>
</TFOOT>
</TABLE>
```

As shown in Figure 4.25, the latest version of Internet Explorer applies the
properties defined in the style sheet to the different sections of the table.

TIP

You can define as many TBODY sections as you want within a single table. The only requirement is that a TBODY section must have at least one table row in it. (You should not define
more than one THEAD or TFOOT section, however.)

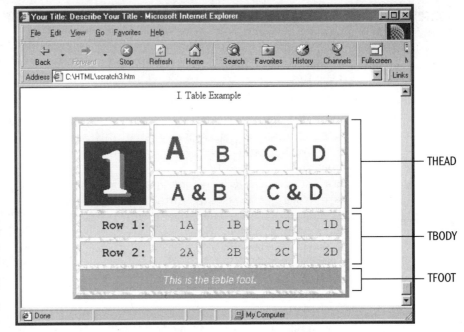

THEAD

TBODY

TFOOT

Figure 4.25

You can define styles that will render the head, body, and foot of your table in the format you prefer.

Other HTML 4.0 Table Tags

HTML 4.0 has added the FRAME, RULES, COLGROUP, COL, and CHAR tags. Only the FRAME and RULES tags are supported, and only by Internet Explorer. Navigator doesn't yet support any of these tags. The COLGROUP and COL tags will allow you to specify formatting for column groups and individual columns, somewhat similar to how the TBODY, THEAD, and TFOOT tags can specify formatting for rows or row sections. The CHAR tag, in conjunction with the COLGROUP or COL tags, will allow vertical alignment within a column on a decimal point, which would definitely be a handy feature. Internet Explorer also supports a number of additional table tags—BORDERCOLOR, BOR-DERCOLORDARK, and BORDERCOLORLIGHT—that have not yet been included in HTML 3.2 or 4.0.

Saving Your Work

Save the HTML file you just created. You can use it later as a reference. When you first saved it, you named it SCRATCH3.HTM. If more than one person is going to be doing this tutorial and you want to make sure it doesn't get overwritten, you might want to give it a new name, such as using your first initial and last name for the file name (JMILLER3.HTM, for instance, if your name is John Miller). After you've saved your scratch pad file, go ahead and exit Notepad.

For your reference, a file, TUTOR3A.HTM, has been included with the sample files that you copied from the CD-ROM. It includes all the previous examples broken out into separate tables, so you can have a reference for each of the features covered here. Feel free to pull it up into Notepad or check it out in your browser.

Creating Icon Link Lists Using Tables

In the Intermediate HTML Tutorial, I showed you how to create indented icon link lists using left-aligned bullet images. That method works fine, except it was limited to indenting only two lines of text. In the following exercise, I'll show you how to create an indented icon link list using tables. That this method is perhaps a bit more difficult to implement than using left-aligned bullet images is compensated for by the lack of any limitation on the number of indented lines.

Loading Your Starting Template

You should start here with a fresh Notepad window. Restart Notepad to get a new empty Notepad window; then load the starting template you saved this morning, C:\HTML\START.HTM. It should look like the following listing (if you didn't save the template, just retype it now):

```
<HTML>
<HEAD>
<TITLE>Your Title: Describe Your Title</TITLE>
</HEAD>
<BODY>
</BODY>
</HTML>
```

Saving Your Scratch Pad File

Save your scratch pad file you'll be using in this brief lesson. In Notepad, select File, Save As. Change the folder where you're going to save your file to C:\HTML and then save your file as SCRATCH4.HTM.

Creating the Icon Link List

To create an icon bullet link list using tables, enter the following HTML:

```
<BODY>
<TABLE WIDTH=100%>
<TR VALIGN="top">
<TD WIDTH="20"><P><IMG SRC="redball.gif" VSPACE="3"> </TD><TD><A
➥HREF="http://www.li.net/~autorent/yoyo.htm">Jon's Yo-Yo Kingdom</A>
➥Claims to have the largest Yo-Yo link list on the Web. This is more
➥text just to show that you can indent as much text as you wish.
➥This is more text just to show that you can indent as much text as
➥you wish.</TD></TR>
<TR VALIGN="top">
<TD><P><IMG SRC="redball.gif" VSPACE="3"> </TD><TD><A
➥HREF="http://pages.nyu.edu/~tqm3413/yoyo/index.htm">Tomer's Page of
➥Exotic Yo-Yo</A> Dedicated to the "little-known, original, unusual,
➥difficult, or otherwise interesting tricks." This is more text just
➥to show that you can indent as much text as you wish. This is more
➥text just to show that you can indent as much text as you
➥wish.</TD></TR>
</TABLE>
```

Figure 4.26 shows what this should look like in your browser.

Figure 4.26

Using tables, you can create an indented icon link list with no limit on the number of indented lines.

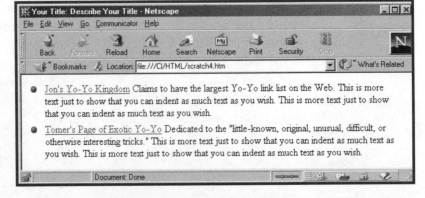

In this example of creating an indented icon link list using tables, you should pay attention to a number of things:

- The TR tags include VALIGN="top" to set the vertical alignment. Without this, the icon bullet images would be middle aligned, which is not what you want. You could also set this attribute value in the TD tag containing the icon bullet graphic.

- A WIDTH attribute value of 20 pixels is set in the first cell of the top row to specify the width of the first column. This width can be increased or decreased to suit your taste.

- A P tag is inserted in the first cell of each row with a space also inserted at the end of the same cell. This makes allowance for older Web browsers that don't support displaying tables. The P tag will cause a non-supporting browser to display the table row as a separate line, and the space will be inserted between the icon graphic and the following text. Note that adding the P tag and inserting the space will not affect the display of the table in a tables-capable Web browser.

- The IMG tags for the icon bullet graphics include a VSPACE (vertical space) attribute of 3 pixels. Rarely will an icon bullet line up evenly with a following line of text. You can add or subtract pixels in the VSPACE attribute in the IMG tag to adjust the position of the icon bullet relative to following text.

Saving Your Work

Save the HTML file you just created. You can use it later as a reference. When you first saved it, you named it SCRATCH4.HTM. If more than one person is going to be doing this tutorial and you want to make sure this file doesn't get overwritten, you might want to give it a new name, such as using your first initial and last name for the file name (JMILLER4.HTM, for instance, if you name is John Miller).

What's Next?

You should now be comfortable including tables in your Web pages. If you completed the entire Tables Tutorial, you not only learned everything you need to know to create effective tables, you also learned how to use some of the latest HTML 4.0 table tags in conjunction with a snazzy style sheet. What's more, you also learned how to create fancy 3-D icon bullet link lists using tables.

If you've managed to complete all three of the Saturday tutorials, you should have a good grasp of all but the more "advanced" HTML features. The Tables Tutorial was the last of the straight HTML tutorials in this book. The remaining tutorials scheduled for Sunday are all software tutorials that show you how to apply shareware and freeware software tools included on the CD-ROM to incorporate more advanced HTML features—frames, forms, Web art special effects, GIF animations, and image maps—in your Web pages.

Even if you've taken the whole weekend to complete the Saturday tutorials, you've still accomplished a great deal. You should know enough now to create a really super-duper Web page or site. Feel free to come back next weekend to try any of the Sunday tutorials at your leisure.

If it's still Saturday night, get a good night's sleep (you deserve it!) so you'll be well rested for the software tutorials scheduled for Sunday.

SUNDAY MORNING

The Frames Tutorial

- ✿ Creating two-row, two-column, and combination frame layouts
- ✿ Creating pages to be displayed in frames
- ✿ Creating hypertext links for frames
- ✿ Using the frames template to create nested frame pages

You've completed both the Basic and Intermediate HTML Tutorials in the Saturday Morning and Saturday Afternoon sessions, and possibly the bonus Tables Tutorial in the Saturday Evening session. It's now Sunday morning and time to begin the Frames Tutorial.

If you weren't able to complete the Intermediate HTML Tutorial yesterday, I recommend that you do that tutorial now before starting this tutorial. You can, however, if you wish, skip the Tables Tutorial for now.

Yes, I know what you're thinking: Frames! Isn't that getting pretty advanced? Well, if you have the right tools, even frames can be easy as pie. In this case, the tool you'll be using is Frame-It, an excellent freeware software program that takes just about all the pain out of creating frames.

Creating a Working Folder

Before you get started doing this tutorial, you should create a working folder where you can save your work. Using Windows Explorer or File Manager, create a Frames folder inside your HTML folder (C:\HTML\FRAMES). If you don't know how to do this, here are some quick instructions:

Windows 3.1

1. Run File Manager. With the C drive selected, click the HTML folder in the window on the left to highlight it.

2. Select File, Create Directory. In the Name box, type **frames**; then click OK. (Leave File Manager open if you want—you'll be using it again a little later on.)

Windows 95/98:

1. Click the Start button and then select Programs, Windows Explorer.

2. Under the C drive, click the HTML folder to highlight it.

3. Select File, New, Folder. Type **frames** as the folder name and press the Enter key. (Leave Windows Explorer open if you want—you'll be using it again a little later on.)

Installing Frame-It

To install Frame-It from the CD-ROM, follow these steps:

1. Insert the *Learn HTML in a Weekend* CD-ROM in your CD-ROM drive.

2. If you are using Windows 95/98, Prima's CD-ROM interface will automatically run, unless you have disabled Autorun. If the CD-ROM interface does not automatically run, from the Start menu, select Run, then type **D:\prima.exe** (where D:\ is your CD-ROM's drive letter) and click OK.

3. If you are using Windows 3.1, select File, Run from Program Manager's menu bar and then type **D:\prima.exe** (where D:\ is your CD-ROM's drive letter). Click OK.

4. With Prima's CD-ROM interface onscreen, click Web Tools, Frame-It, and select Install.

5. For Windows 3.1, select the 16-bit (Windows 3.1x) radio button and click OK. For Windows 95/98 select the 32-bit (Win 96/98/NT) radio button and click OK.

6. In the Winzip Self-Extractor window, click Unzip to unzip Frame-It's program files to C:\FRAME-IT (for Windows 3.1) or C:\FRAME-IT32 (for Windows 95/98).

7. In the message box that states that the files have been successfully unzipped, click OK.

8. A readme text file will open in Notepad telling you that you need to copy a DLL file, IMLIB221.DLL for Windows 3.1 or ILIB95HT.DLL for Windows 95/98, into the Windows System folder. Select File, Exit.

Windows 95/98: Adding Frame-It to Your Start Menu

In Windows 95/98, here's how to add Frame-It to your Start menu:

1. Click the Start button and select Settings.

2. In Windows 95, select Taskbar. In Windows 98, select Taskbar & Start Menu.

3. Click the Start Menu Programs tab and then click Add.

4. Click Browse and go to the *C:\Frame-it32*; then double-click on *Frameit.exe*. Click Next.

5. You can select any location where you want the Frame-It option to be displayed on the Start menu. To display it under Programs, just click Next.

6. Type **Frame-It** as the name for the shortcut; then click Finish. Click OK to exit the Taskbar Properties window.

Windows 3.1: Creating a Program Icon for Frame-It

To add a program icon for Frame-It to the Main window group of Program Manager, perform the following steps:

1. Click the Main program group window to activate it. If the Main group is not already open in Program Manager, select Window, Main (or select More Windows, Main). If you want to add Frame-It's program icon to a different program group, select it instead.

2. Select File, New. Leave the Program Item radio button selected. Click OK.

3. Click Browse, select the C: drive (if you're not already there) and then double-click the *frame-it* folder in the Directories list to open it. Double-click *frameit.exe* in the list of files.

4. In the Description box, type **Frame-It,** and then click OK.

Copying Frame-It's DLL File

Before you can run Frame-It, you need to copy the DLL file mentioned in its readme text file into Windows' system folder. If you don't know how to do this, I've included instructions here on how to do this in Windows 95/98 and Windows 3.1.

Windows 95/98:

Before you can run Frame-It, you need to copy the ILIB95HT.DLL file that was mentioned in the readme text file into Windows' system folder. Here's how to do it:

1. On the Start menu, select Programs, Windows Explorer (if you left Windows Explorer open after creating your working folder, just use Alt+Tab to hop back over to it).

2. Under the C: drive, click the *Frame-it32* folder.

3. In the right window, right-click *ilib95ht.dll* and select Copy.

4. In the left window, click the *Windows* folder to highlight it (if you're running both Windows 3.1 and Windows 95 on your computer, you'll need to click the Win95 folder).

5. In the right window, right-click the *System* folder and then select Paste.

Windows 3.1

Before you can run Frame-It, you need to copy the IMLIB221.DLL file that was mentioned in the readme text file into Windows' system folder. Here's how to do it:

1. From the Main window, double-click the File Manager icon (if you left File Manager open after creating your working folder, just use Alt+Tab to hop back over to it).

2. If the Drive C: icon is not selected, click it to select it.

3. Find the *frame-it* folder; then click on it to highlight it.

4. In the right window, click *imlib221.dll* to highlight this file.

5. From the menu bar, select File, Copy.

6. In the To box, type **c:\windows\system** and then click OK.

7. Select File, Exit to close the File Manager.

Starting Frame-It

In Windows 95/98, click the Start button and then select Programs, Frame-It.

In Windows 3.1, activate the Main window (or the window where you've put the Frame-It icon) and then double-click the Frame-It icon.

NOTE GME Systems has released the version of Frame-It (version 1.23) included on the CD-ROM as freeware. However, when you run Frame-It, you'll still see an opening window telling you that your copy of Frame-It is a 15-day evaluation version. When the 15-day evaluation period is over, just enter the following registration codes:

Name: Registered User

Code: 29700

When you first enter the user name and registration code, you may get an error message. Just rerun Frame-It and it should come up registered to "Registered User."

In the following examples, I'll show you how to create the following three different kinds of frame pages:

○ **A two-row frame page.** This exercise covers dividing the browser window into two horizontal frames (rows), with the top frame including links that control the contents of the bottom frame.

○ **A two-column frame page.** This exercise covers dividing the browser window into two vertical frames (columns), with the left frame including links that control the contents of the right frame.

○ **A combination row-and-column frame page.** This exercise covers creating a frame page that includes a combination of rows and columns. First two rows are defined and then the bottom row is divided into two columns.

NOTE The screen captures and descriptions in this tutorial are all from the Windows 95 version of Frame-It. The Windows 3.1 version, however, is virtually identical to the Windows 95 version. Any differences between the versions should be minor.

Example One: Creating a Two-Row Frame Page

In this example you'll create a simple two-row frame page with links in the top frame controlling what's displayed in the bottom frame. Follow these steps to start creating a two-row frame page:

1. After starting Frame-It, an opening banner will be displayed for a few seconds before Frame-It's opening window appears.

2. Leave the Row Orientated radio button selected. Leave 2 selected in the No. of Rows option. (See Figure 5.1.)

3. Click Next.

Row orientation

Two rows

Figure 5.1

Frame-It's default settings are for a frame page with two rows.

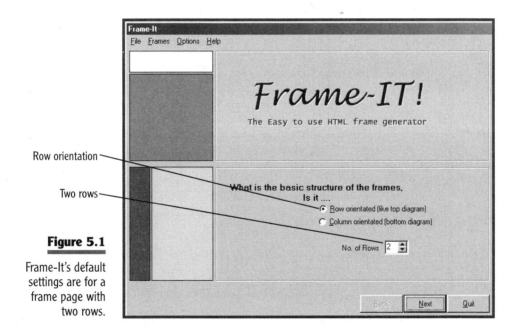

Defining the Top Frame

Here you'll define the settings for the top frame:

1. Click your mouse in the top frame to highlight it. (See Figure 5.2.)
2. Type **Top_Bar** in the Name of the Frame box.
3. Type **top_bar.htm** in the Filename box. (You can also click the file folder icon to the right of the Filename box to browse for the HTML file you want to use in the top row.)
4. In the Frame Dimensions section, change the Height (%) setting to 25. Leave the Width (%) setting unchanged. (See Figure 5.3.)

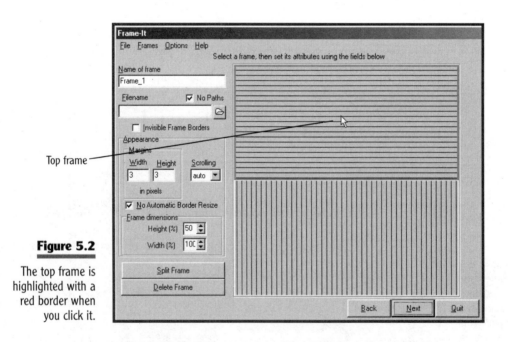

Figure 5.2

The top frame is highlighted with a red border when you click it.

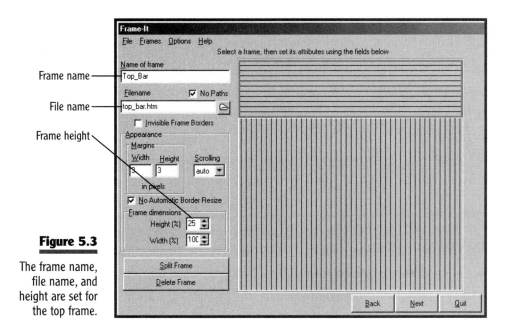

Frame name —

File name —

Frame height —

Figure 5.3

The frame name,
file name, and
height are set for
the top frame.

NOTE

You may be wondering about the other options and controls included on Frame-It's window. The No Paths check box should always be left checked. By unchecking it and then browsing to select a file, you'll insert a full URL that will work on your local hard drive, but not on the Web when you transfer your files onto a server. To turn off the display of the frame borders, check the Invisible Frame Borders check box. You can change the amount of margin space inside a frame by increasing or decreasing the Width and Height settings. (A minimum setting of 1 pixel is required.) In the Scrolling list, you can set a frame to only display scroll bars if required (Auto), to always display scroll bars (Yes), or to never display scroll bars (No). The Split Frame button will be used later when you get around to doing the combination row-and-column frame page example.

Defining the Bottom Frame

Here you'll define the settings for the bottom frame:

1. Click in the bottom frame to highlight it.
2. Type **Window** in the Name of Frame box.
3. Type **window.htm** in the Filename box.
4. Leave all the other settings as they are (see Figure 5.4). Note that the Height (%) setting has been automatically set at 75.

NOTE   The Frames menu on Frame-It's menu bar allows you to add, insert, or delete rows when creating a row-orientated frame page. For instance, selecting Add a Row would add a row at the bottom of the other rows. Selecting Insert a Row would insert a row above the currently selected row. Selecting Delete a Row would delete the currently selected row.

5. Click Next.

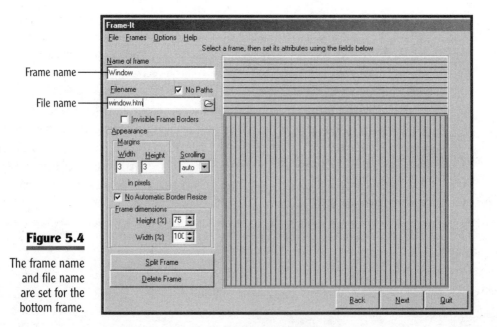

Figure 5.4

The frame name and file name are set for the bottom frame.

Creating the NOFRAMES Text

The NOFRAMES text will be displayed in browsers that can't display frames. In the following steps, you'll assign colors to the background, text, and links, as well as enter the actual text you want to have displayed:

1. Click the Background button. The Color dialog box is displayed, as shown in Figure 5.5.

2. Select a background color. For instance, select black as the color (bottom-left corner) and then click OK. You'll notice that the background of the Colors box has now changed to black.

3. Click the Text button and select a text color. For instance, select white as the color (bottom-right corner) and then click OK. You'll notice that the text in the Colors preview box has now changed to white.

4. Click the Links button and select a color for any links you want to include. For instance, select yellow as the color (second color in the first row) and then click OK. You'll notice that the link representations in the Colors preview box have now changed to yellow.

5. Skip the Background Image setting. (You can use this to specify a background image, if you want, but I hardly think it's worth bothering with.)

Figure 5.5

The Color dialog box is displayed when you select background, text, and link colors for your NOFRAMES text.

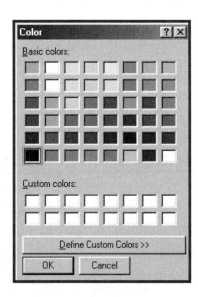

6. In the Text to Be Displayed box, type this:

```
Sorry, this page requires a Frames-capable browser. Feel free to
view the <A HREF="noframe.htm">Non-Frames Version</A> of this
page.
```

Figure 5.6 shows the NOFRAMES text entered in the Text to Be Displayed box.

NOTE NOFRAMES.HTM is just a dummy file name. When you're setting up a real Web page using frames, you'll create and reference your actual nonframes page. One alternative here is to use the initial page that's displayed in your bottom frame (the Window frame) as your "no frames" page as well. However, you need to make sure to also include any of the links from the top frame of your frame page.

7. You're going to want to save this text so that you can use it again in the other frame page examples. To do this, just click and drag to highlight the NOFRAMES text. Press Ctrl+C to copy the text, run Notepad, and then press Ctrl+V to paste in the text. In Notepad, save

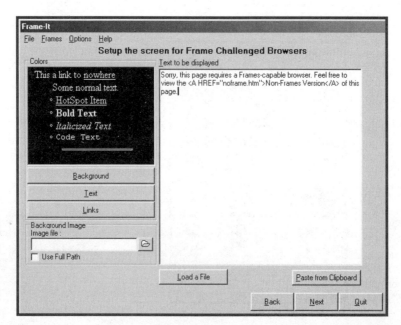

Figure 5.6

The NOFRAMES text will show up only in a browser that can't do frames.

the file as **boiler.htm** in C:\HTML\FRAMES. Exit or minimize Notepad and then return to Frame-It.

8. Click Next.

Copying Your Frame Settings to the Clipboard

The next step is to copy your frame settings to the Clipboard. After you do this, you'll be pasting these settings into Notepad and then saving them out as your actual frame page. To copy your frame settings, follow these steps:

1. Leave the Copy to Clipboard radio button selected (the default). Alternatively, you could save your frame settings to a file rather than to the Clipboard. (See Figure 5.7.)

2. Leave the Include File Paths in Final Output check box unchecked, because you're storing all your files in a single folder.

3. Click the Store button.

4. At the Finished window, click OK. (Don't worry about the imprecation in the message box to "place the information in a secure place as

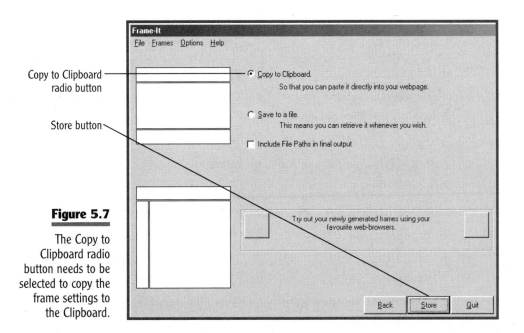

Figure 5.7

The Copy to Clipboard radio button needs to be selected to copy the frame settings to the Clipboard.

soon as possible"—the next thing you'll be doing is pasting it into Notepad.)

You can just leave Frame-It open here and then hop back to it when you're ready to use it again for creating the second frame page example. (Frame-It's program window doesn't have a minimize button, but you can drag it most-ly off the Desktop to get it out of the way and then drag it back when you want to use it again.)

Frame-It allows you to specify the location of two Web browsers that can be used to preview the layout of your frame page. Just select Options, Define Browser Locations and then click the browse icons to specify the location of the program files for one or two Web browsers. I don't find this feature to be very useful, primarily because Frame-It stores your frame codes as a temporary file in the Frame-It folder. This means that, even if you create and save the HTML files that will be displayed in the top and bottom frames of your frame page, your browser will look for these files in the Frame-It folder. If you want to use this feature, one option would be to save all your frame pages in the Frame-It folder. Another option would be to copy Frame-It's program file to the folder where you're saving your frame pages and then run Frame-It from that location.

I much prefer simply pasting the frame codes into Notepad and then saving them out to the folder of my choice. At the same time, I can create and save any HTML files that will be displayed in the frame windows. Then I only need to run my browser and open the frame page to see what it's going to look like. If I want to make any changes to the frame layout, I just have to hop back over to Frame-It, make the changes, and then generate a new set of frame codes.

Creating and Saving FRAME1.HTM

You now need to paste your frame settings into Notepad and then save them as FRAME1.HTM in C:\HTML\FRAMES:

1. Run Notepad.
2. Press Ctrl+V (or select Edit, Paste) to paste the frame settings into Notepad.
3. Turn Word Wrap on by selecting Edit, Word Wrap.

• •

NOTE What you're pasting into Notepad here are the actual HTML codes produced by Frame-It according to the settings you just specified. When you clicked the Store button in Frame-It, those codes were copied to the Clipboard. Now you're just pasting those very same codes from the Clipboard into Notepad.

• •

Your file in Notepad should read as follows:

```
<html>
<! -- Generated using Frame-it v1.23 -- >
<! -- http://www.iinet.net.au/~bwh/frame-it.html -->
<frameset rows="25%,75%">
<frame name="Top_Bar" src="top_bar.htm" marginheight=3 marginwidth=3
➥scrolling=auto noresize>
<frame name="Window" src="window.htm" marginheight=3 marginwidth=3
➥scrolling=auto noresize>
</frameset>
<noframes>
<body bgcolor=#000000 text=#FFFFFF link=#80FFFF>
Sorry, this page requires a Frames-capable browser. Feel free to
➥view the <A HREF="noframe.htm">Non-Frames Version</A> of this
➥page.</noframes>
```

4. Save the file as **frame1.htm** in C:\HTML\FRAMES.

• •

NOTE You'll notice at the bottom of the codes produced by Frame-It that there's no </BODY> or </HTML> end tag. Frames-capable browsers won't bother to read anything beyond the FRAMESET element, and apparently excluding these end tags has no ill effect on browsers that aren't frames capable.

• •

Creating and Saving TOP_BAR.HTM

You've created and saved the HTML file (FRAME1.HTM) that includes your frame settings, but you still need to create and save the HTML files that will be displayed inside the frames. First, create and save the HTML file (TOP_BAR.HTM) that will be displayed in the top-row frame:

1. Clear Notepad's window by selecting File, New.

2. Type in the following:

```
<HTML>
<HEAD><TITLE></TITLE></HEAD>
<BODY>
<H1 ALIGN="center">The Frame Page Title</H1>
<P ALIGN="center">[<A HREF="window.htm"Target=Window>Page 1</A>]
➥[<A HREF="window2.htm" Target="Window">Page 2</A>] [<A
➥HREF="window3.htm" Target="Window">Page 3</A>]
</BODY>
</HTML>
```

3. Save this file as **top_bar.htm** in C:\HTML\FRAMES.

Creating and Saving WINDOW.HTM

You now need to create and save the HTML file that will initially be displayed in the bottom frame of your frame page. This file will also be displayed in the bottom frame when the "Page 1" link is clicked in the top frame (in TOP_BAR.HTM). To create and save this file, follow these steps:

1. Clear Notepad's window by selecting File, New.

2. Type in the following:

```
<HTML>
<HEAD><TITLE></TITLE></HEAD>
<BODY>
<H1 ALIGN="center">This is Page 1.</H1>
</BODY>
</HTML>
```

3. Save the file as **window.htm** in C:\HTML\FRAMES.

Creating and Saving WINDOW2.HTM

Next, you need to create and save the file that will be displayed in the bottom frame when the "Page 2" link is clicked in the top frame (in TOP_BAR.HTM):

1. Clear Notepad's window by selecting File, New.

2. Type in the following:

```
<HTML>
<HEAD><TITLE></TITLE></HEAD>
<BODY>
```

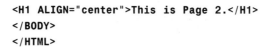

```
<H1 ALIGN="center">This is Page 2.</H1>
</BODY>
</HTML>
```

3. Save the file as **window2.htm** in C:\HTML\FRAMES.

Creating and Saving WINDOW3.HTM

Now, create and save the file that will be displayed in the bottom frame when the "Page 3" link is clicked in the top frame (in TOP_BAR.HTM):

1. Clear Notepad's window by selecting File, New.
2. Type in the following:

```
<HTML>
<HEAD><TITLE></TITLE></HEAD>
<BODY>
<H1 ALIGN="center">This is Page 3.</H1>
</BODY>
</HTML>
```

3. Save the file as **window3.htm** in C:\HTML\FRAMES.

Because you'll be using Notepad quite often in the following exercises, you can just minimize it here if you want, rather than close it. Then, when you need to use Notepad again, just click it in the Windows 95 taskbar or press Alt+Tab until you bring up its window.

Viewing the Two-Row Frame Page in Your Browser

Now that you've created and saved your frame page, as well as the separate pages that will be displayed in the frames, take a look at the frame page in your Web browser:

1. Run your browser and open FRAME1.HTM from the C:\HTML\FRAMES folder. Figure 5.8 shows what your frame page should look like in any frames-capable Web browser.
2. Click the second link, "Page 2," to display WINDOW2.HTM in the bottom frame. (See Figure 5.9.)
3. Click the third link, "Page 3," to display WINDOW3.HTM in the bottom frame. (See Figure 5.10.)

TOP_BAR.HTM

WINDOW.HTM

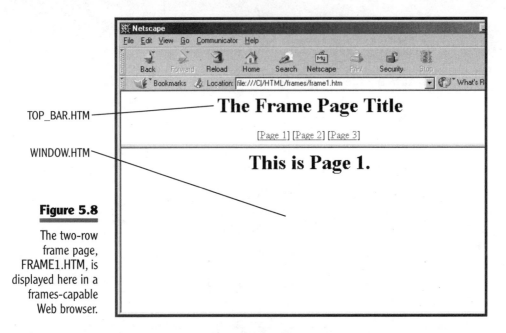

Figure 5.8

The two-row frame page, FRAME1.HTM, is displayed here in a frames-capable Web browser.

"Page 2" link

WINDOW2.HTM

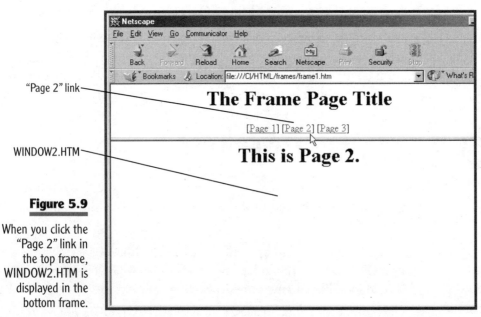

Figure 5.9

When you click the "Page 2" link in the top frame, WINDOW2.HTM is displayed in the bottom frame.

4. Click the first link, "Page 1," to redisplay WINDOW.HTM in the bottom frame.

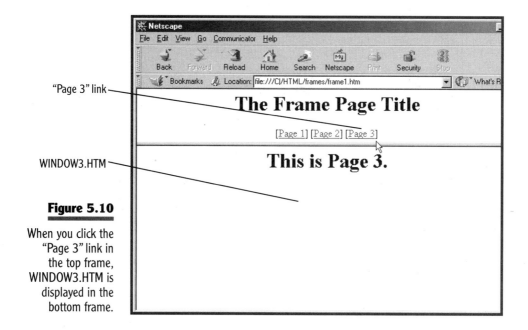

"Page 3" link

WINDOW3.HTM

Figure 5.10

When you click the "Page 3" link in the top frame, WINDOW3.HTM is displayed in the bottom frame.

Example Two: Creating a Two-Column Frame Page

In this exercise, you'll create a frame page that's quite similar to the one you just created, except that it uses two columns rather than two rows.

Starting Frame-It

Follow these steps to start Frame-It for the second frame page example:

1. If you didn't exit Frame-It after generating the frame codes for the last example, use Alt+Tab to bring Frame-It's window back to the foreground. (You may need to drag its window back onto the Desktop if you dragged it off previously.) Click the Back button three times and then click OK at the message "Going back here will undo all work done on this screen."

   If you've exited Frame-It since the last example, rerun Frame-It.

2. Select the Column Orientated radio button. Leave 2 as the setting for the No. of Columns option (the default). (See Figure 5.11.)

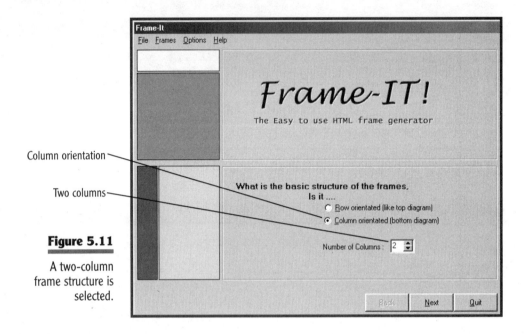

Column orientation

Two columns

Figure 5.11

A two-column
frame structure is
selected.

3. Click Next.

Defining the Left Frame

Here you'll define the settings for the left frame:

1. Click the left frame to highlight it (it will be outlined with a red border).
2. Type **Left_Bar** in the Name of Frame box.
3. Type **left_bar.htm** in the Filename box.
4. Define the frame dimensions: Change the Width (%) setting to 25. Leave the Height (%) setting unchanged. (See Figure 5.12.)

Defining the Right Frame

Next, you'll define the settings for the right frame:

1. Click your mouse in the right frame to highlight it.
2. Type **Window** as the name of the frame.

Frame name ——

File name ——

Frame width ╲

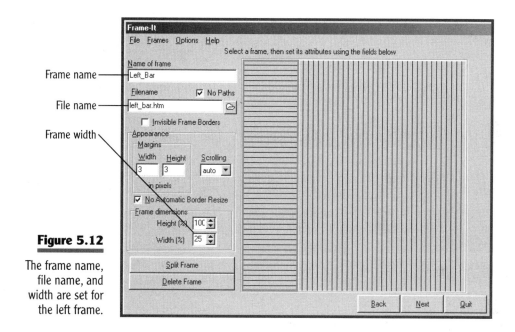

Figure 5.12

The frame name,
file name, and
width are set for
the left frame.

3. Type **window.htm** as the file name. (See Figure 5.13.)

NOTE The Frames option on Frame-It's menu bar allows you to add, insert, or delete columns when creating a column-oriented frame page. For instance, selecting Add a Column would add a third column (Frame_3) to the right of the other columns. Selecting Insert a Column would insert a column to the left of the currently selected column. Selecting Delete a Column would delete the currently selected column.

4. Click Next.

Creating the NOFRAMES Text

If you returned to Frame-It's starting window by using the Back button, your settings and the NOFRAMES text will still be there. Just go ahead and click the Next button now.

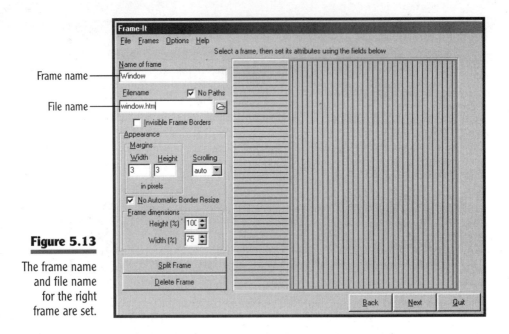

Frame name ——

File name ——

Figure 5.13

The frame name
and file name
for the right
frame are set.

If you've restarted Frame-It from scratch, you'll need to input the background, text, and links settings again. If you're not clear on how to do this, see the instructions for this in the first frame page example. (If you saved the NOFRAMES text as BOILER.HTM in the last example, instead of retyping the text, you can click the Load a File button to open BOILER.HTM from C:\HTML\FRAMES.) After you've input the NOFRAMES settings again, click the Next button.

Copying Your Frame Settings to the Clipboard

At Frame-It's last screen, follow these steps:

1. Leave Copy to Clipboard selected (the default). Leave all other settings as they are.

2. Click Store. At the Finished window, click OK to copy the frame settings to the Clipboard.

Just leave Frame-It open here—you'll be using it again to create the settings for the third frame page example. Because Frame-It doesn't have a minimize button, just drag it off to the side of the Desktop to get it out of the way.

Creating and Saving FRAME2.HTM

If you left Notepad open when you used it in the last example, just use Alt+Tab to activate its window. If you exited, you'll need to run Notepad again (if you're using Windows 95 or 3.1, don't forget to turn Word Wrap on).

In Notepad, press Ctrl+V to paste your frame page settings from the Clipboard.

The text in your Notepad window should match what's shown here:

```
<html>
<! -- Generated using Frame-it v1.23 -- >
<! -- http://www.iinet.net.au/~bwh/frame-it.html -->
<frameset cols="25%,75%">
<frame name="Left_Bar" src="left_bar.htm" marginheight=3
➥marginwidth=3 scrolling=auto noresize>
<frame name="Window" src="window.htm" marginheight=3 marginwidth=3
➥scrolling=auto noresize>
</frameset>
<noframes>
<body bgcolor=#000000 text=#FFFFFF link=#80FFFF>
Sorry, this page requires a Frames-capable browser. Feel free to
➥view the <A HREF="noframe.htm">Non-Frames Version</A> of this
➥page.</noframes>
```

Save the file as **frame2.htm** in C:\HTML\FRAMES.

Creating and Saving LEFT_BAR.HTM

Here, you'll create the file (LEFT_BAR.HTM) that will be displayed in the left frame. Clear Notepad's window by selecting File, New. Type in the following:

```
<HTML>
<HEAD><TITLE></TITLE></HEAD>
<BODY>
<H2 ALIGN="center">Sidebar Menu</H1>
<HR>
<UL>
<P><LI><A HREF="window.htm" Target=Window>Page 1</A>
<P><LI><A HREF="window2.htm" Target=Window>Page 2</A>
<P><LI><A HREF="window3.htm" Target=Window>Page 3</A>
</BODY>
</HTML>
```

Save the file as **left_bar.htm** in C:\HTML\FRAMES.

NOTE Because you already created WINDOW.HTM, WINDOW2.HTM, and WINDOW3.HTM in the last exercise, you don't have to re-create them here. However, remember that if you want to create a frame page using this format from scratch, you'll need to create the initial page (WINDOW.HTM) and any subsequent pages (WINDOW2.HTM, WINDOW3.HTM, and so on) that you want to be able to cycle through in the right frame. Also, when creating a frame page from scratch, you don't need to use these particular file names. You could name the initial file that's displayed in the Window frame FRONT.HTM, for instance, with the following pages displayed in that window named as PAGE1.HTM, PAGE2.HTM, and so on. Just make sure your frame page settings in Frame-It and your hypertext links in LEFT_BAR.HTM agree.

Just leave Notepad open—you'll need to use it again later when you do the third frame page example. Click the minimize button, if you want to get it off the Desktop.

Viewing the Two-Column Frame Page in Your Browser

Now, here's how to check out your new frame page in your browser:

1. Run your browser and then open FRAME2.HTM from C:\HTML\FRAMES. (See Figure 5.14.)
2. Click the first link, "Page 2," to display WINDOW2.HTM in the right frame. (See Figure 5.15.)
3. Click the second link, "Page 3," to display WINDOW3.HTM in the right frame. (See Figure 5.16.)
4. Click the third link, "Home," to redisplay WINDOW.HTM in the right frame.

Take a Break

Ready for a breather? This seems like as good a time as any. Get up and stretch, pour that second cup of coffee, stare out the window at the horizon to relax your eyes—do whatever you feel like. Grab a bite if haven't had breakfast yet.

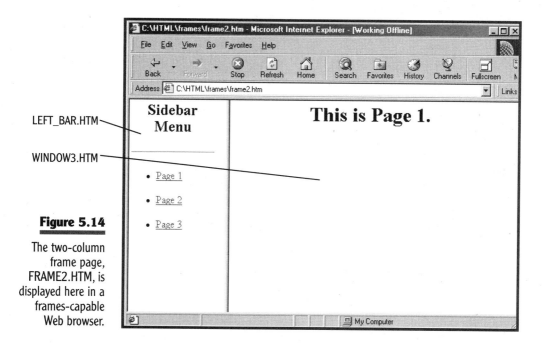

LEFT_BAR.HTM

WINDOW3.HTM

Figure 5.14

The two-column frame page, FRAME2.HTM, is displayed here in a frames-capable Web browser.

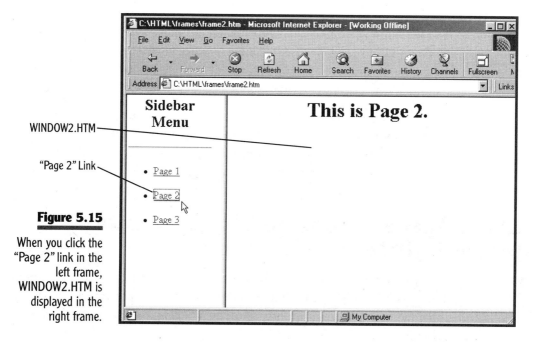

WINDOW2.HTM

"Page 2" Link

Figure 5.15

When you click the "Page 2" link in the left frame, WINDOW2.HTM is displayed in the right frame.

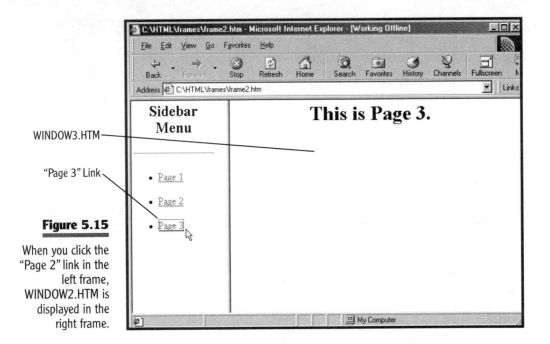

WINDOW3.HTM ——

"Page 3" Link ——

Figure 5.15

When you click the "Page 2" link in the left frame, WINDOW2.HTM is displayed in the right frame.

The remaining example in this tutorial is optional. If you're running short on time this morning, feel free to skip it—you can come back and do it later. Of course, if you want to take the rest of the day to just play around with creating frame pages, that's fine, too.

If you're continuing on, I'll see you back in 10 or 15 minutes, when you'll learn how to create a combination row-and-column frame page. If you've decided to skip the remainder of this tutorial for now, I'll see you after lunch for the start of the Sunday Afternoon session.

Example Three: Creating a Combination Row-and-Column Frame Page

In this example, you'll create a frame page that uses both rows and columns. This example starts out the same as the first example (where you created a two-row frame page), except here you'll be splitting the bottom row into two columns.

Starting Frame-It

Follow these steps to start Frame-It for the third frame page example:

1. If you didn't exit Frame-It after generating the frame codes for the last example, use Alt+Tab to bring Frame-It's window to the foreground (you may need to drag its window back onto the Desktop if you dragged it off previously). Click the Back button three times and then click OK at the message "Going back here will undo all work done on this screen."

    If you've exited Frame-It since the last example, rerun Frame-It.

2. Select the Row Orientated radio button (this will already be selected if you started Frame-It from scratch). Leave 2 as the setting for the No. of Columns option. (See Figure 5.17.)

3. Click Next.

Row orientation

Two rows

Figure 5.17

You start defining a combination row-and-column frame page by first defining row or column orientation (here, row orientation is defined).

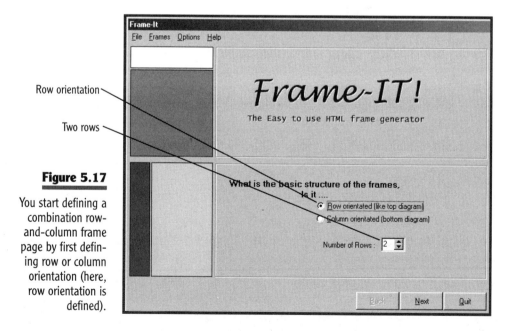

Defining the Top Frame

First, define the top row frame:

1. Click in the top frame to select it.
2. Type **Mast_Bar** as the name of the frame.
3. Type **mast_bar.htm** as the file name.
4. Define the frame dimensions by changing the Height (%) setting to **25**. Leave the Width (%) setting unchanged. (See Figure 5.18.)

Defining the Bottom-Left Frame

To define the bottom-left frame, you'll need to select the bottom frame and then split it. Here's how:

1. Click the bottom frame to select it. (See Figure 5.19.)
2. Click the Split Frame button.
3. Click in the bottom-left frame to select it. (See Figure 5.20.)
4. Type **Left_Bar** as the name of the frame.
5. Type **left_bar.htm** as the file name.

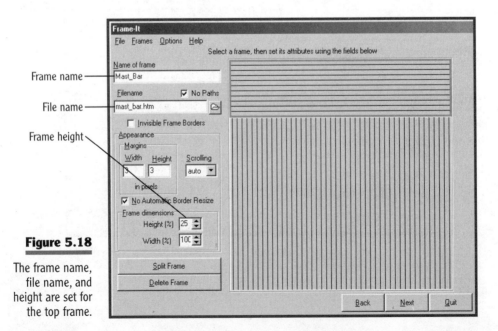

Figure 5.18

The frame name, file name, and height are set for the top frame.

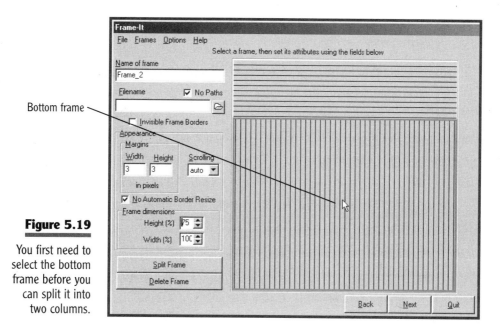

Figure 5.19

You first need to select the bottom frame before you can split it into two columns.

Bottom frame

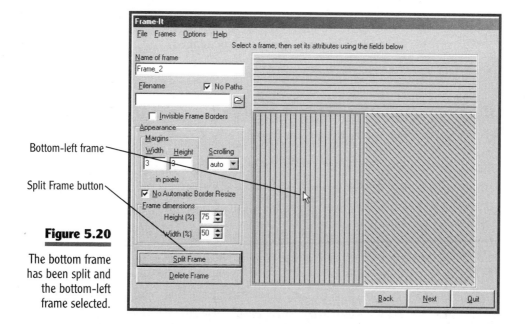

Bottom-left frame

Split Frame button

Figure 5.20

The bottom frame has been split and the bottom-left frame selected.

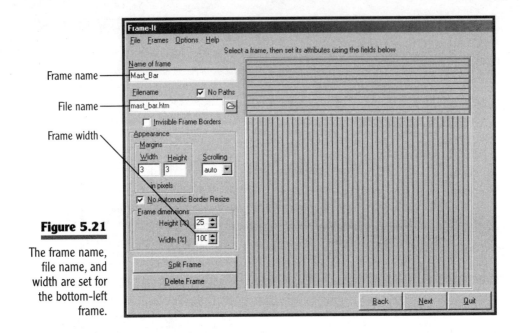

Frame name

File name

Frame width

Figure 5.21

The frame name,
file name, and
width are set for
the bottom-left
frame.

6. Define the frame dimensions by changing the Width (%) setting to **25**. Leave the Height (%) setting unchanged.

7. Leave all the other settings as they are. (See Figure 5.21.)

Defining the Bottom-Right Frame

Next, define the bottom-right frame:

1. Click in the bottom-right frame to select it.

2. Type **Window** as the name of the frame.

3. Type **window.htm** as the file name. Leave all the other settings as they are. (See Figure 5.22.)

NOTE You'll notice that the frame names and file names for the bottom-left and bottom-right frames are the same as in the two-column frame page you created in the second exercise. That's because you'll be reusing those same pages in this exercise.

4. Click Next.

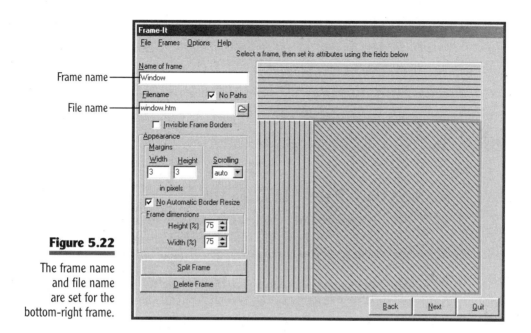

Frame name —

File name —

Figure 5.22

The frame name
and file name
are set for the
bottom-right frame.

Creating the NOFRAMES Text

If you returned to Frame-It's starting window by using the Back button, your settings and the NOFRAMES text will still be there. Just go ahead and click the Next button now.

If you've restarted Frame-It from scratch, you'll need to input the background, text, and links settings again. If you're not clear on how to do this, see the instructions for this in the first frame page example. (If you saved the NOFRAMES text as BOILER.HTM in the last example, instead of retyping the text, you can click the Load a File button to open BOILER.HTM from C:\HTML\FRAMES.) After you've input the NOFRAMES settings again, click the Next button.

Copying Your Frame Settings to the Clipboard

At Frame-It's last screen, follow these steps:

1. Leave Copy to Clipboard selected (the default). Leave all other settings as they are.

2. Click Store. At the Finished window, click OK to copy the frame settings to the Clipboard.

This is the last frame page example, so you can exit Frame-It now if you want to. However, if you think you may want to experiment further with Frame-It at the end of this session, just leave Frame-It open for now. (Because Frame-It doesn't have a minimize button, just drag it off to the side of the Desktop to get it out of the way.)

Creating and Saving FRAME3.HTM

If you left Notepad open after using it in the last example, just use Alt+Tab to activate its window. If you exited, you'll need to rerun Notepad (if you're using Windows 95 or 3.1, don't forget to turn Word Wrap on).

In Notepad, press Ctrl+V to paste your frame page settings from the Clipboard.

The text in your Notepad window should match what's shown here:

```
<html>
<! --- Generated using Frame-it v1.23 --- >
<! --- http://www.iinet.net.au/~bwh/frame-it.html --->
<frameset rows="25%,75%">
<frame name="Mast_Bar" src="mast_bar.htm" marginheight=3
➥marginwidth=3 scrolling=auto noresize>
<frameset cols="25%,75%">
<frame name="Left_Bar" src="left_bar.htm" marginheight=3
margin➥width=3 scrolling=auto noresize>
<frame name="Window" src="window.htm" marginheight=3 marginwidth=3
➥scrolling=auto noresize>
</frameset>
</frameset>
<noframes>
<body bgcolor=#000000 text=#FFFFFF link=#80FFFF>
Sorry, this page requires a Frames-capable browser. Feel free to
➥view the <A HREF="noframe.htm">Non-Frames Version</A> of this
➥page.</noframes>
```

NOTE If you examine the HTML codes you just pasted in, you'll notice that one FRAMESET element is nested inside of another. The first FRAMESET element defines the horizontal rows, whereas the second, nested FRAMESET element defines the two vertical columns that are inside the bottom row (the frame you split).

Save the file as **frame3.htm** in C:\HTML\FRAMES.

Creating and Saving MAST_BAR.HTM

You now need to create and save the HTML file (MAST_BAR.HTM) that will be displayed in the top frame. You'll include links on this page that will display either of the two previous frame page examples in your browser. To create this file, follow these steps:

1. Clear Notepad's window by selecting File, New.

2. Type in the following:

```
<HTML>
<HEAD><TITLE></TITLE></HEAD>
<BODY>
<H1 ALIGN="center">The Frame Page Title</H1>
<P ALIGN="center">[<A HREF="frame1.htm" Target=_top>View Two-Row
➥Page</A>] [<A HREF="frame2.htm" Target=_top>View
Two-Column Page</A>]
</BODY>
</HTML>
```

3. Save the file as **mast_bar.htm** in your C:\HTML\FRAMES folder.

TIP You'll notice the **Target=top** attribute value in the hypertext links in MAST_BAR.HTM. If you didn't include this attribute value, the target links would be displayed in the current frame window, which is not exactly what you want. You want them to be displayed in the full browser window, which is ensured by including the **Target=top** attribute value in the links.

NOTE Because you already created LEFT_BAR.HTM, WINDOW.HTM, WINDOW2.HTM, and WINDOW3.HTM in the previous exercises, you don't have to re-create them here. However, remember that if you want to create a frame page using this format from scratch, you'll need to create these files (you can give them whatever names you wish, as long as your frame page settings in Frame-It and your hypertext links in LEFT_BAR.HTM agree).

Although this is the last example in this tutorial, you may want to experiment further with Frame-It at the end of the tutorial. If you know you're not going to experiment with Frame-It at this time, feel free to exit Notepad now. Otherwise, just leave it open until you are finished working.

Viewing the Combination Row-and-Column Frame Page in Your Browser

Now, to check out your new frame page in your browser, follow these steps:

1. Run your browser and then load FRAME3.HTM from C:\HTML\FRAMES. (See Figure 5.23.)

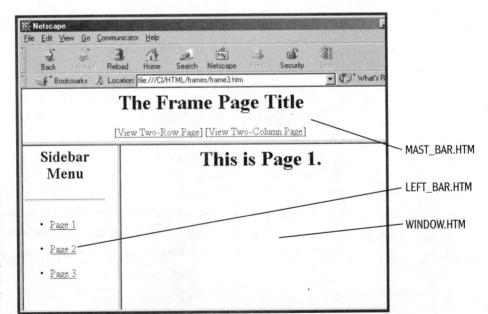

Figure 5.23

The combination row-and-column frame page, FRAME3.HTM, is displayed in a frames-capable Web browser.

2. Click the links in the bottom-left frame (LEFT_BAR.HTM) to cycle through the different pages in the bottom-right frame. For instance, clicking "Page 2" will display WINDOW2.HTM in the bottom-right frame. (See Figure 5.24.)

3. Next, click any of the links in the top frame. For instance, clicking View Two-Row Page will display the two-row frame page example in your browser (refer to Figure 5.8). Click your browser's Back button to return to FRAME3.HTM. Clicking View Two-Column Page will display the two-column frame page example in your browser (refer to Figure 5.14). Click your browser's Back button to return to FRAME3.HTM.

Creating Nested Frame Pages Using the Frames Template

The method I just showed you for creating a combination row-and-column frame page in Frame-It only allows you to control the contents of a single frame from a hypertext link. In many situations this may be just fine, but

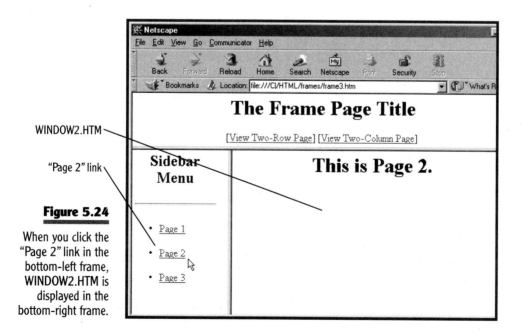

WINDOW2.HTM

"Page 2" link

Figure 5.24

When you click the "Page 2" link in the bottom-left frame, WINDOW2.HTM is displayed in the bottom-right frame.

situations exist in which you may want to be able to control the contents of two or more frames, all from a single hypertext link.

The trick for doing this is not that complicated. You start out by creating a regular two-row or two-column frame page (as in the first and second examples in this tutorial). The difference is that the name of the file to be displayed in one of your frames (which one is up to you) references not a regular HTML file but rather another frame page. For instance, you might first create a two-row frame page that includes in one of its frames another frame page (a two-column frame page). Or you could do it the other way around. This allows you to then use hypertext links to display additional frame pages in the same frame window (thus updating more than one frame, those of the nested frame page, from a single hypertext link).

ON THE

CD

Don't worry about trying to understand exactly how this works right now. If you're interested in creating a nested frame page, I've included a template on the CD-ROM that makes use of a nested frame page to allow for the controlling of two frames from a single hypertext link. You can find the template in the \EXAMPLES\TEMPLATE\FRAMES\3FRAMES folder on the CD-ROM. Just open that folder's INDEX.HTM file in your browser to check out the template.

You can use Prima's CD-ROM interface to install all of the Web page templates to C:\HTML\TEMPLATE. Just select Examples, Templates, then Install. This will install the nested frames template to C:\HTML\TEMPLATE\FRAMES\3FRAMES on your hard drive. The template includes all the instructions you should need to be able to make use of it.

If you would like to just copy the nested frames template to your hard drive, you run Windows Explorer and create a folder for the template under C:\HTML (\3FRAMES, for instance), then copy all of the files from \EXAMPLES\TEMPLATE\FRAMES\3FRAMES on the CD-ROM to that folder.

Before doing so, however, you might want to practice creating more two-row, two-column, and mixed row-and-column frame pages, as covered in the three exercises in this tutorial. After you understand how these types of frame pages work, you shouldn't have much trouble figuring out how to use the template for a nested frame page.

What's Next?

If you don't feel up to tackling creating nested frame pages yet, as detailed in the last section, feel free to go back and experiment further with creating more two-row, two-column, and combination row-and-column frame pages.

You can, of course, do a great deal more to gussy up your frames. Here are some things you can do to make your frames even more attractive:

- ✿ Try creating and inserting graphic icon buttons in place of the links.
- ✿ Use different background colors or images in the different frame pages. Adjust the text and link colors to match.
- ✿ If a frame has scroll bars where you don't want scroll bars, turn scrolling off in the affected frame by using the setting `"scrolling=no"`.
- ✿ Experiment with turning off the borders in Frame-It's main window— just click the Invisible Frame Borders check box so that it's checked for any frame in which you don't want borders. This can be effective if you don't have any scroll bars. It can also be a way of hiding the frames, themselves, if you wish.

PROGRAM DETAILS

Frame-It by GME Systems

Registration: Freeware

URL: http://www.iinet.net.au/~bwh/frame-it.html

Email: bwh@iinet.net.au

Fax number: +61 9 4469413

Other products by GME Systems: SwagMan (shareware HTML editor) and Remove-It (freeware HTML code stripper).

The Forms Tutorial

- ✿ Creating text fields, check boxes, radio buttons, list boxes, comment boxes, and other controls
- ✿ Submitting form responses
- ✿ Indirectly and directly importing form responses
- ✿ Exporting form responses
- ✿ Editing form files

Hey, it's Sunday afternoon! If you've done everything up to this point, you've really come a long way. You've learned basic and intermediate HTML, as well as tables and frames. Now you're ready to tackle creating forms.

Don't worry, however, if you haven't been able to get to everything. Everyone has a different learning style and curve. So, just relax and go at your own speed. If you haven't completed the Intermediate HTML Tutorial yet, you should go back and do that tutorial before attempting to do the Forms Tutorial. If you've skipped doing the Tables Tutorial or the Frames Tutorial, that's fine—you don't have to do those tutorials before doing the Forms Tutorial.

In this tutorial, you'll use a software tool called WebForms to create a customer response form. WebForms is a good deal more than just a wizard for creating forms. It also can retrieve, convert, and organize the responses to your forms. If you're planning to create more than just a couple of forms or expect to receive a significant volume of form responses, registering WebForms can be an excellent investment. Even if you decide not to register WebForms, the forms you've created will continue to function—plus other tools are available for converting the responses to your forms into a more readable format (see the Web Tools section of this book's Web site for links). You'll also find a full rundown of all the form tags in HTML in Appendix A, "HTML Quick Reference." By comparing the HTML file and the descriptions of the HTML tags in Appendix A, the industrious among you shouldn't have too much difficulty figuring out how to create your own forms from scratch.

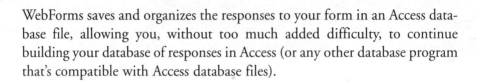

WebForms saves and organizes the responses to your form in an Access database file, allowing you, without too much added difficulty, to continue building your database of responses in Access (or any other database program that's compatible with Access database files).

What You Need to Do the Forms Tutorial

No special requirements exist for creating the sample form in WebForms and viewing it in your browser. However, if you want to test submitting a response to the form you'll create in this tutorial, you'll need to use a Web browser that's compatible with Mailto forms. Any recent version of Netscape Navigator will do (I've personally checked out both the 3.0 and 4.0 versions, but can't vouch for the 2.0 or 1.0 versions), but if you're using Internet Explorer, you'll need to use version 4.0 or greater. You'll also need to have a regular e-mail account at your ISP (not a Web e-mail account) and have the mail program for your browser (Messenger for Netscape or Outlook Express for Internet Explorer) configured at least to be able to send mail to your ISP's outgoing mail server (or SMTP server). If you've sent e-mail messages using Mailto links previously in your browser, then you're configured to send outgoing mail.

NOTE   The WebForms version included on the CD-ROM is an evaluation (or shareware) version. You'll be able to make full use of the program's features for 30 days after installing it. After the evaluation period is over, you will be limited to indirectly importing form responses and will only be able to indirectly import one form response at a time.

Creating a Working Folder

You should create a separate working folder in which you can save all the files created during the Forms Tutorial. I recommend that you go ahead and create a C:\HTML\FORMS folder. (If you're unsure about how to create a new folder in Windows 95/98 or Windows 3.1, see the "Creating a Working Folder" in the Frames Tutorial session.)

Installing WebForms

WebForms is a 16-bit application that can be used with either Windows 95 or Windows 3.1.

If you've installed a previous version of WebForms in C:\WEBFORMS, you should remove or rename that folder before trying to install WebForms 2.7a from the CD-ROM to C:\WEBFORMS.

To install WebForms from the CD-ROM, do the following:

1. Insert the *Learn HTML in a Weekend* CD-ROM in your CD-ROM drive.
2. If you're using Windows 95/98, Prima's CD-ROM interface will automatically run, unless you have disabled Autorun. If the CD-ROM interface does not automatically run, select Run and then type **D:\prima.exe** (where *D* is your CD-ROM's drive letter). Then click OK.
3. If you're using Windows 3.1, select File, Run from Program Manager's menu bar; then type **D:\prima.exe** (where *D* is your CD-ROM's drive letter). Click OK.
4. With Prima's CD-ROM interface onscreen, click Web Tools and then click WebForms.
5. Click Install in the drop-down menu.
6. The WebForms setup screen should be automatically displayed on the screen. Click OK to accept C:\WEBFORMS as the program folder.
7. At the message that installation is complete, click OK.

Starting WebForms

In Windows 95/98, click the Start button and then select Programs, Web-Forms 2.7, and then WebForms 2.7 again.

In Windows 3.1, activate the program group where the WebForms icon has been installed; then double-click the WebForms icon.

When you run WebForms, in either Windows 95/98 or Windows 3.1, a Welcome box is displayed telling you that WebForms must first create its

database. This box is only displayed the very first time you run WebForms. Click OK. Creating the database will take a few seconds. Next, a lengthy window is displayed that informs you about WebForms. Wait until the OK button is no longer grayed-out; then click OK to run WebForms.

When you first run WebForms, the WebForms Tutorial window is displayed on the screen. Just select File, Exit to close the window, or you can click the Close button in the upper-right corner of the window. The WebForms Tutorial window should only be displayed the first time you run WebForms. (If you want to come back and do this tutorial later, just select Help, WebForms Tutorial from WebForms' menu bar.)

NOTE The screen captures and descriptions in this tutorial are all from Windows 98. Because the same 16-bit program runs in both Windows 95/98 and 3.1, it should operate identically in either version of Windows.

Starting a New Form

From the WebForms main window, select File, Forms, New. The Create New Form window opens with the General tab section displayed. Go ahead and maximize the Create New Form window (see Figure 6.1).

Creating the General Settings

The General tab is the tab section that's initially displayed. Fill out the fields as follows (press the Tab key to go to the next field or press Shift+Tab to go back to a field):

1. Form Title: **Visitor Questionnaire**

2. Form Heading: **Visitor Questionnaire**

   Click the Center check box so it is checked. This will cause the form heading to be centered at the top of the form page.

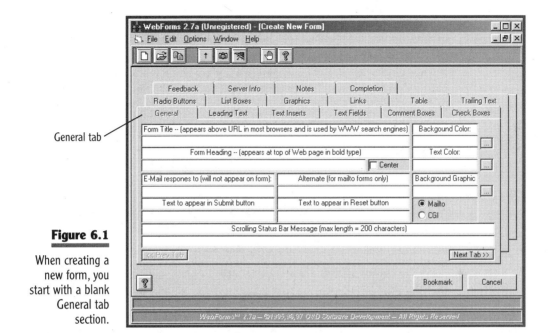

General tab

Figure 6.1

When creating a new form, you start with a blank General tab section.

NOTE

The Form Title content specifies the title of the form page and will be displayed on the title bar of a browser. The Form Heading content specifies the level-one heading (H1) that's displayed at the top of the form page.

Feel free to substitute any other form title or form heading you wish to use here. You should be aware, however, that apostrophes (single quotes) are not allowed; therefore, if you want to include your name here, you'll need to do it in the form of "Visitor Questionnaire of Mary Smith," for instance, instead of "Mary Smith's Questionnaire." You also can't include any double quotes.

3. E-Mail responses to:

   Type the e-mail address where you want responses from your form to be sent. For instance, **myname@myserver.com**. (This e-mail address will not be displayed on the form.)

If you want to be able to test your form over the Internet, you need to enter your actual e-mail address here, not just a dummy address.

4. Alternate:

   For Mailto forms, include an e-mail address here for responses from users without a forms-capable Web browser. Because you *are* creating a Mailto form, you can type in here the same e-mail address you entered in the previous step. (This e-mail address, however, will be displayed on the form.)

5. Text to appear in Submit button: **Submit Form**

6. Text to appear in Reset button: **Reset Form**

7. Background Color: (Leave this blank.)

8. Text Color: (Leave this blank.)

TIP
If you want to add a background or text color, just click the button to the right and select the color you want. The corresponding hexadecimal value will be inserted. Assigning background and text colors here is no different than directly assigning such colors in the BODY tag.

9. Background Graphic: (Leave this blank.)

10. Scrolling Status Bar Message: (I recommend you leave this blank.)

NOTE
The problem with including a scrolling message is that (for what I take to be of very little benefit) your Web browser has to continually access your hard drive as it displays this message over and over again. Do a favor for your visitors and leave this one blank. If you do decide to include a message here, try to keep it short and sweet.

11. You'll create a Mailto form, so leave the Mailto radio button selected (see Figure 6.2).

12. Click the Next Tab button.

Figure 6.2

In the General tab section, a title, a heading, e-mail and alternate e-mail addresses, and the content of the submit and reset buttons have been specified.

Creating Leading Text

The Leading Text tab section allows you to enter a block of introductory text that will be displayed at the top of your form. It should explain the function of the form and any general information the user may require to complete filling out the form. As an example of a leading text block, type the following in the Leading Text window:

```
I'm gathering information about visitors to my site. I'm gathering
this information solely for the purpose of being able to better
serve and respond to the needs and desires of my site's visitors.
Information you provide to me here will not be given or sold to
spammers, nor will you receive any unsolicited e-mail from me. Thank
you for your cooperation and participation.
```

The Leading Text tab section should now look like what is shown in Figure 6.3. Click the Next Tab button.

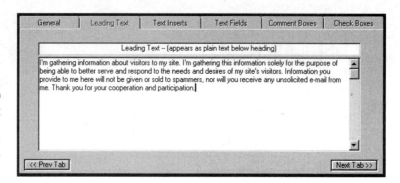

Figure 6.3

The Leading Text
contents will
automatically be
displayed at the top
of your form.

Creating Text Inserts

Text inserts are blocks of text you can insert into your form at any point.
Think of them as being essentially the same as the leading text block you just
filled out, except that you can insert them anywhere you want.

TIP You should always create lead-in text here for any radio button and check box groups as well
as for any list boxes you want to include. The reason is that the name you assign to a group
of radio buttons, check boxes, or pull-down list items is not displayed on the form, but just
the individual group elements (the radio buttons in a radio button group, for instance).

Here, you'll create four text inserts that will be used as lead-ins for the radio
button and check box groups as well as for the list box you'll create later on:

1. Type **What is your age-group?**

   Press the down-arrow key to add another text insert.

2. Type **What is your field or profession? (Check any that apply.)**

   Press the down-arrow key.

3. Type **How did you find out about my site?**

   Press the down-arrow key.

4. Type **Would you like to be notified when this site is updated?**

   (See Figure 6.4.)

5. Click the Next Tab button.

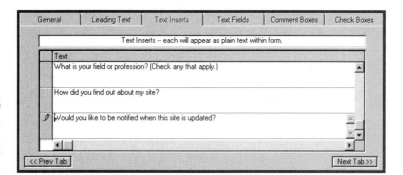

Figure 6.4

The last three entries are shown in the Text Inserts tab section.

Creating Text Fields

Next, you define the text fields you want your visitors to fill out. WebForms includes a total of seven columns that are used to define each text field. Only three of these columns are required to define a text field: Field Name, Size, and Data Type. You'll also use the Default Value column in this tutorial.

The Field Name field specifies the name, or label, for the text field and will be displayed to the left of a text field box.

The Size field specifies the number of characters that can be entered for any one text field—in order to keep your database as compact as possible, you want to make your text field sizes just big enough to allot sufficient room for the user to enter the necessary data.

The Default Value field specifies a default value that will appear in a text field box when it's first displayed. The Data Type field specifies either Freestyle, Integer, or Decimal as the type of data to be entered in a text field. At minimum, a Field Name, a Size, and a Data Type are required for each text field.

You won't use the other three columns—Required, Condition, and Value—in this tutorial. If you want to know more about how to use these columns, go ahead and read the following paragraph. Otherwise, feel free to skip it until later.

The Required field specifies that a text field must be filled out before the form can be submitted—just type **Y** in the column to specify that the field is required. The Condition and Value columns are used in conjunction with the Data Type column. For instance, if Freestyle has been selected in the Data Type column, you can select from Contains, Starts With, or Ends With as the condition. If you've selected either Integer or Decimal as the data type, you can select > (Greater Than), < (Less Than), or Between as the condition. For instance, to specify that a text field must start with a URL, you would specify Freestyle as the data type, select Starts With as the condition, and type **http://** as the value. To specify that a text field contains a whole integer between 1 and 10, you would specify Integer as the data type, select Between as the condition, and type **1;10** as the value. Needless to say, you should make clear in a text field's Name column, or in a preceding Text Insert, any conditions that might affect user input, such as, "(Type a number between 1 and 10)," for instance.

NOTE Text field names in WebForms cannot include any of these characters: space, single quote ('), double quote ("), plus sign (+), and ampersand (&). Indicate a space character by inserting an underscore (_). A colon will automatically be inserted at the end of the text field name when it's displayed in your form, so don't add a colon at the end of the field name.

Follow these steps to create the text fields for your form:

1. With the cursor inserted in the Field Name column, type **First_Name/Middle_Initial** as the name of your first text field; then press the Tab key.

2. Type **30** as the size. You can skip adding a default value at this time.

3. Click the cursor inside the Data Type column, click the drop-down arrow, and then select Freestyle. Press the down-arrow key to add another text field. (You'll notice that an *N* has been automatically inserted in the Required field.)

4. Repeat steps 1 through 3 to create the following text fields:

NOTE You'll need to manually select Freestyle for each data type. Also, note that the Country text field in the following table includes a default value of *USA*.

Field Name	Size	Default Value
Last_Name	30	
Title	30	
Company	30	
Address_1	40	
Address_2	40	
City	30	
State/Province	30	
Country	30	USA
Zip/Mail_Code	30	
E-Mail_Address	30	
URL	40	

◆ ◆

CAUTION After you enter the last text field (following this caution), do *not* press the down-arrow key after selecting Freestyle as the style. (If you do, you'll leave a blank field at the bottom that will make it impossible to generate your form later.) Instead, press the up-arrow key to cause the "N" to be inserted in the Required field (or you can just type **N**, if you wish).

◆ ◆

Figure 6.5 shows the final seven fields filled out.

5. Click the Next Tab button.

Figure 6.5

When entering text fields, only the Field Name, Size, Required, and Data Type fields are required.

	General	Leading Text	Text Inserts	Text Fields	Comment Boxes	Check Boxes

Text Fields -- allow text input from respondent.

Field Name	Size	Default Value	Required	Data Type	Condition	Value
Address_2	40		N	Freestyle		
City	30		N	Freestyle		
State/Province	30		N	Freestyle		
Country	30	USA	N	Freestyle		
Zip/Mail_Code	30		N	Freestyle		
E-Mail_Address	30		N	Freestyle		
URL	40		N	Freestyle		

<< Prev Tab		Next Tab >>

NOTE If you should accidentally add a blank text or other field at the bottom of a list of fields, it can be a bit tricky to get rid of. You can't just highlight it and delete it. Rather, what you should do is retype the data from the above field and then click the mouse on the blank button to the left of the above field and press the Delete key to delete it.

Creating Comment Boxes

Comment boxes allow a user of your form to include a more lengthy response than is possible with text fields. The Comment Boxes tab section allows you to define any number of comment boxes that can be used by a visitor to your site to enter lengthy comments, questions, and so on. To define a comment box, specify its name, width in characters (columns), and height (rows), as shown here:

1. Type **Comments** in the Name column.

NOTE You can use any name you want for the name of your comment box. The same rules apply, however, as for text fields—no spaces (use an underscore instead), single quotes, double quotes, plus signs, or ampersands. Also, don't include a colon at the end (one will be added automatically).

2. Set Columns to **50** and Rows to **4**. Leave the Required column as is (see Figure 6.6).

3. Click the Next Tab button.

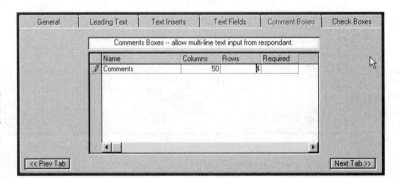

Figure 6.6

A comment box allows a lengthier message to be included in the form response.

Creating Check Boxes

Check boxes allow the users of your form to select from a smorgasbord of options by checking any number of them. The Check Boxes tab section is organized into four input sections. You specify the names of any check box groups you want to include in the upper-left box, adding them to the list of check box groups in the lower-left box. Clicking any of the listed check box groups in the lower-left box locates the cursor in the upper-right box. This is where you type the names for the actual check box items you want to include in the selected group. After typing in a check box item, you then add it to the list of check boxes for that group in the lower-right box.

You can create any number of check box groups, which can then be inserted into your form at any point. (You'll only create one check box group in this tutorial.) To define a check box group, follow these steps:

1. Type the name of the check box group you're adding in the Enter New Check Box Group box (upper left): **Field/Profession**

2. Click the Add Group button. (The Field/Profession check box group has now been added to the list of check box groups.)

NOTE The check box group name in step 1 is not actually displayed on the form. Previously, you created a text insert that will be used as the lead-in for this check box group. Each time you create a check box group, you'll also want to create a text insert to precede it (unless the lead-in text serves that purpose).

3. Click Field/Profession in the Check Box Groups box (lower left). The cursor will be automatically repositioned in the Enter New Check Box Name box (upper right) so that you can start adding the check box items for the group.

4. Type **Executive** as the name of the first check box item; then click the Add Item button to add the check box item to the check box list (lower right). (See Figure 6.7.)

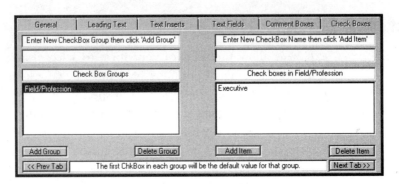

Figure 6.7

The first check box
has been added to
the Field/Profession
check box group.

5. Repeat step 3 for each of the following check box names:

Financial	Manufacturing
Administrative	Retail
Sales/Marketing	Wholesale/Distribution
Technical	Military
Education	Medicine
Government	Legal
Sciences	Internet/Web Professional
Arts	Other
Humanities	

Now take a look at Figure 6.8 to see the new items added to the check box group.

6. Click the Next Tab button.

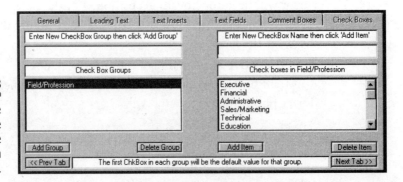

Figure 6.8

The rest of the
check boxes have
been added to the
Field/Profession
check box group.

Creating Radio Buttons

Radio buttons are similar to check boxes, except that only one radio button option can be selected at one time. For your form, you'll create two radio button groups—one allowing the visitors to indicate their age group and the other allowing the visitors to tell you if they want to be notified when your Web site is updated.

You enter information in the Radio Buttons tab section just like in the Check Boxes tab section. Just specify the radio button group name in the upper-left box and then add it to the lower-left box. Select your new group name in the lower-left box and then type the radio button items in the upper-right box, adding them to the lower-right box.

Creating the Age_Group Radio Button Group

This radio button group will allow your visitors to specify their age group:

1. In the Enter New Radio Button Group box, type **Age_Group** and then click the Add Group button.

2. In the Radio Button Groups box, click your new radio button group. The cursor is automatically repositioned in the Enter New Button Name box.

3. With the cursor now in the Enter New Button Name box, type the following radio button names, clicking the Add Item button after each one:

   14 and Under

   15 to 19

   20 to 29

   30 to 39

   40 to 49

   50 to 59

   60 and Over

   Now take a look at Figure 6.9 to see these items added to the radio button group.

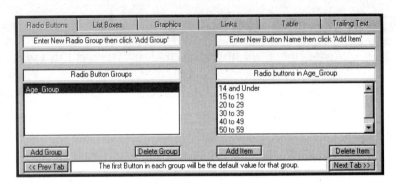

Figure 6.9

The radio buttons
have been named
and added to the
Age_Group radio
button group.

Creating the Notify Radio Button Group

For this group, you'll create a simple two-item (Yes and No) radio button group that enables your visitors to tell you whether they want to be notified when your Web site is updated.

1. Reposition the cursor in the Enter New Radio Button Group box (upper-left box). Type **Notify** and then click the Add Group button.

2. In the Radio Button Groups box, click your new radio button group (Notify). The cursor is automatically repositioned in the Enter New Button Name box.

3. Type the radio button names **Yes** and **No**, clicking the Add Item button after each one (see Figure 6.10).

4. Click the Next Tab button.

Figure 6.10

The Yes and No
radio buttons have
been added to
the Notify radio
button group.

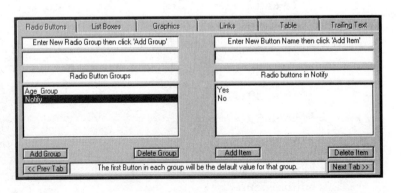

Creating List Boxes

A *list box* is a box that drops down and displays a list when the user clicks its drop-down arrow.

Like the Check Boxes and Radio Buttons tab sections, the List Boxes tab section also uses four input boxes where you can specify list boxes and the list items to be included in each one. List boxes are somewhat similar to radio button groups in that a visitor can only choose one of the items. A list box, however, takes up much less space on your form, and it initially displays only the first item. When the list box's drop-down arrow is clicked, the rest of the list items are displayed.

Create a list box that will enable your visitors to tell you how they found out about your site. Follow these steps:

1. In the Enter New List Box box, type **Where_From**.

The list box name will not be displayed as part of the form—it's used only to identify the list box. Earlier, you created a text insert that you'll use as a lead-in to this list box when you get around to assembling the final form. The same rules that apply to creating text field names also apply here.

2. Click the Add Group button.
3. In the List Boxes box, click the group you just added.
4. With the cursor now in the Enter New List Box Item box, enter the following items, clicking the Add Item button after each one:

Alta Vista	**Yahoo**
Excite	**Other Index/Search Engine**
HotBot	**Friend, Relative, or Associate**
Infoseek	**Another Web Page**
Lycos	**Magazine/Newspaper**
Open Text	**Radio/Television**
Starting Point	**Other**
WebCrawler	

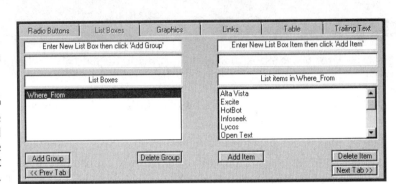

Figure 6.11

The list items have
been named and
added to the
Where_From list
box group.

Now take a look at Figure 6.11 to see these items added to the list box group.

5. Click the Next Tab button.

Adding Graphics

The Graphics tab section enables you to specify any graphics that you want to include on your form.

If the graphics you want to use are saved in the same folder as your form files (that is, C:\HTML\FORMS), you only need to specify their file names. However, if the graphics you want to use are saved in a different folder, you'll have to specify where they are with a relative URL.

For example, it would be nice to specify a logo or banner graphic that is automatically placed at the head of your form. Unfortunately, WebForms does not allow you to place a graphic in front of the form heading and leading text elements, which are automatically inserted by WebForms at the top of the form. What you can do, however, is insert a logo or banner graphic and then move it later after you've created the form.

I've provided a sample logo graphic, named LOGO.GIF, that you can use here. When you copied the sample graphics used in the Basic and Intermediate HTML Tutorials, this graphic was also copied to C:\HTML. You can use a different graphic if you wish, but if you want HEIGHT and WIDTH attributes added, you'll need to know its dimensions. When you get around to assem-

bling the different pieces to create your form, you'll insert your graphic in one place, but later you'll manually move it to where you want it to be.

Follow these steps to specify the sample logo graphic that has been provided:

1. Click the cursor in the Graphic Filename column.

2. Click the File Dialog button; then browse to C:\HTML and double-click LOGO.GIF. The file name will be inserted in the Graphic Filename field.

3. Because LOGO.GIF is not in the same folder where your form file will be, add the relative URL for your graphic file. Edit the Graphic Filename entry so that it looks like this:

   `../logo.gif`

   Now press the Tab key.

4. In the Align field, you enter the alignment you want to use. Type **top** as the alignment. (You can specify "top," "middle," or "bottom," but not "left" or "right.") Press the Tab key.

5. Type **75** as the height, press the Tab key, and then type **75** as the width (see Figure 6.12).

You're only including one graphic in this form. To add additional graphics, you would just press the down-arrow key and then repeat the previous steps for each graphic you want to include. Because you're not adding any more graphics, just click the Next Tab button.

Figure 6.12

A graphics file, LOGO.GIF, has been added to the Graphics tab section.

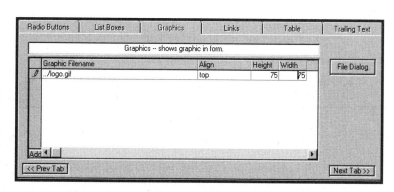

Adding Hypertext Links

This tab section enables you to include any hypertext links you want in your form. For instance, you might want to include a link back to your home page. To add a link back to your home page, do the following:

1. In the Link URL column, type the URL of your home page. For example, type **http://www.mysite.com/mydir/mypage.htm** (or whatever the actual URL of your home page might be, if you have a home page); then press the Tab key.

2. In the Linked Text column, type the text you want to appear as the link. For example, type **Return to My Home Page** (see Figure 6.13).

To add additional hypertext links, just press the down-arrow key and then repeat the first two steps. For this tutorial, however, you're not going to be adding any more links, so just click the Next Tab button.

Creating Tables

The Table tab section allows you to add a table to your form. Most forms do not include a table, so you're not going to bother adding one this time. However, if you do want to add a table to your form, here are the pertinent points to pay attention to:

- You can add only one table in a form.
- Your table cannot have more than 10 columns of data.

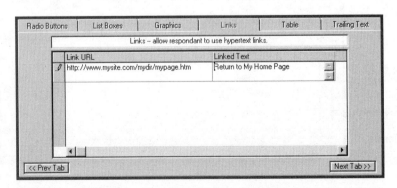

Figure 6.13

A hypertext link back to the home page has been added in the Links tab section.

- The number of rows you can add is unlimited.
- You can include either text or manually inserted hypertext links into table cells.
- You cannot include text fields, comment boxes, or other form controls that take user input.
- You can add a table caption in the Caption box.
- Click the Center check box to center the table.
- Click the Border check box to add borders to the table.
- Insert your column headings in the first row. If you don't want column headings, leave the first row empty.

Click the Next Tab button to proceed.

Creating Trailing Text

The Trailing Text tab section enables you to add trailing text to your Web form. *Trailing text* is similar to leading text except that it's automatically placed at the bottom of your form.

For this tutorial, you're going to skip adding any trailing text. Just click Next Tab.

Providing Feedback

The Feedback tab section is a two-part section that enables you to specify how feedback is to be provided to the users of your form after it has been submitted by them. The CGI Forms part at the top of the tab section is filled out *only* if you're creating a CGI form. The bottom part of the tab section is filled out if you're creating a Mailto form.

Providing CGI Form Confirmation

Because in this tutorial you're not creating a CGI form, you should leave the CGI Forms section blank.

NOTE Although you won't be creating a CGI form in this tutorial, you may want to create one in the future. When creating a CGI form, the Confirmation Pg radio button is automatically selected. When this radio button is selected, you can specify a header (Confirmation Page Header section) and a body (Confirmation Page body) for your confirmation message. The header will be displayed on the browser's title bar, whereas the body will be displayed like a regular HTML Web page. You can manually include any HTML codes you want in the Confirmation Page Body section, but you should not include BODY or HTML tags.

If you select the Jump to URL radio button, you can specify the URL of any Web page that you want to be displayed as your confirmation page.

Providing Mailto Form Confirmation

You create a Mailto form in this tutorial. Therefore, to provide confirmation to users of your form that their form response has been successfully submitted, you'll type a confirmation message in the Confirmation Message Box for Mailto Forms box. You're limited to a total of 200 characters in your message. The confirmation message will be displayed in a pop-up box to any users of your form who have JavaScript-capable browsers. Follow these steps:

1. For the confirmation, type **Thanks for your submission. Have a nice day.** (See Figure 6.14.)

Figure 6.14

A Mailto confirmation message has been added to the Feedback tab section.

| Feedback | Server Info | Notes | Completion | General | Leading Text |

CGI Forms: Confirmation Page Header:

Confirmation Page Body (enter HTML code -- <BODY> tag not necessary)

● Confirmation Pg

○ Jump to URL

Confirmation Message Box for Mailto Forms (max length = 200 characters)

Thanks for your submission. Have a nice day.

<< Prev Tab   Next Tab >>

2. Click the Next Tab button.

Providing Server Info (for CGI Forms)

The Server Info tab section enables you to provide information about where Perl, the Sendmail program, and CGI scripts are stored on your server.

You only need to fill out this tab section if you're creating a CGI form. Because you're creating a Mailto form in this tutorial, you should leave this tab section blank.

If you were creating a CGI script here, you would need to find out from your Web space provider the paths on your server to where the Perl and Sendmail programs are located, as well as where CGI scripts are stored. Click the Next Tab button.

Adding Notes

The Notes tab section allows you to insert any notes you want to keep about your form. These notes are actually inserted into your form file inside of HTML comment tags. For now, just leave this tab section blank. Click the Next Tab button.

Completing Your Form

The Completion tab section is where you assemble and order all the elements (or controls) that are going to be included in your form Then you generate the HTML file for the form.

Refreshing Your Controls

The first step in completing your form is to refresh your controls in the list of controls.

CAUTION ◆

I've had WebForms freeze up on me after clicking the Refresh Controls button, most likely from having too many other programs open at the same time. The result is that all the settings for the form have to be reentered. I recommend that you close any other open programs before continuing on with refreshing your controls and assembling the pieces of your form.

Also, if you want to make any changes in any of the tab sections for your form, you should do so (by clicking the Prev. Tab button) *before* clicking the Refresh Controls button. Once you've clicked the Refresh Controls button, if you want to change any of the controls for your form, you have to click the Bookmark button to save your current settings, exit out to Web-Forms' main screen, and then reopen your form (File, Forms, Open).

◆ ◆

Here's how to refresh your controls:

1. Click the Refresh Controls button. All the controls you created in the previous tab sections should be listed in the Controls List box (see Figure 6.15).

2. If you've failed to fill in a required field or have made some other error, you'll be directed to go back and fix it before the list of controls will be generated.

Moving Your Controls into the Sequence List

Next, you need to move the controls listed in the Controls List box into the Sequence List box in the order in which you want them to appear on your form. Follow these steps:

1. In the Controls List box, click "GRAPHIC - ../logo.gif" to highlight

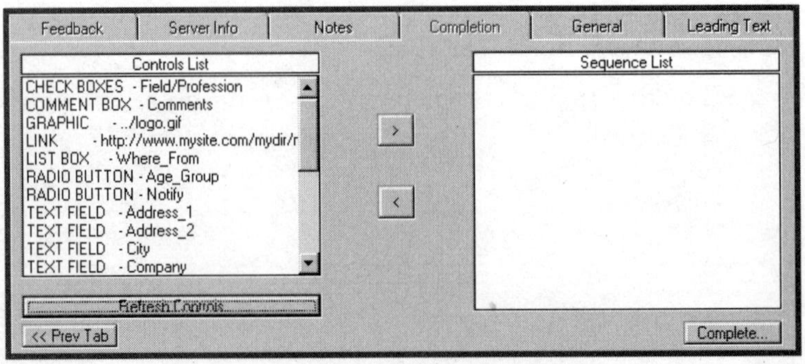

Figure 6.15

When the Refresh Controls button is clicked, all the controls created in the previous tab sections are listed in the Controls List box.

it; then click the right-arrow button (>) to move it into the Sequence List box (see Figure 6.16).

2. Move the text field controls into the Sequence List in the following order:

```
TEXT FIELD - First_Name/Middle_Initial
TEXT FIELD - Last_Name
TEXT FIELD - Title
TEXT FIELD - Company
TEXT FIELD - Address_1
TEXT FIELD - Address_2
TEXT FIELD - City
TEXT FIELD - State/Province
TEXT FIELD - Country
TEXT FIELD - Zip/Mail_Code
TEXT FIELD - E-Mail_Address
TEXT FIELD - URL
```

Now take a look at Figure 6.17 to see these items added to the Sequence List box.

Figure 6.16

The first control, the LOGO.GIF graphic, has been moved into the Sequence List box.

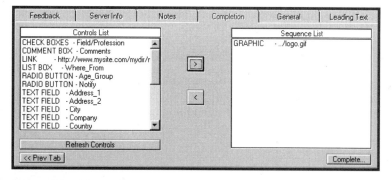

Figure 6.17

The text fields have all been moved into the Sequence List box.

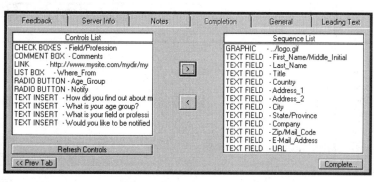

3. Next, you'll need to move the following two controls, which together will comprise the first radio button list:

```
TEXT INSERT - What is your age-group?
RADIO BUTTON - Age_Group
```

4. Now, you'll need to move the following two controls, which together will comprise the check box list:

```
TEXT INSERT - What is your field...
CHECK BOXES - Field/Profession
```

5. Next, move the list box into the Sequence List box:

```
TEXT INSERT - How did you find out about...
LIST BOX - Where_From
```

6. Move the comment box into the Sequence List box:

```
COMMENT BOX - Comments
```

7. Now, you'll need to move the following two controls, which together will comprise the second radio button list:

```
TEXT INSERT - Would you like to be notified...
RADIO BUTTON - Notify
```

8. Last, move the link control that provides a link back to your home page:

```
LINK - http://www.mysite.com/mydir/mypage.htm
```

The Controls List box should now be completely empty, with all the controls now listed in the Sequence List box in the order in which you want them to appear in your form (see Figure 6.18).

Figure 6.18

All the controls have been moved from the Controls List box to the Sequence List box.

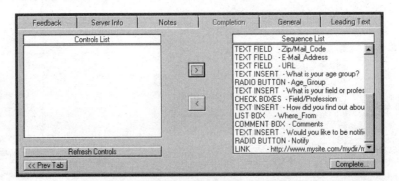

Generating Your Form

The last step is to save your data in the WebForms database and then generate the HTML file for your form:

1. Click the Complete button in the lower-right corner. At the "Ready to generate HTML file?" message, click Yes.

2. After a second or so, you'll be informed that your data has been saved and that WebForms will now create the HTML form. Click the OK button.

3. In the Generate HTML File dialog box, go to the C:\HTML\FORMS folder. Type **MYFORM.HTM** as the file name (see Figure 6.19). Click OK.

4. WebForms will now create your form. After awhile, you'll be told that the creation of the form is complete. Click OK. You'll be at the WebForms main window.

Viewing Your Form in Your Browser

Minimize WebForms and then run your Web browser and load C:\HTML\FORMS\MYFORM.HTM.

As I'm sure you'll notice, the logo graphic is not where you want it. Unfortunately, as shown in Figure 6.20, WebForms does not position this for you above the heading and leading text paragraphs, but rather it places the graphic below these paragraphs.

Figure 6.19

The form is being saved as MYFORM.HTM in C:\HTML\FORMS.

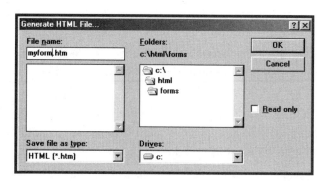

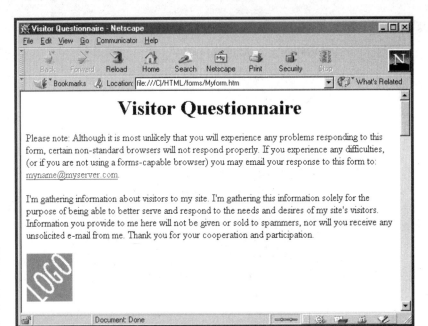

Figure 6.20

The LOGO.GIF
graphic is not
where you want
it to be.

Moving the Logo Graphic

To put the logo graphic in the right place, you need to edit the HTML file created by WebForms. Follow these steps:

1. Run Notepad and open C:\HTML\FORMS\MYFORM.HTM. (If you're using Windows 3.1 or 95, turn Word Wrap on by choosing Edit, Word Wrap.)

2. Locate the code `<IMG src="../logo.gif" ALIGN="top" HEIGHT=75 WIDTH=75>` and then highlight and cut it to the Clipboard (Ctrl+X).

3. Look back up through the file until you see the `</SCRIPT>` tag. Just underneath it, position the cursor after the `<H1>` tag (but in front of "Visitor"). Press Ctrl+V to paste in the code you just cut.

4. To create some extra separation between your logo graphic and your heading, add an `HSPACE=30` attribute value to the IMG tag. This line of your file should now look like this:

```
<center><h1><IMG src="../logo.gif" ALIGN="top" HEIGHT=75 WIDTH=75
HSPACE=30>My Visitor Questionnaire</h1></center>
```

5. Save your file (File, Save).

6. Hop back to your Web browser and reload C:\HTML\FORMS\MYFORM.HTM (press Ctrl+R in either Navigator or Internet Explorer). Your logo graphic should now be up on the first line in front of your heading, as shown in Figure 6.21.

 NOTE
- -
When editing your form file, you want to be careful not to change the order of any of the form elements that take user input. Otherwise, WebForms is liable to stick data from the Last Name field in the Company field, for instance.
- -

For more guidance on other ways in which you can edit your form file, see the section "Editing Form Files Created with WebForms" later in this session.

Figure 6.21

The LOGO.GIF graphic has been moved to a better place.

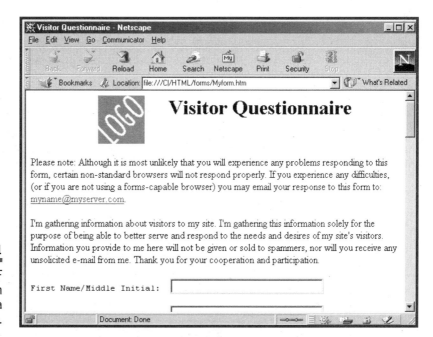

Testing Your Form

To test your form, you need to be connected to the Internet. If you haven't already logged onto the Internet, do so now.

First, scroll down so the first text field (First Name/Middle Initial) is visible at the top of your browser window. Go ahead and fill out the first three text fields (see Figure 6.22).

Next, experiment with selecting radio buttons, checking check boxes, clicking items in the list box, filling out the comment box, and so on. Make sure you check several check boxes, so you can check out how multiple field responses are handled once you've imported your response into WebForms' database. When you are done, send your response by clicking the Submit button on your form (you'll need to be connected).

Submitting a Response

The form you've created is a Mailto form that uses JavaScript. Therefore, to be able to fully test out submitting a response from your form, you need to be using a Web browser that's compatible with both Mailto forms and

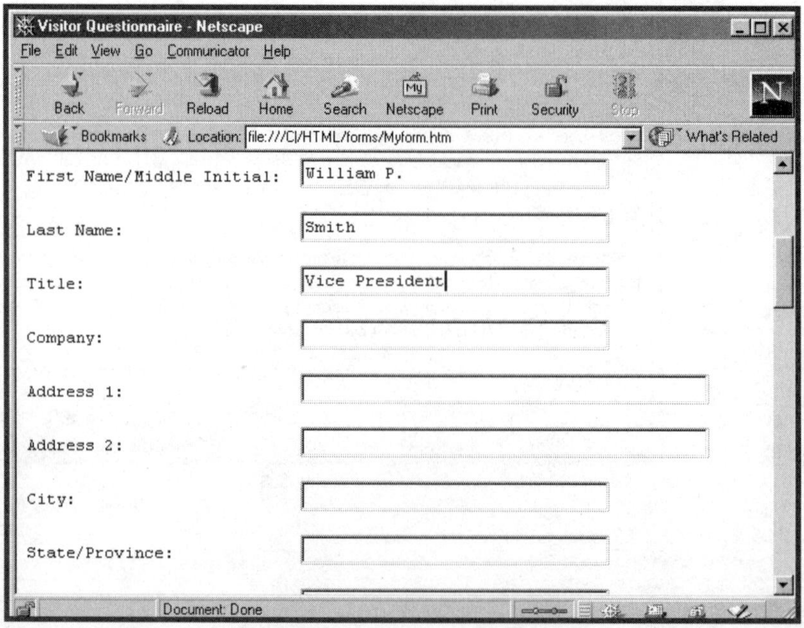

Figure 6.22

The first three text fields have been filled out.

JavaScript—Netscape Navigator 3.0 and higher or Internet Explorer 4.0 and higher. Earlier versions of Navigator that are not JavaScript compatible can also be used, but you won't receive a confirmation message after submitting the form response.

For Internet Explorer 4.0 or higher, you'll also need to have Outlook Express configured as your mail program. Outlook 97 or 98 may also work fine for this, but I haven't actually checked them out. Versions of Outlook configured to work with Internet Explorer 3.0+ will not work. If you're using Microsoft Exchange as your mail program, you won't be able to test out submitting a form response.

For Netscape Navigator, you'll need to have Netscape Messenger (or Navigator's built-in mail program for versions earlier than 4.0) configured as your mail program.

 NOTE   At minimum, to be able to submit a Mailto form response, Outlook Express or Messenger needs to be configured to send mail to your outgoing mail server (your SMTP mail server). If you haven't set this up, you'll have to find out from your Internet access provider how to configure your mail programs to send mail.

To submit your response, click the Submit button on your form. This will send the response to the e-mail address you specified when creating the form.

NOTE   If you used a dummy e-mail address when creating the form, you won't be able to test submitting a response to your form. Instead, you'll get an error message.

After successfully submitting your form, you should receive a pop-up confirmation that your submission has been made—the same text you created in the Feedback tab section (see Figure 6.23).

Figure 6.23

A confirmation message is returned after the form has been successfully submitted (if the browser is JavaScript capable).

Depending on how your browser is configured, upon submitting your response you may receive a message warning that your message is being sent unencrypted. If so, just click OK.

Submitting a Second Response

To be able to demonstrate importing multiple responses into the WebForms database, you need to send one more response.

To clear your form, click the Reset button. Fill out the form's fields again using different dummy information (try using a friend's name and information, for instance). When finished, click the Submit button to send a second response.

Mailto versus CGI Forms

So, which type of forms should you use—Mailto or CGI? Well, both have advantages and disadvantages, as detailed in the following sections.

Mailto Forms

- **PRO:** Client-side (no server support or Perl or Sendmail access required).
- **PRO:** Single-file solution (no CGI script required).
- **PRO:** You can fully test your form on your local drive before posting it to your site.
- **CON:** Not all Web browsers support sending Mailto form responses.

CGI Forms

- **CON:** Server-side (access to Perl and Sendmail programs on server required).
- **CON:** CGI script required.
- **CON:** You can't test out your form on your local drive before posting it to you site.
- **CON:** Not all ISPs support CGI scripts fully (or at all).

✪ **PRO:** Supported by all Web browsers that support forms.

So, what's right for you? Quite frankly, that depends. No one simple answer exists. The only real problem with Mailto forms is that they're not universally supported by all Web browsers. Internet Explorer 3.0, for instance, even with Internet Mail installed and configured, doesn't support Mailto forms. Internet Explorer 4.0 does support Mailto forms, but only if Outlook Express is designated as its mail program (and not Microsoft Exchange). All versions of Netscape Navigator support Mailto forms. My recommendation is that you start out first with a Mailto form, simply because it's easier to create and set up, and you can fully test it on your own hard drive before putting it up on your site. That way, you can get a form up and going on your site right away. Then, if you want, you can investigate putting a CGI form up, which would mean finding out what your server's policies and procedures are for using CGI scripts (they might need to be tested and approved first), where to put your CGI script on the server, where the Perl and Sendmail programs are located, and so on.

Take a Break

I've waited this long to ask you if you need a break because the form responses you just sent may take a little bit of time to get posted to your mail box. Different mail servers vary on how fast they post your messages. So, get up and walk around, catch a breath of fresh air if you want, grab a quick bite or a soda. You deserve it! I'll see you back in about 10 minutes or so, when I'll show you how to edit your form file, as well as how to use WebForms to retrieve the form responses you just sent. Finally, I'll also show you how to use WebForms to manage your form responses after you've retrieved them.

Managing Form Responses

After you've created a form and tested it out by sending off a couple of responses to your e-mail address, you can use WebForms to do the following:

✪ Indirectly or directly import form responses into WebForms' database

✪ View and track form responses in WebForms' database

✪ Export form responses to an Access or Access-compatible database

Indirectly Importing Form Responses

The default setting for WebForms is to indirectly import your form responses. During your evaluation period, and after registering the WebForms program, you can also directly import your form responses. However, primarily because you don't have to do anything to set it up, I recommend that you try indirectly importing your responses first. (If you want to try directly importing your form responses later, see the "Directly Importing Your Responses into WebForms" section, later in this session.)

Indirectly importing your form responses is a two-step process. First, you retrieve your mail messages and save your form responses; then you import your responses into WebForms' database.

Retrieving and Saving Form Responses

You retrieve your form responses right along with any other e-mail messages you might have. Form responses sent by Netscape Navigator will have "Form from Mozilla" in the subject line, whereas form responses sent by Internet Explorer will have "Form from Microsoft Internet Explorer" in the subject line.

To save form responses in Netscape Messenger, follow these steps:

1. Click the message to display it in the lower window.
2. For forms sent by Navigator, you'll see a "Part 1" link. Double-click it to open it in a new window; then select File, Save As.
3. For forms sent by Internet Explorer, you'll see a POSTDATA.ATT link. Double-click on it to bring up the Save As dialog box.
4. Save your form response to C:\WEBFORMS as a text file (resp1.txt, for instance).
5. Repeat these steps for the second test form response you sent, but this time give it a different file name (resp2.txt, for instance).

Here's how to save a form response in Outlook Express:

1. Double-click the message to display it in a separate window.

2. You'll see an icon in the lower-left corner (labeled "Form posted from Mozil..." (for forms sent from Navigator) or "POSTDATA" (for forms sent from Internet Explorer). Double-click it and then click OK to bring up the Save Attachment As dialog box.

3. Save your form response to C:\WEBFORMS, using .txt as the file extension (resp1.txt, for instance).

4. Repeat these steps for the second test form response you sent, but this time give it a different file name (resp2.txt, for instance).

Importing Your Saved Responses into WebForms

Next, you need to import the form responses you just saved into WebForms:

1. Run WebForms if you've exited it. Select File, Responses, Import.

2. Click the first file (resp1.txt) you saved from your e-mail program; then click the right-arrow button (>) to move the file into the window on the right.

3. Click the second file (resp2.txt) you saved from your e-mail program; then click the right-arrow button to move the file into the window on the right (see Figure 6.24).

4. Click OK to import the responses; then click OK again when told the responses have been imported.

Figure 6.24

Resp1.txt and resp2.txt have been moved into the list of form responses to be indirectly imported.

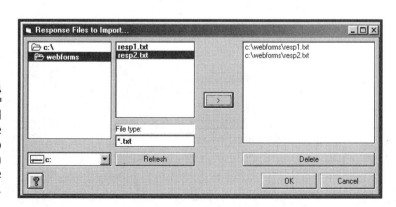

NOTE If you're still in your evaluation period, you can select multiple form responses to import. Just click the files you have saved out of your e-mail program and then click the right-arrow button to move them into the window on the right. If you are no longer in your evaluation period and have not registered WebForms, you'll be able to indirectly import only one response at a time.

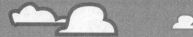

Viewing Form Responses

To view your responses (after you've imported them), select File, Responses, View. Double-click the name of your form. The Responses window will then display the responses to your form (see Figure 6.25). You can view all the responses to your form, or just new or old responses.

Directly Importing Form Responses

During WebForms' evaluation period or after registering the software, you can set up WebForms to directly import form responses from your mail server.

NOTE Because you still have a lot to do and learn this weekend, I recommend that you forego checking out directly importing form responses (for the time being, anyway). If you want to skip ahead at this point, that's fine. You can come back and read this section if you decide later that you want to try directly importing your form responses.

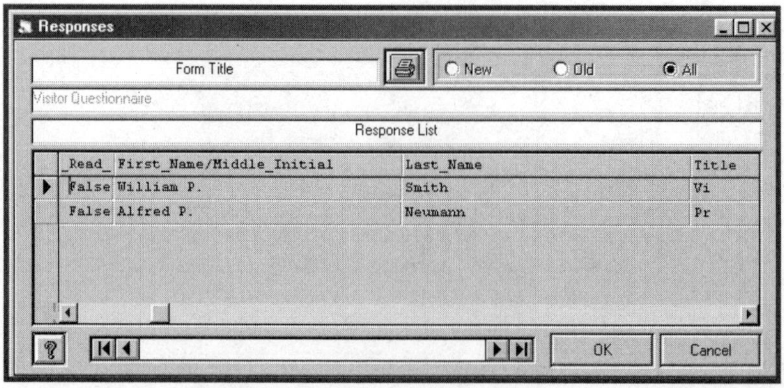

Figure 6.25

The imported responses are being viewed in WebForms' database for the Visitor Questionnaire form.

Editing WebForms' Preferences to Allow Direct Importing

To edit WebForms' preferences to enable direct importing, follow these steps:

NOTE In order to be able to directly import your form responses into WebForms, you need to have a POP3 e-mail box, where your retrieved messages are stored on your own local drive, and not an IMAP e-mail box (where your retrieved massages are stored on the server). If you have an IMAP e-mail box, you'll have to indirectly import your form responses.

1. In WebForms, select Options, Preferences. In the message box that tells you that you'll only be able to use this feature during the evaluation period, click OK.

2. With the Importing tab selected, click the Direct Import check box so that it's checked. Fill in the name of your mail host in the Mail Host field. This is the mail server that handles your outgoing mail (sometimes also called a *POP3 server*).

NOTE If you don't know the name of your mail host, you can check the e-mail program you're using for this information. For instance, if you're using Netscape Navigator 4.0 or higher, select Edit, Preferences and then double-click Mail and Groups and click Mail Server. The information you want is in the Incoming Mail Server field. If you're using Netscape 3.0, select Options, Mail and News Preferences and then click the Servers tab. The information you want is in the Incoming Mail (POP3) Server field.

3. Fill in your user name in the UserName field. This is your login name. (This is often the first part of your e-mail address.)

4. Fill in your password in the Password field. This is usually the same password you use when logging onto the Internet. If you have a different password for your e-mail account, you'll need to use it instead.

5. Click OK.

Directly Importing Your Responses into WebForms

To directly import form responses, you'll need to be connected to the Internet.

In short, in order to directly import the responses you just sent, select File, Responses, Import. In the message box that tells you that this feature will only be available during the evaluation period, click Yes. At the Direct Import window, click the Begin Import button. If the import is successful, you'll be told how many responses have been found and imported.

Exporting Form Responses

WebForms automatically creates its database as a Microsoft Access database. Therefore, you can view the WebForms database in Access at any time. This can, however, prove to be a bit unwieldy, in that the WebForms database includes the data for all the forms you may have created.

A better idea is to first export the data for the particular form that you want to view or manipulate in Access:

1. In WebForms, choose File, Responses, Export.
2. Click the down-arrow control on the right of the Form to Export box; then select the name of the form you want to export.
3. Leave the Export to Access Database radio button selected (the default). You could also select the Export to Text File (CSV) radio button, which would export your data as comma-separated values in a regular text file.
4. Leave the Purge Responses from Original Table check box unchecked, unless you also want to purge the data from your WebForms database. Click OK.
5. Retrieve C:\WEBFORMS\WFRESP.MDB in Microsoft Access (or into any other database program that can read Access database files).

Editing Form Files Created with WebForms

You got a taste of editing your form file earlier when you relocated your logo graphic to the top of the form.

NOTE If you are running short on time or are just all "formed out," feel free to skip this section. You can come back and read it later. However, if you later plan on doing any editing or fixing up of forms (other than just moving a logo or banner image, as shown previously) that are generated by WebForms, you should return and read this section *before* proceeding.

When editing your form file, be careful not to alter the sequence and order of any form elements that receive user input, such as text fields, radio button groups, and so on. Also, don't delete or add any such elements. If you like (or if it makes you feel more comfortable), experiment with making changes to a *copy* of your form file rather than the original generated by Web-Forms. At this point, however, I don't think that is really necessary.

NOTE At this point, right after generating your form, you can always regenerate your form if you should screw up editing it, so I don't see any need to work on a copy of your form file. However, once you've built up a database of responses in WebForms, you won't be able to regenerate your form file without replacing your database of responses. So once you've created a database of responses, you should *always* make any editing changes to a copy of your form file (unless you don't care about holding onto your prior responses).

Here's what you can do without adversely affecting the ability of WebForms to accurately retrieve the responses to your form:

✿ Edit any tags that affect the layout of your form.

✿ Edit any tag attributes that can affect how different form elements might appear on the page.

Changing the Layout of Your Form

When creating your form, WebForms actually makes quite a few layout decisions for you. Just for the sake of showing you a fairly straightforward example, WebForms lays out radio button groups with a BR (break) tag between each group item, displaying each item on a separate line. Nothing is stopping you from simply deleting these BR tags in order to have your radio button group display all on one line.

You also might have noticed that following the check box group on the form is a message in italics reading, "Multiple items may be chosen." This message has been automatically inserted by WebForms, whereas you inserted the lead-in text to the group: "(Check any that apply)." It would be nice if you could tell WebForms not to insert its message in the first place, but you can't. However, nothing is stopping you from deleting it, if you wish.

You could also make quite a few changes in how the text fields are displayed at the start of your form, although I personally don't think you should spend a lot of effort doing this. For instance, WebForms inserts text fields inside of PRE tags, causing the text to be displayed in Courier, and spaces and returns to be displayed "as is," which allows the boxes to be vertically aligned. If you get rid of the PRE tags, the text will be displayed in Times, and text boxes will no longer be vertically aligned but will immediately follow after the preceding text. By also getting rid of the separating P tag, you can display the City and State text fields on the same line, but you'll have to reduce the SIZE attribute for one or both of these fields if you want them both to fit on one line. (It's okay to reduce any of these sizes, just don't *increase* them.)

You could also insert FONT size and color changes in order to gussy up your form. I wouldn't, however, spend a whole lot of effort trying to redesign a form using fonts and colors, because, if you choose to regenerate your form in WebForms, all your changes will go right down the drain.

Changing the Appearance of Form Elements

WebForms automatically selects (turns on or checks) the first item of a radio button or check box group. If you don't want the first item in one of these groups to be selected, just delete the CHECKED attribute in the first INPUT tag in these groups.

TIP If pressing Ctrl+R in Navigator does not update changes you've made to your form file (deleting the CHECKED attributes is apparently one of those instances), hold down the Shift key while clicking the Reload button on Netscape's toolbar or hold down the Shift key, click the right mouse button in Netscape's window, and then select Reload.

There really aren't any other attribute values that you could change here that you can't just as easily control from within WebForms, such as assigning default values to text fields. Nothing is stopping you, however, from making a last minute change, such as changing `Value="USA"` in the Country text field to `Value=""` (or vice versa).

What's Next?

Wow, you've really come a long way now! If you've managed to complete both the Frames and Forms Tutorials, you're really doing great. Even if you've only completed this Forms Tutorial—leaving the Frames Tutorial for another time—that's still excellent.

You should now know enough about creating forms with WebForms that you can create just about any kind of form you want. Not only that, but you can also automate the handling and maintenance of all of the responses to your forms.

You can learn more about creating forms by looking at the tags and attributes used in the HTML file generated by WebForms and then comparing them with their descriptions in Appendix A, "HTML Quick Reference."

PROGRAM DETAILS

WebForms 2.7a by Q&D Software Development

Registration: $34.95 (WebForms Pro)

URL: http://www.q-d.com/

E-Mail: dversch@q-d.com

Phone: (908) 626-9224

Other programs by Q&D Software Development: WebMania (HTML editor), Bookmark Magician, WinBrowse, and Adaptable Applets

The Graphics Tutorial

(Bonus Session)

- ✿ Creating interlaced and transparent images
- ✿ Creating transparent drop shadow effects
- ✿ Creating solid, pattern, and gradient fill effects
- ✿ Creating 3-D buttons
- ✿ Creating GIF animations
- ✿ Creating image maps

Wow, it's Sunday evening! It has been a long haul, if you've managed to follow the schedule so far. I really haven't expected you to do everything up to this point, but if you have, you're doing just fantastic.

I've put this Graphics Tutorial last for a couple of reasons. First, much of what's covered in this session is not strictly focused on HTML, but on using graphics to enhance and add to your Web publishing efforts using HTML. Second, graphics, as I've stressed previously in this book, are a value-added enhancement for your Web pages and should be thought of as the frosting on the cake, not as the cake itself. Don't go hog-wild trying to create really eye-popping graphics for your Web pages, at least until you've managed to develop their content. Bake the cake first, in other words, and then add the frosting.

At this point, you should have at least completed the Basic and Intermediate HTML Tutorials that were scheduled for Saturday morning and afternoon. If you haven't yet completed both of those tutorials, you should return and do them first before attempting to do the Graphics Tutorial.

This session is divided up into three main sections:

- Creating Special Effects with Paint Shop Pro 5
- Creating GIF Animations with GIF Construction Set
- Creating Image Maps with Mapedit

In the "Creating Special Effects with Paint Shop Pro" section, you'll use Paint Shop Pro to learn how to create various "special effects" graphics. Next, in

293

the "Creating GIF Animations with GIF Construction Set" section, you'll use GIF Construction Set to learn how to create GIF animations. Then, in the "Creating Image Maps with Mapedit" section, I'll show you how to easily create image maps using Mapedit. Feel free to leave either or both of the other sections (GIF animations and image maps) until later. However, you should do the first section on creating special effects first before trying the second and third sections.

NOTE   The Paint Shop Pro, GIF Construction Set, and Mapedit versions included on the CD-ROM are all 30-day evaluation versions. If you want to continue using the programs beyond the evaluation periods, you'll need to register them. (The good news is that they are all relatively inexpensive.) You may want to wait to install these programs until you're ready to use them in their section in this tutorial. For information on how to register the programs, see the Program Details boxes at the end of each mini-tutorial.

What You Need to Do the Graphics Tutorial

For the first mini-tutorial, "Creating Special Effects with Paint Shop Pro," you'll need to use Windows 95 or 98. Most of the special effects and other techniques demonstrated in that section are not available in the Windows 3.1 version of Paint Shop Pro. Besides the instructions for installing the Windows 95 version of Paint Shop Pro, I've also included installation instructions for the Windows 3.1 version (Windows 3.1 users will need to use it in the GIF animation mini-tutorial).

For the second mini-tutorial, "Creating GIF Animations with GIF Construction Set," both Windows 3.1 and Windows 95/98 versions of the software are available on the CD-ROM. The steps for creating GIF animations are identical in both. The instructions for creating the images for the animation frames use the Windows 95/98 version of Paint Shop Pro—however, I've also included a couple of special tips for Windows 3.1 users as a guide for using the 16-bit version of Paint Shop Pro to create animation frames.

For the third mini-tutorial, "Creating Image Maps with Mapedit," both Windows 3.1 and Windows 95/98 versions are included on the CD-ROM.

These versions differ somewhat, with the Windows 95/98 version of Maped-it streamlining the process considerably. The basic process, however, is still pretty much the same for both versions—in the instruction steps I've indicated where and how the two versions differ.

Creating a Working Folder

You should create a separate working folder where you can save all the files created during the Graphics Tutorial. I recommend that you go ahead and create a C:\HTML\GRAPHICS folder. (If you're unsure about how to create a new folder in Windows 95/98 or Windows 3.1, see the "Creating a Working Folder" section in the Frames Tutorial session.)

Creating Special Effects with Paint Shop Pro 5

Paint Shop Pro is the most popular shareware paint program on the Web—and for good reason. It has features that rival, and even in some respects surpass, those of heavyweight commercial products (such Adobe Photoshop), which cost hundreds of dollars more.

In this mini-tutorial, you'll learn how to create the following special effects:

- Interlaced GIF images
- Transparent GIF images
- Drop shadow effects
- Fill and pattern effects
- 3-B buttons

Installing Paint Shop Pro

Although this is a Windows 95 only section, I've included instructions here for installing and running both the Windows 95 and Windows 3.1 versions of Paint Shop Pro.

If you're a Windows 3.1 user, after installing the 16-bit version of Paint Shop Pro here, you should skip ahead to the next main section in this tutorial, "Creating GIF Animations with GIF Construction Set." In that section, you'll find a Windows 3.1 tip for a workaround for creating drop shadow effects in the Windows 3.1 version of Paint Shop Pro. After that, to install Paint Shop Pro from the CD-ROM, follow these steps:

1. Insert the *Learn HTML in a Weekend* CD-ROM in your CD-ROM drive.

2. If you're using Windows 95/98, Prima's CD-ROM interface will automatically run, unless you have disabled Autorun. If the CD-ROM interface does not automatically run, from the Start menu, select Run and then type **D:\prima.exe** (where *D* is your CD-ROM's drive letter) and click OK.

3. If you're using Windows 3.1, select File, Run from Program Manager's menu bar and then type **D:\prima.exe** (where *D* is your CD-ROM's drive letter). Click OK.

4. With Prima's CD-ROM interface onscreen, click Multimedia, Paint Shop Pro.

5. Click Install in the drop-down menu.

6. Select the 32 bit (Win 95/98/NT) radio button if you're using Windows 95/98. Select the 16 bit (Windows 3.x) radio button if you're using Windows 3.1. Click OK.

7. Follow the instructions on Paint Shop Pro's setup screen to install Paint Shop Pro. If you're installing the Windows 95 version, it will be installed in the C:\Program Files\Paint Shop Pro 5 folder. If you're installing the Windows 3.1 version, it will be installed in the C:\PSP folder.

8. For Paint Shop Pro 5.01, you'll be asked if you want to view important information about Paint Shop Pro. Click Yes to view the release notes for the program, or click No to skip this.

9. For Paint Shop Pro 3.11, at the end of the installation routine, you'll be asked if you want to run the program. Because you won't be doing the remainder of this section, just click No.

10. If Prima's CD-ROM interface is not onscreen, use Alt+Tab to bring it back to the front. Click Exit.

Starting Paint Shop Pro

To run Paint Shop Pro 5.01 (Windows 95/98), click the Start button and then select Programs, Paint Shop Pro 5, and then Paint Shop Pro 5 again.

To run Paint Shop Pro 3.11 (Windows 3.1), double-click its icon in the Program Group that has been created for it.

(If you're using Windows 3.1, you should skip ahead to the next main section, "Creating GIF Animations with GIF Construction Set.")

Setting File Associations

When you run Paint Shop Pro 5 for the first time, you're prompted to specify the file types you want to be associated with Paint Shop Pro. Starting out, the initial selections are Kodak Digital Camera File (.KDC), Paint Shop Pro Image (.PSP), SciTex Continuous Tone (.SCT, .CT), and Windows Enhanced Meta File (.EMF). To add any additional file types, just click their check boxes to select them. To unselect a file type, just click its check box so that it's unchecked. Click OK to accept the current selections.

Turning Off or Moving the Controls and Layers Palettes

When you first run Paint Shop Pro, the Controls and Layers palettes are displayed in the middle of Paint Shop Pro's window. To get them out of the way, go ahead and turn the display of these palettes off (you can also just drag them off to the side or bottom of the screen if you're running in 800-by-600 or higher screen resolution):

1. Select View and Toolbars.
2. Click the Controls Palette check box so it's unchecked.
3. Click the Layer Palette check box so it's unchecked.
4. Click OK.

You'll turn the Controls Palette back on later in this mini-tutorial when defining a pattern fill. The Layer Palette is used to define image layers, which won't be covered in this mini-tutorial.

Starting a New Image

Here's how to start a new image in Paint Shop Pro:

1. Select File, New. In the New Image dialog box, type **450** as the Width and **150** as the Height.

2. Set the Background color to White. Set the Image Type to 16.7 Million Colors (24 Bit). Click OK. (See Figure 7.1.)

Repositioning the Tool Palette

When you run Paint Shop Pro for the first time, the toolbar is arrayed along the top of the window, whereas the tool palette is arrayed along the left side of the window. However, if you're running in a 640-by-480 screen resolution, you won't be able to see all the tools on the tool palette unless you move it. To move the tool palette, click and hold the mouse on the double bars at the top; then drag it up until you see its outline overlapping the toolbar. Let go of the mouse button to insert the tool palette into the indicated position (see Figure 7.2). You may need to try this a few times before you get it into the right position (it may also pop into place on the same line but following the toolbar, or it may drop in as a separate window).

If you're running in an 800-by-600 or greater screen resolution, you can leave the tool palette arrayed along the left side of Paint Shop Pro's window, if you like. However, I'll refer to the tool palette in this mini-tutorial (and showing it in the figures) as positioned at the top of Paint Shop Pro's window, underneath the toolbar.

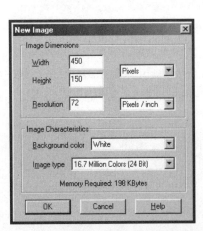

Figure 7.1

In the New Image dialog box, you specify the dimensions, background color, and the number of colors.

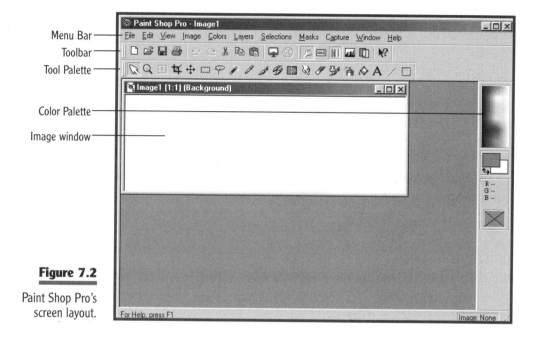

Menu Bar
Toolbar
Tool Palette
Color Palette
Image window

Figure 7.2

Paint Shop Pro's
screen layout.

Paint Shop Pro's Screen Layout

Let's pause for a moment right now and go over Paint Shop Pro's screen layout. This is important because throughout this section, I'll refer to different parts of Paint Shop Pro's screen simply by their names instead of describing them in detail. As you go through this tutorial, you can use Figure 7.2 and the attendant call-outs, or "labels," as a quick reference to what is what on Paint Shop Pro's screen.

The following list describes the call-outs to Figure 7.2:

✪ **Menu bar.** The menu bar is the pull-down menu (File, Edit, View, and so on) at the top of Paint Shop Pro's screen. When referencing a menu, I'll always say "Select File," for instance.

✪ **Toolbar.** The toolbar is the top row of buttons, which are primarily shortcuts for operations that can be carried out using the menu bar. For instance, instead of selecting File, New to create a new image, you can just click the first toolbar button (New). The toolbar also includes four icons grouped at the right that you can use to toggle on and off the display of the tool palette, style bar, and color palette.

- **Tool palette.** The tool palette is the second row of buttons. These buttons will be used heavily in manipulating your image. They allow you to zoom in or out, move your image in the image window, select part of the image, paint, erase, fill, add text, and so on. When referring to one of these buttons, I'll always say something like "Click the Paint Bucket button on the tool palette," for example.

- **Color palette.** The color palette is located on the right side of Paint Shop Pro's screen. The color palette has three parts: the Select Color panel, the Active Colors panel, and the Current Color panel. When you move the mouse pointer into the Select Color panel, the pointer turns into the Dropper tool—you can select a color and assign it as the foreground color by clicking it with the left mouse button. To assign a color as the background color, click the right mouse button. The Active Colors panel contains two overlapped rectangles that display the currently selected foreground and background colors—you can assign foreground and background colors by clicking either of the rectangles. The Current Color panel displays the current color when you select a color from the Select Color panel or when you use the Dropper tool to pick a color from the image window. The palette settings for the color are also displayed here, either as HSL (hue, saturation, and luminance) or RGB (red, green, and blue) palette values.

- **Image window.** This is the window that contains the actual graphic you're creating. Note that you can have more than one image window open at a time, but only one of them will be the active image window.

Creating Interlaced GIFs

GIF images can be either noninterlaced or interlaced. In a noninterlaced GIF image, all the lines of the image are progressively displayed in sequence from top to bottom in a single pass. An interlaced GIF image, on the other hand, is displayed in several passes—in the first pass, only one in three lines might be displayed, with the remainder displayed on subsequent passes. The advantage of using interlaced GIF images on Web pages is that the viewer can see what the image is long before it has been entirely downloaded and displayed. Saving all GIF images to be displayed on Web pages as interlaced is a good idea.

Saving a GIF image is actually very simple and easy in Paint Shop Pro. However, before you can save an image, you have to create one. In the following section, you'll select a foreground color and then insert some text that will be displayed in that color.

Selecting a Foreground Color

To select a foreground color that will be used for the text, follow these steps:

NOTE   When you run Paint Shop Pro 5 for the first time, the foreground color rectangle is set as white, and the background color rectangle is set as black. If you've used this copy of Paint Shop Pro, the most recently selected foreground and background colors will be displayed in the color rectangles (rather than white and black).

1. Click the foreground color rectangle in the color palette. The Color dialog box is displayed, as shown in Figure 7.3.

2. Click the color red (the first color in the first row of basic colors).

3. Click OK. You'll now see that the foreground color rectangle has changed to red.

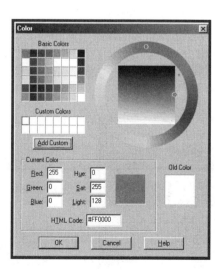

Figure 7.3

In the Color dialog box, you can select from a wide range of colors.

Go ahead and leave the background color rectangle (colored black) as it is for right now (you'll change it later, however, when you get around to creating a GIF image with a transparent background color).

Adding Some Text

Next, add some text to your image:

NOTE If you're running in 640-by-480 screen resolution and you haven't repositioned the tool palette, you won't be able to see or access the Text tool (the "A" button). You should return to and follow the instruction in the "Repositioning the Tool Palette" section and then come back and execute the following steps.

1. Click the Text tool (the "A" button) on the Tool Palette and then click in the middle of your image window.
2. Select Arial as the font name, Bold as the style, and 72 points as the size. Type **Headline** as the text. Leave all the other settings as they are (see Figure 7.4). Click OK.

Your "Headline" text, colored in red, is now inserted in the image window. The letters of your text are surrounded by a dashed line, meaning that the text is selected. Click and hold down the mouse button on the "Headline"

Figure 7.4

The text, "Headline," is set in a 72-point, bold, Arial font.

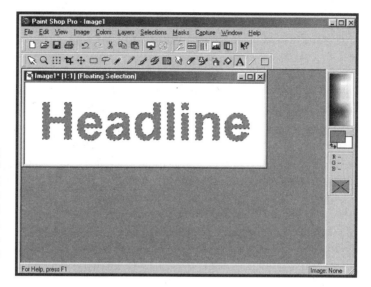

Figure 7.5

The "Headline" text is inserted in the current foreground color and positioned in the middle of the image window.

text; then drag your text to position it as close to being in the center of the image window as you can manage (see Figure 7.5).

Saving an Interlaced GIF

Now that you've created an image with something in it, you can save it as an interlaced GIF. Follow these steps:

1. Select File, Save (or Save As). The Save As dialog box is displayed.
2. In the Save In text box, change the folder to C:\HTML\Graphics.
3. In the Save as Type box, select CompuServe Graphics Interchange (*.GIF) as the file type.
4. Type **headline.gif** in the File Name box.
5. Click the Options button. The Version 89a and Interlaced radio buttons should be selected. Click OK.

NOTE GIF files have two variants—version 89a and version 87a. You should always save your GIF files as version 89a files, which is the more recent version. The main limitation of version 87a is that it does not allow for GIF animations.

6. Click Save and then click Yes to allow Paint Shop Pro to reduce the number of colors to 256 (GIFs can only have up to 256 colors).

NOTE You may wonder why we started out creating an image using 16.7 million colors, only to reduce it here to 256 colors. First, I wanted to show you that Paint Shop Pro will automatically reduce the number of colors in an image when saving to a format that allows fewer colors than are included in the image being saved. Second, in order to apply any of Paint Shop Pro's special effects, deformations, or other filters, the number of colors in an image must be set to 16.7 million colors.

That's it. You've just created and saved an interlaced GIF file. A very simple one, admittedly, but you'll do more with it as you go along.

Creating Transparent GIFs

A *transparent GIF* is a GIF file with one of the colors, usually the background color, set to be transparent. This can allow you, for instance, to create a banner or logo graphic that will display transparently against a Web page's background color or image.

Selecting a Background Color

You'll set the background color as transparent, but first you have to select the color for the background color rectangle that you want to be transparent. Because the background of your image is white, select white as the color of the background color rectangle:

1. Click the background color rectangle in the color palette. The Color dialog box is displayed.

2. Click the color white (the bottom-right color in the Basic Colors area).

3. Click OK. You'll now see that the background color rectangle has changed to white.

Setting the Background Color to Transparent

Now, you need to set the background color (the color displayed in the background color rectangle) to transparent:

1. Select Colors from the menu bar and then select Set Palette Transparency.

2. Click Yes to reduce the image to one layer and 256 colors.

3. Leave the Optimized Median Cut radio button selected. Leave the Nearest Color radio button selected. Click OK.

NOTE   The Optimized Median Cut palette includes those colors that occur most frequently in the image, while excluding those colors that occur least frequently. The Optimized Octree palette works similarly to the Optimized Median Cut palette but does not weigh color frequency. The Standard palette selects colors based on the standard 256-color palette, including the 16 standard Windows colors.

Selecting the Optimized Median Cut palette will result in better image quality. If you have multiple images that you want to share the same palette, you should select the Standard palette. The Optimized Octree palette should probably be avoided.

Of the three reduction methods listed, selecting Ordered Dither or Error Diffusion can result in better image quality, with one large reservation. If you're going to apply a drop shadow effect or other "blur" effect against a transparent background, you should always choose Nearest Color as the reduction method, because if you use an ordered dither or error diffusion effect, your background color might get dithered (and is therefore no longer transparent).

4. In the Set Palette Transparency dialog box, select the second radio button, Set the Transparency Value to the Current Background Color. Click OK.

5. If you want to view the transparent color, press Shift+V (or select Colors, View Palette Transparency). The transparent color should be displayed in a checkerboard pattern. Press Shift+V again to return to the normal viewing mode.

NOTE   With Paint Shop Pro 5, you have to set the transparency color for each image you want to save as transparent. With previous versions, color transparency was included in the save options, and you had to remember to turn it off if you didn't want it for subsequent GIF images.

Saving Your Transparent GIF

Because you've already saved the file, just select File and Save to resave the file (or press Ctrl+S).

Viewing Your Transparent Image

To view your transparent image, you need to create an HTML file using your transparent image and a background image to show it off; then you need to load it into your Web browser. To save you some time, I've already created the following HTML file for you and included it with the example files you copied from the CD-ROM to C:\HTML earlier:

```
<HTML>
<HEAD><TITLE>Graphic Headline</TITLE>
</HEAD>
<BODY BACKGROUND="backgrnd.gif">
<P ALIGN="center"><IMG SRC="graphics/headline.gif" WIDTH="450"
➥HEIGHT="150">
</BODY>
</HTML>
```

The background image here, BACKGROUND.GIF, is the same you used in the Intermediate HTML Tutorial in the Saturday Afternoon session.

To view HEADLINE.HTM in your Web browser, follow these steps:

1. Run your Web browser.
2. Open HEADLINE.HTM from the C:\HTML folder (in Internet Explorer, select File, Open, Browse; in Netscape Navigator, select File, Open Page, and Choose File).

As shown in Figure 7.6, the "Headline" image is displayed transparently against the background image.

Figure 7.6

The text in the transparent GIF image seems to float on top of the background image.

Creating Drop Shadows

One of the easiest and most effective special effects you can add to your graphic is a drop shadow. To add a drop shadow to the "Headline" text, follow these steps:

1. Special effects such as drop shadows cannot be performed on 256K GIF files. In Paint Shop Pro, select Colors, Increase Color Depth, 16 Million Colors (24 bit).

2. Click the foreground color rectangle in the color palette. Choose any color, other than red, that you think might look good (for instance, try selecting the blue-green color—the fourth color down in the third column). Click OK.

3. Select Image, Effects, Drop Shadow.

4. In the Drop Shadow dialog box, select Foreground Color for the Color setting, 90 for the Opacity setting, 10 for the Blur setting, and 6 for both the Vertical and Horizontal Offset settings. Click OK.

Figure 7.7 shows your text now with a drop shadow added.

Resetting the Image As Transparent

The number of colors in the image was increased back to 16 million colors when you added the drop shadow. Because the transparency effect can only

Figure 7.7

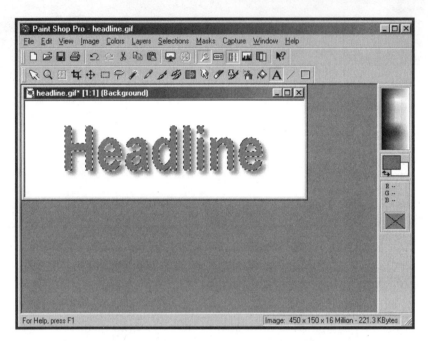

Figure 7.7

A drop shadow
is a good way to
add a 3-D touch
to an image.

be used in images with a maximum of 256 colors, you need to reset the background color as transparent (and change the number of colors in the image back to 256):

1. Select Colors, Set Palette Transparency; then click Yes to reduce the number of colors in the image to 256 colors.

2. Click OK to accept the Decrease Color Depth settings (they should be unchanged from when you last set the color transparency).

3. In the Set Palette Transparency dialog box, select the second radio button, Set the Transparency Value to the Current Background Color. Click OK.

Viewing Your Drop Shadow in Your Web Browser

First, press Ctrl+S to resave your image (or select File, Save).

Hop back over to your Web browser where HEADLINE.HTM should still be displayed. Reload the page in order to display your new transparent image

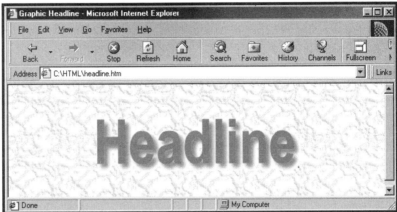

Figure 7.8

Both the text and
the drop shadow
seem to float on
top of the
background image.

using the drop shadow effect (in Netscape Navigator or Internet Explorer, just press Ctrl+R). Because you reset the background color of your image to transparent, both the text and the drop shadow appear to be floating on top of the background image, as shown in Figure 7.8.

Creating Transparent Drop Shadows Against a Black Background

When you use a blur effect such as a drop shadow, the background of your image will only appear to be transparent if the background color in Paint Shop Pro closely matches the background color or the predominant color in a background image displayed in your Web browser. The blur effect actually blurs from its color to the color of the background, and only the non-blurred background color will actually be transparent.

If the background color (or other color set as transparent) in Paint Shop Pro is very different from the background color or predominant color in a background image displayed in your Web browser, you'll see a very noticeable cookie-cutter effect surrounding your drop shadow. Figure 7.9 shows an example of this (with the colors in the background image reversed).

(I've included both the HTML file and background image with the reversed colors with the example files in C:\HTML. If you want to see what this looks like in your own browser, just open HEADLIN2.HTM in your browser.)

Figure 7.9

If the background color of your image and the background color (or the predominant color in a background image) don't match, you'll get a cookie-cutter effect around the drop shadow.

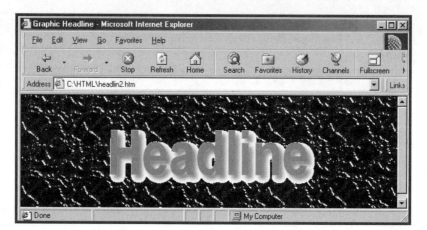

Because the predominant color in the HEADLIN2.HTM file's background image (BACKGRN2.GIF) is black, you would just need to start with a black background before adding your text and drop shadow to have it appear to meld seamlessly into the browser's background image.

Matching Background Colors in Your Browser and Paint Shop Pro

You can, of course, just guess when trying to match a background color in Paint Shop Pro to a background color in your browser, but it's far more effective if you can match the colors exactly.

If the background color is specified as a RGB hex code in your HTML file's BODY tag, matching the background color in Paint Shop Pro is as simple as clicking the background color rectangle and typing the corresponding hex code in the Color dialog's HTML Code box. For instance, if the BODY tag in your HTML file includes the code, BGCOLOR="#FF8000" (setting the background color to orange), you would match that color simply by typing **#FF8000** in the Color dialog box's HTML Code box.

Now, if the background color is specified in your HTML file as a color name (BGCOLOR="olive", for instance), finding the matching color in Paint Shop Pro is not quite so quick and easy. In that case, you'll just have to make the best match you can by means of trial and error.

Matching Background Colors Using the Dropper

What if the background image in your HTML file has many color gradations? Which color do you try to match and how do you go about matching it in Paint Shop Pro? The answer is to load the background image into Paint Shop Pro and then use the Dropper tool to pick up the predominant color of the background. Then you drop the color onto the background color rectangle. If you want to see how to do this, the following steps walk you through the process:

● ●

NOTE The following steps are optional. You're not required to do them before continuing on with the remainder of this mini-tutorial.

● ●

1. Open the background image that you want to match into Paint Shop Pro. (Try 3DGREEN1.GIF, which is a background image I've included with the example files in C:\HTML.)

2. You might want to zoom in on the background image to get a closer look at it. Select View, Zoom In, 2:1.

3. Select the Dropper tool (sixth button from the left on the tool palette) and position its pointer on what you see as the predominant or most common color in the image.

4. Right-click to assign the Dropper color to the background color rectangle.

5. Start a new image (File, New) and select Background Color in the Background color box.

That's it. The background color of your new image will match the predominant or most common color in the background image. Just add your text and drop shadow (setting suitable colors for both) and then set the background color as transparent before saving your file. Any drop shadow using a blur (or any other blur effect) should appear to blend seamlessly into your browser's background image.

Before continuing on with the rest of the mini-tutorial, close the last two image windows you opened (3DGREEN1.GIF and the image window with the green background).

Using Fill Effects

You can also use a variety of different *fill effects*—effects you can create using the Flood Fill tool (the "paint bucket" button) on the tool palette.

Before trying out some of these effects, however, you first need to do a few things with the HEADLINE.GIF image:

1. With HEADLINE.GIF as the one image window remaining on the screen, select Colors, Increase Color Depth, 16 Million Colors.

2. If you changed the background color in the last section, click the background rectangle and reselect white as the background color.

3. Select Selections and Select None to "unselect" the "Headline" text (you'll see the dotted line around the letters disappear).

Selecting Just the "H"

1. To reselect just the letter H, click the Magic Wand tool (fifth button from the left) on the tool palette.

2. Position the pointer so that the crosshairs (the cross-shaped cursor) are inside the letter H. Click the left mouse button. You'll notice the letter H is now selected (it's surrounded by dashed lines).

Using a Solid Fill Effect

1. Click the foreground color rectangle and then select a color with which to fill the letter H (try blue, the fifth color down in the first column). Click OK.

2. Click the Flood Fill tool (the "paint bucket" button) on the tool palette.

3. Turn on the display of the controls palette: select View, Toolbars and then click the Control Palette check box (it should be checked). Click OK. On the controls palette, Solid Color should already be selected as the Fill Style setting. Leave the other settings as they are.

4. Click the left mouse button on the letter H. It will now be filled with the foreground color you just selected, as shown in Figure 7.10.

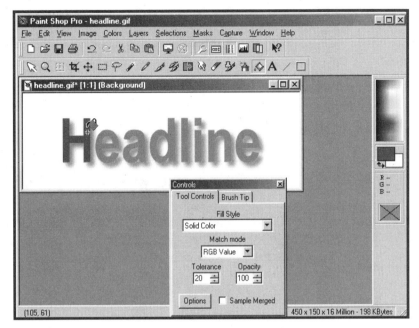

Figure 7.10

The letter "H" has been filled with a solid color using the Flood Fill tool.

Using a Pattern Fill Effect

Another neat effect is to fill an object with a pattern. You can use any image currently loaded in Paint Shop Pro as a pattern. The best images to use are background images that contain a pattern or texture. Any image that you want to use as a pattern, however, must first be opened in Paint Shop Pro. To open a background image to use as a fill pattern, follow these steps:

1. Select File, Open. Then open 3DGREEN1.GIF from C:\HTML.

2. Click the title bar of the HEADLINE.GIF image window to bring it to the front.

3. Click the Flood Fill tool (the "paint bucket" button) on the tool palette. On the controls palette, select Pattern as the Fill Style setting.

4. Click the Options button on the controls palette. In the Flood Fill Options window, select 3DGREEN1.GIF from the New Pattern source drop-down list. Click OK.

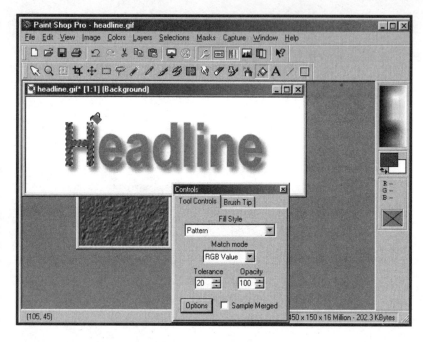

Figure 7.11

You can create a
pattern fill based
on any image
loaded in Paint
Shop Pro—here
the letter "H" has
been filled with a
pattern based on a
background image,
3DGREEN1.GIF.

5. Click the letter H in "Headline." As shown in Figure 7.11, the letter H has been filled with the pattern you just selected.

Using a Gradient Fill Effect

Another very effective fill effect you can use that works great for text is a *gradient fill effect*. You can create four different gradient fill effects in Paint Shop Pro: linear, rectangular, sunburst, and radial. The following steps walk you through adding a linear gradient fill to your image:

1. Leave the blue color selected in the foreground color rectangle. It will be one of the colors in your gradient fill. Also, leave white selected in the background color rectangle. It will be the other color in your gradient fill.

2. Click the Magic Wand tool (eighth tool from the left) on the tool palette; then click the mouse on the letter "e" to select it. Hold down the Shift key and click the mouse on each of the remaining letters ("a," "d," "l," "i," "n," and "e"). Leave the dot on the "i" unselected,

however. The last seven letters of the "Headline" text should now be selected (surrounded by dotted lines).

3. Click the Flood Fill tool (the "paint bucket" button). On the controls palette, select Linear Gradient as the Fill Style setting.

4. Click the Options button on the controls palette. In the Degree box, type **180**. Click OK.

5. Click the mouse on the "e" letter, filling it with the gradient fill. Repeat for the remaining letters.

The last seven letters of "Headline" (except for the dot on the "i") should now be filled with the gradient fill, as shown in Figure 7.12.

 TIP

If you mess up or just want to back up and try something different, you can undo any steps you've performed by selecting Edit, Undo. You can back up through as many steps as you want by just continuing to click the Undo option. (You can also undo multiple steps you've performed with the Undo History option.)

Figure 7.12

The last seven letters in "Headline" are filled with a linear gradient fill.

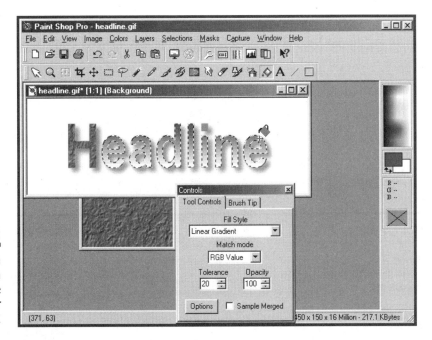

Viewing the Gradient Fill Effect in Your Web Browser

Before you resave HEADLINE.GIF, you'll need to reset the background as transparent. Select Colors and Set Palette Transparency, click Yes to decrease the number of colors to 256, click OK to accept the Decrease Color Depth settings, select the second radio button (Set the Transparency Value to the Current Background Color), and then click OK.

NOTE Remember that *current background color* refers to the background color rectangle, not the background color in your image. The background color in your image must match the background color rectangle if it's to be transparent.

Hop back over to your Web browser and reload HEADLINE.HTM (press Ctrl+R) to see what your image now looks like (see Figure 7.13).

Creating 3-D Buttons

Paint Shop Pro has a "buttonize" effect that makes it a breeze to create 3-D buttons. In this section, you'll create a 3-D wood grain "Home" button that can be used as a loop-back image link to your home page.

Figure 7.13

Using a transparent background, a drop shadow, a pattern fill, and a gradient fill, the finished "Headline" image is displayed in a Web browser.

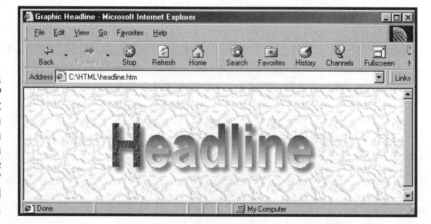

Starting a New Image

To create the 3-D button example, you'll need to start a new image. Just follow these steps:

1. Clear the previous image windows.

2. Select File, New. Type **125** as the width and **60** as the height. Select white as the background color. Leave the number of colors set to 16.7 million colors. Click OK.

3. Select the Zoom tool (the "magnifying glass" button) on the tool palette. Click the mouse twice inside the image window to increase the zoom factor to 3:1.

Adding the Wood Grain Fill

I've included a wood grain background image, WOOD1.GIF, with the example files in C:\HTML that you can use to create a wood grain pattern fill. Follow these steps:

1. Select File, Open. Double-click WOOD1.GIF in C:\HTML to open it.

2. Reselect your blank image window by clicking its title bar to bring it to the foreground.

3. Select the Flood Fill tool (the "paint bucket" button); then select View, Toolbars. Click the Control Palette check box so it's checked. Click OK.

4. Select Pattern as the Fill Style setting and then click the Options button.

5. From the New Pattern Source drop-down list box, select WOOD1.GIF as the pattern source. Click OK. (Move the controls palette out of the way so that it isn't blocking your image window, but don't close it yet—you'll use it later to add a gradient fill.)

6. Click the mouse inside your blank image window. The image window should now be filled with the wood grain pattern fill (see Figure 7.14).

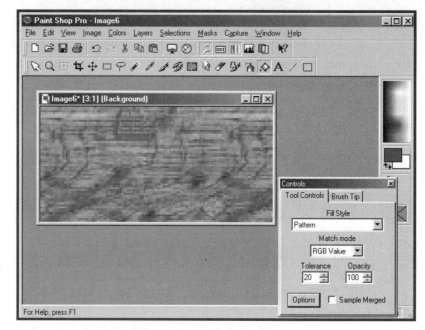

Figure 7.14

The image has been filled with a wood grain pattern.

Creating the Button Effect

Now, "buttonize" the image:

1. First, you need to select a dark color in the background color rectangle that will be the color of the shadow of the button effect. Click the background color rectangle, select the dark brown color (second color in the first row), and then click OK.

2. Select Image, Effects, Buttonize. In the Buttonize window, set the height as 15, the width as 15, and the opacity as 80. Leave the Transparent Edge radio button selected. Click OK.

The wood grain fill should now have a very noticeable 3-D button look (see Figure 7.15).

Adding the Text and Drop Shadow

Now, add the text for the button (Home), fill it with a gradient fill, and then add a drop shadow to provide some relief between the text and the button:

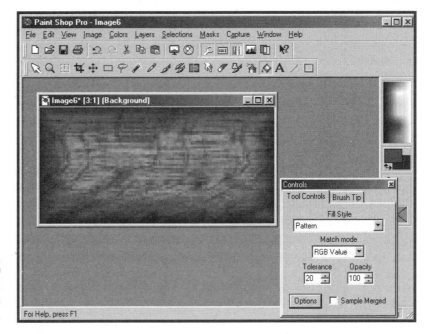

Figure 7.15

The wood grain background has been buttonized.

1. First you need to add the text. Click the Text tool (the "A" button) and then click the center of the image. Select Arial as the font, Bold as the style, and 26 as the size.

2. Type **Home** as the text (in the Enter text here box). Click OK.

3. Select the gradient fill colors: Click the foreground color rectangle and type **#FF8000** in the HTML Code box to specify orange as the color; then click OK. Click the background color rectangle and select bright yellow (second down in the first column) and then click OK.

4. Click the Flood Fill tool (the "paint bucket" button). In the controls palette, select Linear Gradient as the Fill Style setting and then click Options. Leave the Degree setting at 180. Click OK. Click the mouse inside of each of the letters ("H," "o," "m," and "e") to fill them with the linear gradient.

5. To add the drop shadow, click the background color rectangle, select the dark brown color (second color in first row), and click OK. Select Image, Effects, Drop Shadow. Select Background Color as the color,

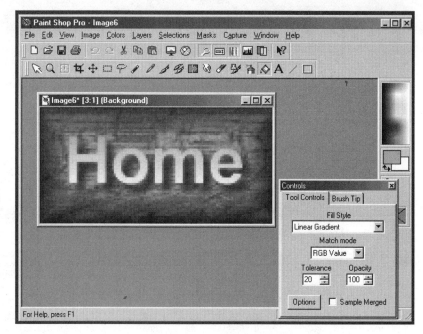

Figure 7.16

The "Home" text, filled with a gradient fill and backed with a drop shadow, is superimposed on top of the 3-D button.

90 as the opacity, 5 as the blur, and 4 as the vertical and horizontal offsets. Click OK. Select Selections and Select None to get a good look at your 3-D button (see Figure 7.16).

If you want to see your 3-D wood grain button at its true size, just select the Zoom tool and right-click in the image window twice to return the zoom aspect to 1:1.

Saving Your 3-D Button

Go ahead and save your 3-D button:

1. Select File, Save. You should already be at the C:\HTML\GRAPHICS folder (if not, go there).

2. Select "JPEG - JIFF Compliant" in the Save as Type list box; then type **home_btn.jpg** as the file name.

3. Click Options. Standard Encoding should be selected. Decrease the compression level setting to 10. Click OK.

4. Click Save to save the image.

TIP It is a good idea to compress JPG images when saving them. Just setting the compression level to 10 for the HOME_BTN.JPG file reduces its size from 8K to 4K, for instance. That can represent a big bandwidth saving if you're going to include several buttons or other JPG images on a Web page.

Unlike with previous versions of Paint Shop Pro, in version 5, retrieving and resaving a previously compressed JPG image will not add the two compressions together but rather will resave the image only at the currently selected compression level (unless the selected compression level is less than the previously saved compression level, in which case, the saved compression level will be retained).

You'll need to do some experimenting to find the optimum compression level for a particular JPG image. The way to do it is to first save your JPG image with 1 set as the compression level and then resave it under different file names with the compression levels set at progressively higher numbers (you might want to include the compression number in the file name as a handy way of keeping track). Then retrieve the compressed versions of your image and compare them in Paint Shop Pro to your original. To check on the relative file sizes run Windows Explorer (with View, Details selected) to view the folder where you've saved your images.

Exiting Paint Shop Pro

You need to exit Paint Shop Pro before installing the software for the next mini-tutorial (for creating GIF animations). To exit Paint Shop Pro, click File, Exit.

PROGRAM DETAILS

Paint Shop Pro 5 by JASC, Inc.

Registration: $69

URL: http://www.jasc.com/

Email: order@jasc.com

Phone: 1-800-622-2793

FAX: 1-612-930-9172

Other software by JASC, Inc.: ImageCommander (image manager), Pixel 3D (3D rendering), Media Center (file manager/slide show), and Image Robot (batch image processor).

ON THE

CD

Look on the CD-ROM for additional programs and utilites for creating images for display on the Web. LVIEW Pro is a great image viewer with quite a few image editing tricks up its sleeve. Check out some of the other image viewing/manipulation utlities included on the CD-ROM as well, including ACDsee, Flashview, Image Commander, Media Center, and PolyView. Also included on the CD-ROM are demo versions of NetSketch, an object-drawing program, and WebPainter, a full-feature paint program, which you might want to try out.

Creating GIF Animations with GIF Construction Set

The graphics special effects covered in the last section on using Paint Shop Pro are effective ways to really "juice up" a Web site, but they don't do one thing—they don't move. That's where GIF animations come in. A GIF animation is simply a GIF file that contains two or more individual frames that are played in succession, either in a sequence, once or several times through, or in an unending loop. Players or plug-ins aren't needed to enable a visitor to your site to see your GIF animations—any browser that can display GIF files should also be able to display GIF animations without any trouble.

You don't need to create a separate folder for this mini-tutorial. Just use C:\HTML\GRAPHICS, which you created earlier, to save any files that you create here. The following sections include instructions for installing and running GIF Construction Set.

Installing GIF Construction Set

You can install GIF Construction Set directly from the CD-ROM using Prima's interface:

1. Insert the *Learn HTML in a Weekend* CD-ROM in your CD-ROM drive.

2. If you're using Windows 95/98, Prima's CD-ROM interface will automatically run, unless you have disabled Autorun. If the CD-ROM interface does not automatically run, select Run and then type **D:\prima.exe** (where *D* is your CD-ROM's drive letter) and click OK.

3. If you're using Windows 3.1, select File, Run from Program Manager's menu bar and then type **D:\prima.exe** (where *D* is your CD-ROM's drive letter). Click OK.

4. With Prima's CD-ROM interface onscreen, click Multimedia, GIF Construction Set.

5. Click Install in the drop-down menu.

6. Select the 32-bit (Win 95/98/NT) radio button if you are using Windows 95/98. Select the 16-bit (Windows 3.x) radio button if you are using Windows 3.1. Click OK.

7. Follow the instructions on GIF Construction Set's installation windows to install the software. If you're installing the 32-bit (Windows 95/98/NT) version, it will be installed in the C:\GIFCONSTRUC-TIONSET folder. If you're installing the 16-bit (Windows 3.1) version, it will be installed in the C:\GIFCON folder.

8. The "What's New" file will be automatically displayed in WordPad (Windows 95/98) or Write (Windows 3.1). Feel free to read through it if you wish, or you can print it out on your printer for future reference. When you're done, select File, Exit.

9. If Prima's CD-ROM interface is not onscreen, use Alt+Tab to bring it back to the front. Click Exit.

Creating GIF Animations

Creating GIF animations is a two-step process. First, you use Paint Shop Pro to create the individual "frames" that will be included in your animation; then you use GIF Construction Set's Animation Wizard to turn your separate frames into a GIF animation.

Reviewing the Example Animation Frames in Paint Shop Pro

For this tutorial, in order to save some time, I've already created for you the images for the animation frames and included them with the example files in C:\HTML. You could, at this point, just run GIF Construction Set and assemble your animation, but then you wouldn't be getting a feel for how the whole process works. Go ahead and run Paint Shop Pro to review the animation frames before importing them into GIF Construction Set.

To run Paint Shop Pro 5.01 (Windows 95/98), click the Start button and then select Programs, Paint Shop Pro 5, and then Paint Shop Pro 5 again.

To run Paint Shop Pro 3.11 (Windows 3.1), double-click its icon in the Program Group that has been created for it.

The example images for the animation frames were created using the Windows 95/98 version of Paint Shop Pro. Many of the effects used cannot be directly duplicated in the Windows 3.1 version of Paint Shop Pro. In discussing the individual frames and the methods used to create them, however, I've also included a series of tips for workarounds that can be done in the Windows 3.1 version of Paint Shop Pro to achieve similar effects.

Opening the Example Animation Frames

In either the Windows 95/98 or Windows 3.1 version of Paint Shop Pro, follow these steps:

1. Select File, Open. Go to the C:\HTML folder and double-click the *click4.gif* file to open it.
2. Repeat step 1 for *click3.gif, click2.gif,* and *click1.gif.*
3. In Windows 95, select Window, Tile Horizontally. In Windows 3.1, select Window, Tile (see Figure 7.17).

 NOTE The screen capture for Figure 7.17 was done using the Windows 95/98 version of Paint Shop Pro. If you're using the Windows 3.1 version, what you see should be similar to, but not exactly the same as, what is shown in that figure.

Previewing the First Frame

CLICK1.GIF is the image that will be used as the first frame in the animation. Here are the effects that were used to create the image:

○ The "CLICK" text was added using the Text tool (with red selected as the foreground color).

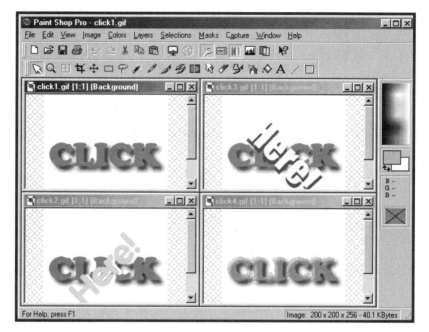

Figure 7.17

The four example images used for the GIF animation are displayed in Paint Shop Pro.

○ The drop shadow effect was added behind the text (with navy blue selected as the foreground color).

If you are a Windows 95/98 user, then you've already had practice in the previous mini-tutorial. If you are a Windows 3.1 user, you're probably wondering, "How do I do that?"—for a workaround method for creating drop shadows in Paint Shop Pro 3.11, see the sidebar, "Creating Drop Shadows in Windows 3.1."

NOTE You may have noticed in the description of CLICK1.GIF that no mention was made of setting the background color to transparent. That's because, for GIF animation files, you have to specify transparency for the image frames in GIF Construction Set and not in Paint Shop Pro.

CREATING DROP SHADOWS IN WINDOWS 3.1

This is a method for creating drop shadow effects in the Windows 3.1 version of Paint Shop Pro (this also works in the Windows 95 version):

1. In Paint Shop Pro 3.11, select File, New. Type 200 for both the Width and the Height settings. Make sure that the 16.7 Million Colors setting is selected. Click OK.

2. Double-click the foreground color rectangle to pick a color for the drop shadow effect. Choose whatever color you want and then click OK. (If you're having trouble finding the foreground color rectangle, you'll find it on the Select tool palette.)

3. Select the Text tool (the "T" button) and then click inside your blank image window. Choose whatever font you want. Try setting it to 36 points. Type CLICK as the text. Click OK and position the text so that it's off-center somewhat to the left (you need to leave room on the right for the Wind effect).

4. Choose Image, Deformations, Wind. Choose the From Left radio button. Choose 5 as the Strength setting. Click OK.

5. Double-click again on the foreground color rectangle and select a different color. Click OK.

6. Click the Text tool in the image window again. Leave all the text settings as they are and just click OK. Position the text so that it's overlapping the text you just applied the Wind effect to, but up and to the left.

That's it. The first text to which the Wind effect was applied now looks like a shadow extending down and to the right from the second text you added. You can also try using Motion Blur under Deformations (or Blur under Normal Filters) to create the drop shadow effect.

Previewing the Second Frame

CLICK2.GIF is the image that will be used as the second frame in the animation. Here are the effects that were used to create the image:

✪ The "Here!" text was superimposed over "CLICK" using the Text tool (with lime green selected as the foreground color).

✪ The "Here!" text was rotated 45 degrees to the left (select Image, Rotate).

✪ The drop shadow effect was added behind the "Here!" text (with yellow selected as the foreground color)

If you are a Windows 95/98 user, the only thing that wasn't covered here was rotating text. It's pretty simple, though. Just make sure the text you want to rotate is selected, and then select Image, Rotate, and specify the degree and direction of rotation. (As long as you do this immediately after adding a drop shadow, both the text and drop shadow should be selected and rotated.) If you are a Windows 3.1 user, you can't do this as easily as in the Windows 95/98 version of Paint Shop Pro, but I've included a sidebar, "Rotating Text in Windows 3.1," which will show you how to "spoof" this in Paint Shop Pro 3.11.

Previewing the Third Frame

CLICK3.GIF is the image that will be used as the third frame in the animation. Here are the effects that were used to create the image:

✪ The "Here!" text was superimposed over "CLICK" using the Text tool (with bright yellow selected as the foreground color).

✪ The "Here!" text was rotated 45 degrees to the right (select Image, Rotate).

✪ The drop shadow effect was added behind the "Here!" text (with blue selected as the foreground color and Blur set to 0).

Previewing the Fourth Frame

CLICK4.GIF is the image that will be used as the fourth frame in the animation. Here are the effects that were used to create the image:

✪ The cutout effect (Image, Effects, Cutout) was used to create the 3-D text effect.

ROTATING TEXT IN WINDOWS 3.1

In the Windows 3.1 version of Paint Shop Pro, although you can rotate an entire image, you cannot rotate an object within that image (let alone rotate an image that's on top of another image). What you can do, however, is this:

1. In Paint Shop Pro 3.11, select File, New. Type 200 for both the Width and the Height settings. Make sure that the 16.7 Million Colors setting is selected. Click OK.

2. Add the text "CLICK" with the Wind effect drop shadow behind it (see the previous Windows 3.1 section).

3. Select the rectangle selection tool (just below the "magnifying glass" button on the Select tool palette); then click and drag the mouse around the "CLICK" text to be rotated. A dashed line should now surround your text. Note: You don't want to select the whole image window, just the area immediately surrounding the text and drop shadow).

4. Choose Edit, Copy; then choose Edit, Paste, As New Image. A second image window now contains the part of the first image you copied and pasted.

5. Rotate your new image 45 degrees to the left: Choose Image, Rotate. Choose the Left and Free radio buttons. Type 45 as the degree amount. Click OK.

6. Select a new color in the foreground color rectangle and then click the Text tool on the text you just rotated. Type Here! as the text (if you want to select a different font, go ahead). Click OK.

7. Rotate you image 15 degrees back to the right: Choose Image, Rotate. Choose the Right and Free radio buttons. Type 45 as the degree amount. Click OK.

8. To create a second frame with the "Here!" text rotated the other way, just paste your initial image again (Ctrl+V); then

> **repeat steps 5 through 7 but reverse the directions of the rotations (select Right as the direction in step 5 and Left as the direction in step 7). If you want, you can select a different font and color for the "Here!" text when you create it.**

✪ The drop shadow effect was added behind the "Here!" text (with blue selected as the foreground color and Blur set to 0).

✪ The number of colors was reduced to 256.

The cutout effect wasn't covered previously in the Paint Shop Pro 5 mini-tutorial. The following section details how to create the cutout effect that was used in CLICK4.GIF.

Creating the Cutout Effect

If you want to later try duplicating the effect used in CLICK4.GIF, just add some text, define different foreground and background colors, and then select Image, Effects, Cutout. Specify these settings:

Effect	Setting
Fill Interior with Color check box	checked
Interior Color	Foreground Color
Shadow Color	Background Color
Opacity	255
Blur	36
Vertical Offset	4
Horizontal Offset	4

The cutout effect is not available in the Windows 3.1 version of Paint Shop Pro. And, unlike with the drop shadow and the text rotation effects, you can't "spoof" it either. If you are a Windows 3.1 user, you could try using one of the Deformation effects (such as one of the Perspective deformations or maybe the Skew deformation) to add a different look.

LOADING THE NETSCAPE PALETTE

GIF images can contain a total of 256 colors. However, when 256 Colors is the display mode, Netscape Navigator uses a palette of 216 colors to display images. This can cause a problem when the colors in your 256-color GIF file do not match the 216 colors in Netscape's palette. Color substitution or dithering may then cause your graphics to come out looking rather icky when displayed in Navigator on a system that can only display 256 colors. The problem is magnified with each additional inline image you want to display at the same time, each of which might have a different set of 256 colors. Matters are even worse when it comes to GIF animations, which combine several GIF images into a single multiframe file.

The solution is to apply in Paint Shop Pro the same palette to each of your animation frames before importing them into GIF Construction Set for assembly. An even better solution is to apply the Netscape palette to all your frames.

I've already applied the Netscape palette to the animation frame images, so you don't have to do this now. The following instructions are for future reference only.

Paint Shop Pro 5 includes a copy of the Netscape palette. To attach it to an image, first make sure the image you want to attach it to is selected; then select Colors, Load Palette. Paint Shop Pro should default to the C:\PROGRAM FILES\PAINT SHOP PRO 5\PALETTES folder. Double-click *safety.pal* to load it. To check out the new palette, just click either of the color rectangles.

If you're using the Windows 3.1 version of Paint Shop Pro, I've included a copy of the Netscape palette, NETSCAPE.PAL, with the example files in C:\HTML. Just select the image you want to attach it to and then select Colors, Load Palette. Go to the C:\HTML folder and double-click *netscape.pal* to load the palette. To check out the new palette, just click either of the color rectangles.

Creating the Animation

Now that you've got all the frames created, you're ready to put together the actual GIF animation file. Run GIF Construction Set by following these steps:

1. In Windows 95, click the Start button. Then click Programs, GIF Construction Set 32, and then GIF Construction Set 32 again.

2. In Windows 3.1, double-click the GIF Construction Set icon in the GIF Construction Set program group.

Follow these steps to assemble the image files for your GIF animation:

1. Select File, Animation Wizard. Click Next.

2. Leave the Yes, for Use with a Web Page option selected. Click Next.

3. Leave Loop Indefinitely selected. Click Next.

4. Select the second radio button, Matched to First Palette (the Netscape palette has already been attached to each of the images). Click Next.

5. Change the Delay setting to 20 hundredths. Click Next.

6. Click the Select button to choose the files to be included in your animation.

7. Go to C:\HTML and click CLICK1.GIF once to highlight it; then hold down the Shift key and click CLICK4.GIF. All four of your animation frame files should now be highlighted. In Windows 3.1, just click OK. In Windows 95, you need to click Open, then click Cancel (to let the program know you don't need to open any more images).

8. Your four animation frame GIF files should now be listed in the Selected Files list box (see Figure 7.18). Click Next and then click Done.

9. When GIF Construction Set is finished creating the GIF animation, a listing of all the components in your animation is displayed (see Figure 7.19).

10. To see what your animation is going to look like, click View. Press the Esc key to return to the main window.

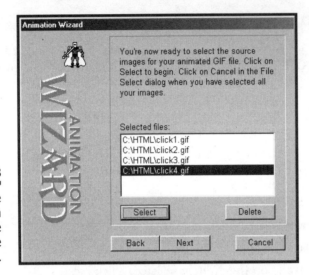

Figure 7.18

Figure 7.18

The four example images have been selected to be included in the animation.

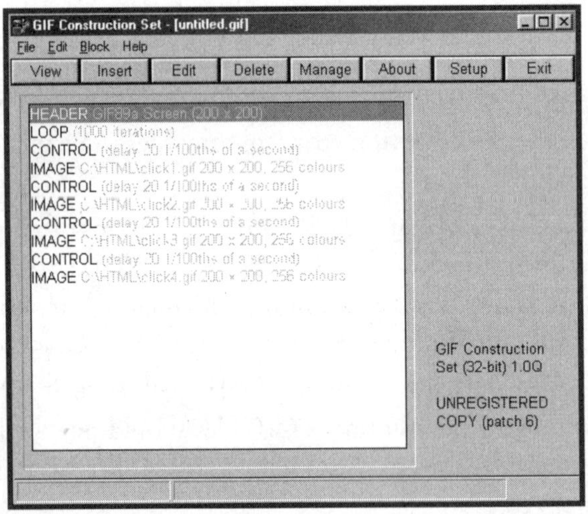

Figure 7.19

The Animation Wizard has created the animation.

Editing the Frame Controls

The frames of your animation still need to have the transparent color set:

1. Click the first instance of CONTROL (third line) to highlight it.

2. Click Edit. In the Edit Control Block dialog box, click Transparent Color to check it. In the Remove By drop-down list, select Background (see Figure 7.20). Click OK.

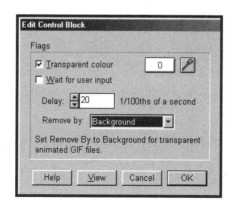

Figure 7.20

To create a
transparent GIF
animation, you
need to edit the
CONTROL blocks.

3. Repeat steps 1 and 2 for each of the other CONTROL blocks.

Saving Your GIF Animation

To save your GIF animation, select File, Save. Change the folder to
C:\HTML\GRAPHICS and then save your image as CLICK.GIF.

Exiting GIF Construction Set

You need to exit GIF Construction Set before installing the software for the
next mini-tutorial (for creating image maps). To exit GIF Construction Set,
click File, Exit.

Creating the HTML File

To view your GIF animation file in your Web browser, you need to create an
HTML file with it included as an inline image. In order to show off the
transparency, you'll also include a background image. Here's how to create
the HTML file:

1. Run Notepad and type the following:

```
<HTML>
<HEAD>
<TITLE>GIF Animation</TITLE>
</HEAD>
<BODY BACKGROUND="../backgrnd.gif">
<P ALIGN="center"><IMG SRC="click.gif" WIDTH="200" HEIGHT="200">
</BODY>
</HTML>
```

2. Save your file as CLICK.HTM in C:\HTML\GRAPHICS.

Viewing Your GIF Animation in Your Web Browser

Now, finally, you can see your GIF animation fully in action:

1. Run (or hop over to) your Web browser.

2. Open CLICK.HTM from C:\HTML\GRAPHICS. Your GIF animation should now load and run.

Hey, creating GIF animations with GIF Construction Set is really easy! Don't go hog-wild, however, adding GIF animations to your Web pages. A few strategically placed, small GIF animations can go a long way.

PROGRAM DETAILS

GIF Construction Set by Alchemy Mindworks, Inc.

Registration: $20

URL: http://www.mindworkshop.com/alchemy/gifcon.html

Email: alchemy@mail.bconnex.net

Other software by Alchemy Mindworks, Inc.: Graphic Workshop for Windows (graphic viewer/manipulator/manager).

Required Notice:

The GIF Construction Set software included with this publication is provided as shareware for your evaluation. If you try this software and find it useful, you are requested to register it as discussed in its documentation and in the About screen of the application. The publisher of this book has not paid the registration fee for this shareware.

ON THE

CD

Other GIF animation programs are available for you to try out on the CD-ROM. I chose to use GIF Construction Set for the GIF animation mini-tutorial because I still think it is the easiest program to use for creating GIF animations, plus it is available for both Windows 95/98 and Windows 3.1. If you want to try out some of the other GIF animation programs on the CD-ROM, check out Animation Shop (installed with Paint Shop Pro 5) and GIF MovieGear. Both are Windows 95/98 programs.

You'll also find some programs on the CD-ROM for creating dynamic Java animation applets that can easily be added to your Web pages, including BannerShow, FreeCast of Characterz, J-Perk, and Texter.

Creating Image Maps with Mapedit

An *image map* is an inline image, either a GIF or JPG file, in which hotspots have been defined. A *hotspot* is an area in the image that works as a link— click the hotspot and the object of the link is activated. The object of the link can be anything that can be linked to (for example, a Web page, a graphic, a WAV sound file, and so on).

Installing Mapedit

You can install GIF Construction Set directly from the CD-ROM using Prima's interface:

1. Insert the *Learn HTML in a Weekend* CD-ROM in your CD-ROM drive.

2. If you're using Windows 95/98, Prima's CD-ROM interface will auto-matically run, unless you have disabled Autorun. If the CD-ROM interface does not automatically run, from the Start menu, select Run and then type **D:\prima.exe** (where *D* is your CD-ROM's drive letter) and click OK.

3. If you're using Windows 3.1, select File, Run from Program Manager's menu bar; then type **D:\prima.exe** (where *D* is your CD-ROM's drive letter). Click OK.

4. With Prima's CD-ROM interface onscreen, click Web Tools and then click Mapedit.

5. Click Install in the drop-down menu.

6. Select the 32-bit (Win 95/98/NT) radio button if you are using Win-dows 95/98. Select the 16-bit (Windows 3.x) radio button if you are using Windows 3.1. Click OK.

7. Follow the instructions on Mapedit's installation windows to install the software. When asked whether you want to start Mapedit, click No.

8. On Prima's interface for the CD-ROM, click Exit.

Creating Image Maps

Creating a client-side image map with Mapedit is a four-step process:

1. Creating the graphic you want to use for your image map
2. Creating an HTML file containing the graphic as an inline image
3. Creating your image map in Mapedit
4. Testing your image map in your Web browser

Creating the Graphic for the Image Map

To save you time, I've already created the graphic, NAVBAR.GIF, that you'll be using for creating your image map. You can find it with the other example files in C:\HTML.

After doing this tutorial, feel free to create your own graphic to use as the basis for an image map—no requirements exist, other than it must be a JPEG or GIF graphic.

Creating the HTML File

Once you have a graphic to use for your image map, you need to create an HTML file with the graphic you're using inserted as an inline image:

1. Run Notepad and type the following:

```
<HTML>
<HEAD>
<TITLE>Navigation Bar Image Map</TITLE>
</HEAD>
<BODY BACKGROUND="../backgrnd.gif">
<P ALIGN="center"><IMG SRC="../navbar.gif" BORDER="0" WIDTH="450"
➥HEIGHT="75">
<P ALIGN="center">
[<A HREF="../back.htm">Back</A>]   [<A
➥HREF="../home.htm">Home</A>]   [<A HREF="../next.htm">Next</A>]
</BODY>
</HTML>
```

> **NOTE** BORDER="0" is included in the IMG tag to turn off the border around the image map.

2. Save this file as NAVBAR.HTM in C:\HTML\GRAPHICS.

3. Exit Notepad. (Mapedit is going to write changes to this file, so you don't want to leave an old copy sitting here.)

Creating the Image Map

To start Mapedit in Windows 95/98, click the Start button and then select Programs, Mapedit, and then Mapedit again. In Windows 3.1, just double-click its icon in the program group that has been created for it.

The opening windows for Mapedit are a bit different, depending on whether you are using the Windows 95/98 or Windows 3.1 version. In the following steps, I've singled out the Windows 3.1 steps (the figure examples, however, are all from the Windows 95 version):

1. The first time you run Mapedit, the First Time Hints window is displayed. Go ahead and read it and then click OK.

2. Windows 3.1 only: In the Open/Create Map window, leave the NCSA radio buttons selected. Click the upper Browse button (Map or HTML File). In the Open dialog box, change the folder to C:\HTML\GRAPHICS. In the List Files of Type, select HTML Pages (*.HTM). Click *navbar.htm* to select it. Click OK and then click OK again.

3. Windows 95/98 only: In the Open dialog box, change the folder to C:\HTML\GRAPHICS. Click *navbar.htm* to select it (see Figure 7.21). Click OK.

4. In the Select Inline Image window, click "../navbar.gif" to select it; then click OK.

5. You'll now see the image for the navigation bar, NAVBAR.GIF, displayed in the Mapedit's main window (see Figure 7.22). Feel free to pull the bottom of Mapedit's window down a bit so that you have a little more room to work.

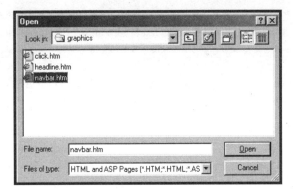

6. Mapedit has three tools—the Rectangle, Circle, and Polygon—that can be used to draw hotspots on your graphic image. The Rectangle tool is selected by default.

NOTE A *hotspot* is an area in an image map that has been defined as a link. When you click the hotspot in the image map, the Web browser will activate the object of the link, just as with a regular hypertext link.

In the examples shown in Figures 7.23 and 7.25, I've drawn the hotspot rectangles on purpose so that they extend out beyond the buttons, just to help ensure that the rectangles will be visible. You can draw your hotspots as close to the margins of the buttons as you like. If you want to draw them slightly inside of the button margins, go ahead.

7. Draw the first hotspot: Just click the mouse slightly to the left and above the first button on the navigation bar and then pull the mouse to just below and to the right of that button (see Figure 7.23).

Mapedit
File Tools Help
? REGISTER UNLOCK

Figure 7.23

A rectangle has been drawn around the first button to define it as a hotspot.

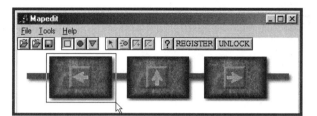

8. With the hotspot drawn around the first button, click the mouse again to bring up the Object URL window. Type **../back.htm** in the first field (URL for Clicks on This Object). Type **Back** in the second field (Alternate Text). Leave the other fields blank. Click OK. (See Figure 7.24.)
9. Draw the second hotspot: Click the mouse slightly to the left and above the second button and then pull the mouse to just below and to the right of that button. Click the mouse again to bring up the Object URL window. Type **../home.htm** as the URL in the first field and **Home** as the alternate text in the second field. Click OK.
10. Draw the third hotspot: Click the mouse slightly to the left and above the second button and then pull the mouse to just below and to the right of that button. Click the mouse again to bring up the Object URL window. Type **../next.htm** as the URL in the first field and **Next** as the alternate text in the second field. Click OK. (See Figure 7.25.)

Object URL
URL for clicks on this object:
../back.htm
OK
Cancel
Alternate text:
Back
Target (For frames; usually left blank!)
JavaScript Attributes for Advanced Users
OnMouseOver
OnMouseOut

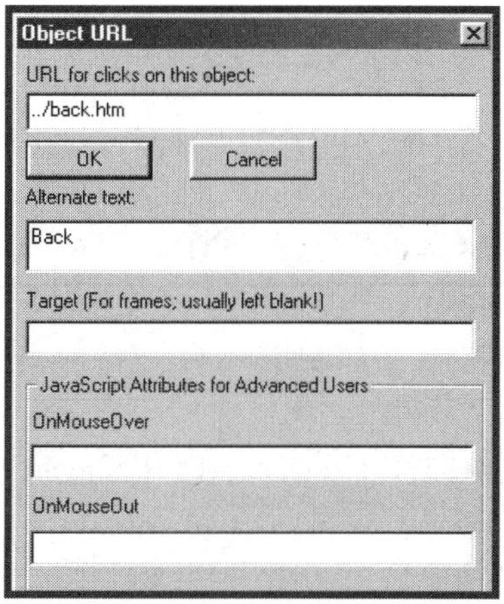

Figure 7.24

When you're drawing the hotspot, clicking the mouse a second time pops up the Object URL window, where you specify the URL and alternate text for the hotspot.

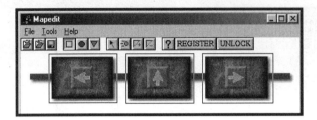

Figure 7.25

Hotspots have been defined for all three buttons.

Saving the Image Map

Go ahead now and save your image map:

1. Select File, Save As.

2. In the Save As dialog box, NAVBAR.HTM should already be selected. (Windows 3.1 version: Make sure the Client Side Map (HTML) radio button is selected.)

3. Click Save to save the file. Click Yes to okay overwriting the previous file.

Exiting Mapedit

Go ahead and exit Mapedit (select File, Exit).

Testing Your Image Map in Your Web Browser

Next, you need to test your new image map in your Web browser to make sure it works properly.

1. Run (or hop over to) your Web browser and open C:\HTML\GRAPHICS\NAVBAR.HTM (see Figure 7.26).

2. Experiment with clicking the buttons in the image map. (I've created some dummy files, BACK.HTM, HOME.HTM, and NEXT.HTM, that are included with the example files in C:\HTML.) Just click the Back button in Navigator or Internet Explorer to return to NAVBAR.HTM.

Note that BACK.HTM, HOME.HTM, and NEXT.HTM are dummy files used merely to illustrate how this works. When creating a real image map that you want to use, you'll need to substitute hotspot URL references that point to the actual Web pages that you would want the image map to hop to.

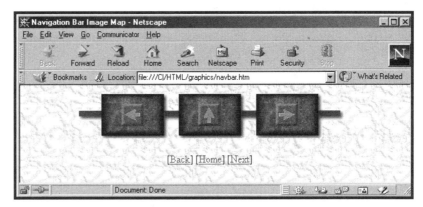

Figure 7.26

The finished image
map is displayed in
a Web browser.

Feel free to open NAVBAR.HTM into Notepad, if you want to, and check out the codes that have been added to the file to enable the image map. Because this image map is a navigation bar, you may want to reuse it on more than one page. You could just re-create a fresh image map, specifying a different HTML file (and hotspot URL references) for each. A shortcut, however, is to just make copies of the final image map file, and then edit the URLs to point them to the files to which you want to link.

That's it—you've created your very first image map. As you can see, creating image maps with Mapedit is really easy. Experiment with creating front-end image map menus for your Web pages or navigation bars like the one demonstrated in this section. Any graphic you can create in Paint Shop Pro can be turned into an image map, almost as easy as 1-2-3.

PROGRAM DETAILS

Mapedit by Boutell.Com, Inc.

Registration: $25

URL: http://www.boutell.com/

Email: mapedit@boutell.com

Phone/Fax: +1 (206) 325-3009

Other software by Boutell.Com, Inc.: WebLater (URL manager), Wusage (Web server statistics), Baklava (Java sprite toolkit).

ON THE

CD

Besides Mapedit, a Windows 95/98 image map editor, LiveImage, is also available on the CD-ROM. Also check out Carouselle and HTMLedPro, both of which include image mapping modules (Windows 95/98 only).

What's Next?

If you've completed all three of the Graphics Tutorials, you should be well on your way to becoming a real graphics whiz! True, you've only scratched the surface of what can be done, but you should at least now know enough to be able to create some pretty neat graphic effects, design a super-cool GIF animation to add just the right dynamic touch to a Web page, and roll your own image maps as well. Hey, not bad for a weekend!

The Sunday Evening Graphics Tutorials end your weekend. Feel free to go back at your leisure and cover any of the sessions that you may have chosen to skip, such as the Tables, Frames, or Forms Tutorials.

Be sure to check out the Web site for this book, at **http://www.calli-han.com/learn2/**. You'll find additional information and resources there to help you further your Web publishing endeavors, including a rundown on Dynamic HTML and a tutorial for using WS-FTP to post your finished Web pages up onto a server. You'll also find links there to where you can find out about low-cost or free Web space providers, many additional Web publishing tools, and other online Web publishing resources, tutorials, and documentation.

Remember, whether you've managed to complete everything in a single weekend or even if you just completed the Basic HTML Tutorial, you can still say with confidence, "I know HTML!"

APPENDIX A

HTML Quick Reference

HTML 4.0 was officially approved as the current standard version of HTML in December of 1997. Full support for HTML 4.0 by current Web browsers, however, is very much still a work in progress. Some HTML 4.0 elements, such as those for creating frames, were already widely supported by current browsers before the advent of HTML 4.0. The new HTML 4.0 table elements, however, are currently only supported by the latest versions of Internet Explorer, but not by Navigator. Many of the other new HTML 4.0 elements, however, have yet to be supported by the latest versions (at the time of this writing) of either of the two main Web browsers. Because support for these elements in current browsers is still quite uneven, I've marked all HTML 4.0 elements with "(4.0)" so you can easily tell which ones they are. Before posting any Web pages using HTML 4.0 elements (other than the frame elements) on the Web, you should check them out in current browsers first. You should also realize that even if future browser versions support all of HTML 4.0, many users will continue to use older browsers that do not. Therefore, even if they're supported by future

343

browsers, the new HTML 4.0 elements (except for the frame elements) should still be used with caution. For the full specification for HTML 4.0, see **http://www. w3.org/TR/REC-html40/** at the World Wide Web Consortium's Web site.

Quick Reference Organization

I've organized the HTML elements according to this order of precedence:

- ✿ Document, HTML, and HEAD elements
- ✿ BODY elements
- ✿ Text markup elements
- ✿ FRAMESET elements
- ✿ HTML general attributes

Throughout this quick reference, I refer to the HTML "tags" as "elements." The term *"element"* refers to the *whole* tag, including both start and end tags, as well as the bracketed content of the tag. I also refer to a single, standalone tag (such as <BR>) as an *empty* element.

Attribute Legend

To help you understand the attribute references that follow (and so I won't have to explain them each and every time), here's a legend of what these references refer to:

`ATTRIBUTE="url"`	An absolute or relative URL
`ATTRIBUTE="text"`	A text string (including character entities)
`ATTRIBUTE="n"`	A number of one or more digits
`ATTRIBUTE="n%"`	A percentage (for example, "75%")
`ATTRIBUTE="#rrggbb"`	A hexadecimal color code
`ATTRIBUTE="MIME type"`	Internet Media Type

DOCTYPE Construct

This can be placed at the top of an HTML document to specify the version of HTML to which the document conforms. The HTML 4.0 specification recommends that authors *should* include a DOCTYPE declaration in HTML documents. However, as far as current browsers are concerned, it doesn't make any difference whether you include this declaration or not. At this time, there are three levels of conformance to HTML 4.0 that can be specified using the DOCTYPE construct: Strict, Transitional, and Frameset. *Strict* conformance excludes all deprecated elements or attributes (the FONT and BASEFONT elements, for instance), as well as framesets. *Transitional* conformance includes deprecated elements and attributes, but excludes framesets. *Frameset* conformance includes deprecated elements and attributes, but includes framesets.

If your HTML document does not include any deprecated elements or attributes, or any framesets, you could include the following DOCTYPE construct at the top of the document:

```
<!DOCTYPE HTML PUBLIC "-//W3C//DTD HTML 4.0//EN"
"http://www.w3.org/TR/REC-html40/strict.dtd">
```

If your HTML document does include deprecated elements or attributes, but does not include any framesets, you could include the following DOCTYPE construct at the top of the document:

```
<!DOCTYPE HTML PUBLIC "-//W3C//DTD HTML 4.0 Transitional//EN"
"http://www.w3.org/TR/REC-html40/loose.dtd">
```

If your HTML document does include both deprecated elements or attributes and framesets, you could include the following DOCTYPE construct at the top of the document:

```
<!DOCTYPE HTML PUBLIC "-//W3C//DTD HTML 4.0 Frameset//EN"
"http://www.w3.org/TR/REC-html40/frameset.dtd">
```

The "EN" in the above DOCTYPE constructs specifies English as the language type of the document. For information on creating HTML documents in languages other than English, see the full HTML 4.0 specification at the Web address provided at the head of this appendix.

HTML

This is the top-level HTML element. All other elements must be nested inside this element.

HEAD

The HEAD element contains any header information to be included in the document, such as the title, keywords for search engines, and other information. The TITLE, BASE, ISINDEX, LINK, META, SCRIPT, and STYLE elements are nested inside the HEAD element.

TITLE

The TITLE element is the only required element within the HEAD element. It identifies the title of the HTML document and is usually displayed by a browser in its top title bar.

BASE

This is an "empty" element that specifies the *base* URL for an HTML document. It's used primarily to indicate the original location of a moved document in order to preserve relative links.

Attributes

HREF="*url*"	Required
TARGET="*frame name*" (4.0)	Optional

In HREF, the URL must be an absolute URL, not a relative URL. For TARGET, see the FRAMESET element.

ISINDEX

This is an empty element that prompts the user to perform a keyword search. This element requires a gateway program to which the user query can be passed and is therefore of little use to the average user. It's also deprecated (although not obsoleted) in HTML 4.0, which is an added reason to avoid using it.

Attributes

PROMPT="*text*"	Optional

PROMPT provides a substitute prompt (such as "Enter keywords:" and so on) in place of the default prompt.

LINK

The LINK element is an empty element that specifies the relation of the current document to other documents. Multiple LINK elements can be included to describe multiple relations.

Attributes

HREF="*url*"	Required
REL="*text*"	Optional
REV="*text*"	Optional
TITLE="*text*"	Optional

REL=`"next"` would identify the link as the next document in a series, whereas REV=`"previous"` would identify it as the previous document.

META

The META tag is an empty element that specifies meta-information not included in other HEAD elements. Multiple META elements can be included.

Attributes

NAME=`"text"`	See below
HTTP-EQUIV=`"refresh"`	See below
CONTENT=`"text"`	Required

NAME names the meta-information ("author," "date," "keywords," and so on). Search engine robots commonly recognize "keywords" here. HTTP-EQUIV is mainly used to cause another document to load after a set interval, which can be handy if you've moved your page and want to switch visitors automatically from your old URL to your new one. CONTENT is required, in combination with either NAME or HTTP-EQUIV. For instance, if the NAME value is "keywords," then the CONTENT value would contain the list of keywords, like the following:

```
<META NAME="keywords" CONTENT="accounting, finance, tax, savings,
➥deduction, economy, economics, audit, books, ledger, cpa, balance
➥sheet">
```

With HTTP-EQUIV, the CONTENT value would include the refresh interval and the URL of the file to be loaded, like this:

```
<META HTTP-EQUIV="refresh" CONTENT="5;URL=http://www.someserver.
➥com/mynewfile.html">
```

SCRIPT

The SCRIPT element was first introduced with HTML 3.2 to allow the inclusion of client-side scripts, such as those created by JavaScript or VBScript. SCRIPT elements can be placed any number of times in the HEAD or BODY of an HTML document.

Attributes

LANGUAGE=`"script language"`	Optional
TYPE=`"MIME type"` (4.0)	Optional
SRC=`"url"`	Optional

LANGUAGE has been deprecated in favor of TYPE in HTML 4.0. LANGUAGE takes the values of "javascript" and "vbscript". TYPE, however, utilizes the Internet Media Type (or MIME type) that has been established by the W3C: "text/javascript", "text/vbscript", "text/tcl", and so on. SRC specifies the script location. In the absence of an SRC attribute, the script is assumed to be included inside the current SCRIPT element.

Shielding Scripts from Nonsupporting Browsers

Two methods exist for dealing with browsers that don't run scripts (either script-aware browsers that for one reason or another are unable to run a script or browsers that are not script aware).

NOSCRIPT (4.0)

The NOSCRIPT element provides alternate text in case a script is not executed by an otherwise script-aware browser. This is a new element that's not supported by current browsers.

Commenting Out Scripts

Script-aware browsers will ignore comment tags that are placed above and below a script. Browsers that are not script aware, on the other hand, will ignore anything included within the comment tags. In the case of a JavaScript script, anything on a line beginning with a `<!--` tag will be seen as part of the comment, whereas anything on a line starting with `//` will also be seen as a comment. Here's an example:

```
<SCRIPT TYPE="text/javascript">
<!-- to hide script from old browsers
JavaScript code...
// end hiding script from old browsers -->
```

STYLE

The STYLE element attaches a style sheet to an HTML document. Cascading Style Sheets (CSS1) is assumed, but other style sheet languages are possible. When inserted in the HEAD element, it affects the whole document; when inserted in the BODY element, it has an effect from that point until contravened by another STYLE element. The STYLE element was first defined in HTML 3.2, but only as a placeholder. The following attributes have all been defined as part of HTML 4.0.

Attributes

TYPE="*MIME type*" (4.0)	Optional
MEDIA="*media type*" (4.0)	Optional
TITLE="*advisory title*" (4.0)	Optional

TYPE overrides the default style sheet language (CSS1) with another style sheet language, with its Internet Media Type (or MIME type) used as the TYPE value. MEDIA specifies the destination medium or media, such as "screen", "print", "projection", "braille", "speech", and "all". Multiple media are comma separated. TITLE specifies a title for the style sheet. It is common to nest the contents of the STYLE tag inside of a comment, to shield them from search engine robots or from browsers that don't support the STYLE element. Here's an example of using the STYLE element to display all level-one, level-two, and level-three headings in a red Helvetica or sans serif font:

```
<STYLE TYPE="text/css">
<!--
H1, H2, H3 { font-family: "helvetica", sans-serif; color: red }
-->
</STYLE>
```

The STYLE *attribute*, not to be confused with the STYLE *element*, can be used to apply STYLE effects to a specific element. If you want to learn more about using style sheets in HTML documents, you can find the full text of the W3C Recommendation for Cascading Style Sheets, Level 1 (CSS1) at **http://www.w3.org/TR/REC-CSS1-961217**.

BODY

The BODY element contains the body of an HTML document. With the exception of the FRAMESET element, everything not included in the HEAD element must go inside the BODY element.

Attributes

BACKGROUND="url"	Optional
BGCOLOR="#rrggbb|colorname"	Optional
TEXT="#rrggbb|colorname"	Optional
LINK="#rrggbb|colorname"	Optional
VLINK="#rrggbb|colorname"	Optional
ALINK="#rrggbb|colorname"	Optional

BACKGROUND specifies the URL of a background image. BGCOLOR assigns a background color using either a hexadecimal color code or a color name. TEXT, LINK, VLINK, and ALINK assign colors to the base text font, hypertext links, visited links, and activated links, respectively.

A

The A (Anchor) element provides a means to insert hypertext links into HTML documents.

Attributes

HREF="*url*"	See below
NAME="*targetname*"	See below
REL="*url*"	Optional
REV="*url*"	Optional
TARGET="*framename*" (4.0)	Optional
ACCESSKEY="*character*" (4.0)	Optional

HREF or NAME is required. HREF specifies the link URL. NAME specifies a target anchor that another link can jump to (either from the same or another Web page). TARGET targets a frame, causing the linked document to be retrieved in the named frame (see the FRAMESET element). ACCESSKEY allows you to assign a shortcut key to a link.

ADDRESS

The ADDRESS element is used to add author and contact information at the end of a document. In most cases, text in an ADDRESS element is italicized. It's common to precede the ADDRESS element with an HR element. Name, email Mailto link, URL, and last date updated are commonly included.

APPLET

The APPLET element is an HTML 3.2 element that can run a Java applet from within an HTML document.

Attributes

CODE="*classfile*"	Required
WIDTH="*n*"	Required
HEIGHT="*n*"	Required
CODEBASE="*url*"	Optional

ALT="*text*"	Optional
NAME="*applet name*"	Optional
ALIGN="top|middle|bottom|left|right"	Optional
HSPACE="*n*"	Optional
VSPACE="*n*"	Optional

CODE references the file name for the applet's compiled subclass, which must be relative to the applet's base URL. CODEBASE specifies the applet's base URL (if other than the HTML document's URL). ALT provides alternate text. NAME allows applets on the same page to communicate with each other. Here's an example:

```
<APPLET CODE="Spirals.class" WIDTH="300" HEIGHT="300">
```

Java applet that draws multicolored spirals.</APPLET>

PARAM

The PARAM (Parameter) element is an empty element used to pass named parameters to an applet. It's nested inside the APPLET element.

Attributes

NAME="*name*"

VALUE="*text*"

NAME specifies a name token, which must start with a letter (A to Z or a to z) and can be followed by any number of letters, digits, hyphens, or periods. Character entities cannot be included. VALUE contains the parameter that's being passed to the applet. Here's an example:

```
<APPLET CODE="AnimalHouse" WIDTH=20 HEIGHT=20>
<PARAM NAME="snd" VALUE="Bark.au¦Meow.au">
Java applet that plays animal sounds.</APPLET>
```

BDO (4.0)

The BDO (Bi-Directional Orientation) element is an HTML 4.0 element that allows authors to override the bi-directional algorithm for text phrases.

Attributes

DIR="ltr|rtl"	Required
LANG="*language code*"	Optional

DIR sets either left-to-right ("ltr") or right-to-left ("rtl") direction. LANG specifies the language (see "Code for the Representation of the Names of Languages" by Robin Cover at **http://www.sil.org/sgml/iso639a.html**, part of the SGML Web Page, or RFC1766, "Tags for the Identification of Languages," by H. Alvestrand at **ftp://ds.internic.net/rfc/rfc1766.txt**.

BASEFONT

The BASEFONT element is used to reset the base font size. You can either specify an absolute or a relative value. Multiple BASEFONT elements can be inserted into an HTML document—the new base font size will apply until a new BASEFONT element is inserted. Although the BASEFONT element has been deprecated in HTML 4.0 in favor of using style sheets, it hasn't been obsoleted and is just too handy to ever be obsoleted.

Attributes

SIZE=`"n"` or `"-n|+n"`   Required

SIZE specifies an absolute or a relative base font size. Seven absolute font sizes are available (1 through 7, with 3 as the default). Relative font sizes are set relative to the current base font size (+3 would equal a font size of 6 relative to the default font size of 3).

BLOCKQUOTE

The BLOCKQUOTE element displays a block of text indented in from the left and right margins. It can be used to display an actual block quote or simply as a means of indenting text in from the margins.

BR

The BR (Break) element inserts a line break. This can be used for formatting lists or lines of poetry—anywhere you want a single line break between lines. (Most "block" elements, such as the P element, are followed by *two* line breaks.)

Attributes

CLEAR=`"left|right|all"`   Optional

CLEAR stops text from wrapping around a left- or right-aligned image. CLEAR="left" breaks text past a left-aligned image. CLEAR="right" breaks text past a right-aligned image. CLEAR="all" breaks text past both a right-aligned image and a left-aligned image.

CENTER

The CENTER element causes any included text or elements to be centered. HTML 3.2 specifies this element as a shortcut for `<DIV ALIGN="center">`. See the DIV element later in this appendix.

(COMMENT)

In HTML, a "comment" can be inserted by preceding the comment with `<!--` and ending it with `-->`.

DIR

The DIR element is deprecated in HTML 4.0—and for good reason. Browsers display it indistinguishably from the UL element, which should be used instead.

DIV

The DIV (Division) element is an HTML 3.2 element that can be used to apply formatting within a "division" of an HTML document.

Attributes

ALIGN="left|right|center"   Optional

The DIV element, by itself, can only be used to align (using the ALIGN attribute) multiple lines of text and elements. In combination with style sheets, however, it becomes much more powerful. The DIV element should not be nested inside any element other than the BODY element.

DL

The DL (Definition List) element allows you to create a "glossary" list.

Attributes

COMPACT   Optional

COMPACT, which is supposed to display a "compacted" definition list, is currently supported only by Navigator and therefore should probably be avoided.

DT

The DT (Definition Term) element specifies the "term" element in a definition item. It's always nested inside the DL element. The DT element is not an empty element, but a container element that has an implied end tag.

DD

The DD (Definition Data) element specifies the "data" element in a definition item; it contains the actual "definition" that's included in the list. It's displayed indented under the DT item. Normally, it follows a DT element, but can be included by itself. The DD element is not an empty element, but a container element that has an implied end-tag. Here's an example of using the DL, DT, and DD elements:

```
<DL>
<DT>List 1
<DD>This is the definition.
<DT>List 2
<DD>This is the definition
</DL>
```

FORM

The FORM element allows you to create a form to allow users to input text and select various options, such as check boxes, radio buttons, and selection lists. Once the form has been filled out, the user can submit his response.

Attributes

ACTION="*url*"	Required
METHOD="GET|POST"	Optional
ENCTYPE="MIME type"	Optional

ACTION specifies the URL used to carry out the action of the form, either a CGI script for a server-side form or a Mailto URL for a client-side form. Internet Explorer 3.0 does not support Mailto forms. METHOD specifies the HTTP method for sending the form data. The GET method adds the content of the form to the end of the ACTION URL. The POST method sends the content of the form to the server as a separate message. GET is the default. CGI forms use either the GET or the POST method, depending on server support, whereas Mailto forms always use the POST method. ENCTYPE specifies the MIME type of the data being sent when the POST method is used. The default is **application/x-www-form-urlencoded**.

These elements are nested inside the FORM element: INPUT, SELECT, TEXTAREA, BUTTON (4.0), LABEL (4.0), and FIELDSET (4.0).

INPUT

The INPUT element is a kind of general-purpose, user-entry element; with it, you can define text fields, buttons, check boxes, radio buttons, and so on.

Attributes

TYPE="*control type*"	Required
NAME="*control name*"	Required*
VALUE="*text|selection*"	Optional*
CHECKED	Optional
ALIGN="left|right|top|middle|bottom"	Optional
SIZE="*n*"	Optional*

*NAME is not required with TYPE="reset" or TYPE="submit". VALUE is required for check boxes and radio buttons. SIZE is required for text fields.

TYPE identifies the input control that is being created—the most commonly used being "checkbox", "radio", "text", "submit", and "reset" values.

❖ TYPE="checkbox"—One check box per INPUT element is defined; a list of check boxes is created by using multiple INPUT elements, with the same NAME value assigned to each. Including the CHECKED attribute will cause a check box to appear checked.

❖ TYPE="radio"—One radio button per INPUT element is defined; a list of radio buttons is created by using multiple INPUT elements, with the same NAME value assigned to each. To have one of the radio buttons in the list default to "on" (filled), include the CHECKED attribute in the relevant INPUT element.

❖ TYPE="text"—Defines a single-line text field into which the user can enter information, such as his name, address, email address, and so on. A SIZE attribute is used to specify the length of the text field in characters. A VALUE attribute is used to specify default text for the text field.

❖ TYPE="submit"—Defines the button that's used to submit the form's content. The VALUE attribute defines the button's label.

❖ TYPE="reset"—Defines a button that can be used to reset the form, clearing it of former responses. The VALUE attribute defines the button's label.

❖ TYPE="file"—Prompts for the name of a file. When the form is submitted, the file contents are submitted to the server along with other user input.

❖ TYPE="hidden"—Specifies a hidden field. When used in conjunction with a VALUE attribute, it can be used to filter form responses.

❖ TYPE="image"—Used to create graphical submit buttons. The URL is provided in the SRC attribute value. The ALIGN attribute aligns the image in the form.

- TYPE="password"—Instead of the text being echoed back to the user in the text field, asterisks (*) are echoed in place of the typed password (to keep prying eyes from seeing it).
- TYPE="button"—Creates a push button in HTML 4.0. The action of the button is determined by client-side scripts (JavaScript or VBScript) which are triggered by button events (the button being clicked and so forth).

Here's an example:

```
<INPUT TYPE="button" VALUE="Click Here" ONCLICK="verify()">
```

SELECT

The SELECT element allows you to create a list box. The user can pull down the list and choose an option.

Attributes

NAME="*controlname*"	Required
SIZE="*n*"	Optional
MULTIPLE	Optional

NAME specifies the list box's name. SIZE specifies the number of rows to be displayed in the list (the default is 1). MULTIPLE allows multiple selections from a list box.

OPTION

The OPTION elements are nested inside a SELECT element to create a list box. Every SELECT element must contain at least one OPTION element, and they often will contain several.

Attributes

SELECTED	Optional
VALUE="*optiontext*"	Optional

SELECTED specifies the default selected item; otherwise, the first item is selected. Only one OPTION element can be "selected." VALUE assigns a value to be returned other than the option's content.

OPTGROUP (4.0)

The OPTGROUP (Option Group) element is always nested inside of the SELECT element and is used to specify a group of options (specified by OPTION elements nested inside the OPTGROUP element.

Attributes

DISABLED	Optional
LABEL="*labeltext*"	Required

DISABLED renders an option group as unavailable. LABEL specifies the label to be displayed with the group.

TEXTAREA

The TEXTAREA element creates a multi-line text area into which a user can type a comment or other message.

Attributes

NAME="*controlname*"	Required
COLS="*n*"	Required
ROWS="*n*"	Required

NAME assigns a name to a TEXTAREA element. COLS specifies the width of the TEXTAREA in text characters. ROWS specifies the number of rows (lines).

BUTTON (4.0)

The BUTTON element combines the functions of the INPUT element's TYPE="submit" and TYPE="reset" attribute values. In addition, it can trigger a script. You can also utilize a graphic image as the button by inserting an IMG element within the BUTTON element.

Attributes

NAME="*controlname*"	Required
TYPE="submit|reset|button"	Required
VALUE="*buttontext*"	Required

NAME names a BUTTON control. Multiple buttons may be included in a form, with the TYPE attribute specifying the type of button that's being created. VALUE specifies the text that's displayed on the button. Here's an example:

```
<BUTTON NAME="subbut" TYPE="submit" VALUE="Send It">
<IMG SRC="../buttons/subbut.gif" ALT="Submit"></BUTTON>
```

LABEL (4.0)

The LABEL element allows you to create a label for a control.

Attributes

FOR="*fieldID*"   Optional

ACCESSKEY="*character*"   Optional

FOR associates a label with the ID value of another control in the document; otherwise, the label will be associated with its contents. ACCESSKEY assigns a shortcut key that will activate the control.

FIELDSET (4.0)

The FIELDSET element allows you to group related controls (radio buttons, check boxes, and so on) together in a "set." The LEGEND element can optionally be nested inside of the FIELDSET element.

LEGEND (4.0)

The LEGEND element is nested inside a FIELDSET element and allows you to create a caption for a FIELDSET control set.

Attributes

ALIGN="top|bottom|left|right"   Optional

ALIGN aligns the LEGEND caption relative to the FIELDSET group.

H*n*

The H*n* elements, H1 through H6, allow you to define different heading levels.

Attributes

ALIGN="center|right"   Optional

ALIGN center- or right-aligns a heading. Left alignment is the default.

HR

The HR (Horizontal Rule) element allows you to insert a horizontal rule.

Attributes

SIZE="*n*"   Optional

WIDTH="*n*|*n*%"   Optional

ALIGN="left|right"   Optional

NOSHADE   Optional

SIZE specifies the height in pixels. WIDTH specifies the width, either in pixels or as a percentage. ALIGN aligns the rule (center alignment is the default). NOSHADE turns off any 3-D shading.

IFRAME (4.0)

The IFRAME (Inline Frame) element is a new HTML 4.0 element that lets you insert and dimension an inline frame in a Web page. Although Navigator 4.0 does not yet support this element, Internet Explorer 3.0 does.

Attributes

SRC="*url*"	Required
HEIGHT="*n*"	Optional
WIDTH="*n*"	Optional
NAME="*framename*"	Optional
ALIGN="*horizontal or vertical*"	Optional
FRAMEBORDER="*0*"	Optional
MARGINHEIGHT=""*n|n%*"	Optional
MARGINWIDTH="*n|n%*"	Optional
SCROLLING="yes|no|auto"	Optional

SRC gives the inline document URL. HEIGHT and WIDTH specify the dimensions (the default in Internet Explorer is 300 pixels wide by 150 pixels high). NAME assigns a name to the frame that can be targeted by an external link's TARGET attribute (see the FRAMESET element). FRAMEBORDER turns the border off ("0"). MARGINHEIGHT and MARGINWIDTH set the frame's margins. SCROLLING turns scrolling "on" or "off" (the default is "auto").

IMG

The IMG (Image) element allows you to insert an inline image in your Web page.

Attributes

SRC="*url*"	Required
ALT="*alternate text*"	Advised
ALIGN="*vertical and horizontal*"	Optional
HEIGHT="*n*"	Advised
WIDTH="*n*"	Advised
BORDER="*n*"	Optional

`HSPACE="n"`	Optional
`VSPACE="n"`	Optional
`USEMAP="#map name"`	Optional
`ISMAP`	Optional

SRC specifies the URL for a GIF, JPEG, or PNG image. ALT provides alternate text for browsers that don't display images. ALIGN specifies vertical alignment ("top", "middle", or "bottom") relative to the baseline of the element, or it specifies horizontal alignment ("left" or "right") with text or other elements wrapping along the other side. The default is "bottom". HEIGHT and WIDTH specify the image dimensions. If the image is inside of an A (Anchor) element (an "image link"), the BORDER attribute can increase or decrease the width of the border around the image. Setting `BORDER="0"` will turn the border off. HSPACE and VSPACE add space to the left and right or above and below the image, respectively. USEMAP specifies the name of a MAP element that defines the hotspots for a client-side image map. (See the MAP element section.) ISMAP causes the clicked location in the image to be passed to the server, activating a server-side image map.

MAP

The MAP element defines the hotspots in a client-side image map.

Attributes

`NAME="map name"`	Required

NAME specifies the name of the MAP element that's called by an IMG element being used as an image map.

AREA

The AREA element nested in the MAP element. It's an empty element that defines a hotspot within a MAP element.

Attributes

`SHAPE="shape"`	Optional
`COORDS="coords"`	Optional
`HREF="url"`	Optional
`ALT="alternate text"`	Advised
`NOHREF`	Optional
`TARGET="text"`	Optional
`TABINDEX="n"`	Optional

SHAPE specifies the shape of the hotspot ("rect", "circle", or "poly"). The default is "rect" (rectangle). COORDS specifies the coordinates of a hotspot, like this:

```
SHAPE="rect" COORDS="left-x,top-y, right-x, bottom-y"
SHAPE="circle" COORDS="center-x, center-y, radius"
SHAPE="poly" COORDS="x(1),y(1),x(2)y(2),x(3),y(3),..."
```

If COORDS is absent, the image coordinates are used. HREF specifies the URL that's activated by the hotspot. If HREF is absent, the document URL is used. Use of ALT is strongly recommended to provide alternate text for browsers that don't display images. NOHREF specifies that the area has no action. TARGET targets a frame name (see the FRAMESET element). TABINDEX specifies the hotspot's tabbing order position. Here's an example:

```
<P ALIGN="center"><IMG SRC="../navbar.gif" BORDER="0" WIDTH="450"
➥HEIGHT="75" USEMAP="#navbar">
<MAP NAME="navbar">
<AREA SHAPE="rect" ALT="Back" COORDS="59,10,141,65"
➥HREF="../back.htm">
<AREA SHAPE="rect" ALT="Home" COORDS="180,10,268,66"
➥HREF="../home.htm">
<AREA SHAPE="rect" ALT="Next" COORDS="307,9,390,66"
➥HREF="../next.htm">
<AREA SHAPE="default" NOHREF>
</MAP>
```

MENU

The MENU element, like the DIR element, is deprecated in HTML 4.0—and with good reason. Use the UL element instead.

SCRIPT

The SCRIPT element can be inserted either in the HEAD or BODY element. For more information on the SCRIPT element, see its listing under the HEAD element.

OBJECT

The OBJECT element is intended to provide a single source for inserting different objects into an HTML document, including image, sound, video, animation, program (such as Java and ActiveX), and other files. Currently, only Internet Explorer supports the OBJECT element. To find out more about using the

OBJECT element, see the W3C's working draft, "Inserting Objects into HTML," at **http://www.w3.org/pub/WWW/TR/WD-object.html**.

OL

The OL (Ordered List) element creates a numbered list. OL elements can be nested inside each other to create a multilevel numbered list. OL elements can also be nested inside of UL (Unordered List) elements, and vice versa.

Attributes

TYPE="1|a|A|i|I"	Optional
START="*n*"	Optional

TYPE specifies the type of ordered list. START specifies where the list is to start, other than at 1, a, A, i, or I (such as 2 or C, for instance).

LI

The LI (List Item) element is used in combination with the UL element (and the OL element) to specify the items in a list. The LI element, despite appearances, is not an empty element, but a container element with an implied end tag. Adding the end tag currently has no effect, although HTML 4.0 has specified that adding the end tag should cause additional space to be added following a list item.

Attributes

TYPE="1|a|A|i|I"	Optional
VALUE="*n*"	Optional

These attributes force a type and value for any list item, with ensuing list items conforming to the new type and number values. You could, for instance, create a list numbered 1, 2, 4, 5 (skipping past 3)—but why would you want to?

P

The P (Paragraph) element defines a text paragraph. The P element is a container element, although adding the end tag (</P>) is considered optional.

Attributes

ALIGN="center|right"	Optional

ALIGN specifies that the paragraph is either center- or right-aligned. Left alignment is the default.

PRE

The PRE (Preformatted Text) element is used to include a block of text displayed in a monospaced font with all spaces and line breaks translated literally. Prior to the TABLE element, the PRE element was the only way to display tabular or columnar data or information. The IMG, BIG, SMALL, SUB, SUP, and FONT elements are not allowed within a PRE element. Because line breaks are translated literally, you don't need to use P or BR elements, but you should be aware that <P> and <BR> codes will be parsed by a browser, rather than presented literally. Also, B, I, EM, STRONG, U, and other text markup elements, as well as character entities, will also be parsed.

TABLE

The TABLE element allows data to be displayed in a tabular format. Tables can also include lists (DL, OL, and UL), paragraphs, forms, images, preformatted text (PRE), and other tables. HTML 4.0 has added a number of additional capabilities to its table model, including decimal alignment in columns, column and row grouping, more flexibility in displaying borders and rules, incremental ("streaming") display of large tables, scrollable tables with fixed headers, better multipage printing support, as well as backward compatibility with Netscape's current implementation of tables.

Attributes

`ALIGN="left|right"`	Optional
`WIDTH="n|n%"`	Optional
`BORDER="n"`	Optional
`CELLSPACING="n"`	Optional
`CELLPADDING="n"`	Optional
`VALIGN="top|bottom"`	Optional
`BGCOLOR="#rrggbb|colorname"` (4.0)	Optional
`COLS="n"` (4.0)	Optional
`FRAME="frame display"` (4.0)	Optional
`RULES="rules display"` (4.0)	Optional

ALIGN aligns a table to the left or right (left alignment is the default). WIDTH specifies the width of the table in pixels or as a percentage of a browser window. BORDER sets the thickness in pixels of the border around the table. CELLSPACING sets the space in pixels between cells. CELLPADDING sets the space in pixels within cells. VALIGN specifies whether text in a table is to be top or bottom aligned. BGCOLOR assigns a background color. This works exactly the same as in the BODY element. COLS specifies the number of columns in a table. This is intended to assist browsers to start rendering a table prior to receiving all the data. FRAME specifies which parts of the frame surrounding a table will be visible. Allowed values are "void", "above", "below", "hsides", "vsides", "lhs" (left), "rhs" (right), "box", and "border". RULES specifies which rules within a table will be visible. Allowed values are "none", "groups" (between THEAD, TFOOT, TBODY, and COLGROUP), "rows", "cols", and "all".

These elements are nested inside the TABLE element: CAPTION, TR, TH, TD, COLGROUP (4.0), THEAD (4.0), TBODY (4.0), and TFOOT (4.0).

CAPTION

The CAPTION element is an optional element that can be nested inside a TABLE element. It specifies a caption for the table.

Attributes

ALIGN="bottom|left|right"   Optional

ALIGN aligns the caption relative to the top, bottom, left, or right of a table. The default is "top".

TR

The TR (Table Row) element defines a table row. Every row in a table should start with <TR> and end with </TR>.

Attributes

ALIGN="left|center|right"   Optional
VALIGN="top|middel|bottom"   Optional

TH

The TH (Table Heading) element defines a heading for a table row. The TH element is displayed by a browser in a bold, center-aligned font. The allowable attributes for the TH element are the same as for the TD element that follows.

TD

The TD (Table Data) element defines a cell within a table. It takes the same attributes as the TABLE element.

Attributes

ALIGN="*left|center|right*"	Optional
VALIGN="*top|middle|bottom*"	Optional
HEIGHT="*n*"	Optional
WIDTH="*n*"	Optional
BGCOLOR="*#rrggbb*"|*colorname*"	Optional
COLSPAN="*n*"	Optional
ROWSPAN="*n*"	Optional
NOWRAP	Optional
AXIS="*heading name*"	Optional
AXES="*list of axis names*"	Optional

ALIGN, VALIGN, HEIGHT, WIDTH, and BGCOLOR all work as described previously. COLSPAN and ROWSPAN in the TR element allow you to create a cell that spans (encompasses) more than one column or row. COLSPAN and ROWSPAN can be used in the same cell (TH or TD). NOWRAP turns wrapping off. AXIS names a header cell. AXES provides a comma-separated list of row and column header names that pertain to a cell.

COLGROUP (4.0)

COLGROUP (Column Group) defines column groups in a table to which styles can be applied.

Attributes

SPAN="*n*"	Optional
WIDTH="*n|n%|0**"	Optional
ALIGN="left|center|right"	Optional
VALIGN="top|middle|bottom"	Optional

SPAN specifies the number of columns in a group (the default is "1"). WIDTH specifies the width for each column in a group. This can be set either in pixels, as a percentage of the table width, or by assigning a value of "0*", which specifies that the width of any column in the group should be the minimum necessary to display its contents. ALIGN and VALIGN work the same as in the TABLE element.

COL (4.0)

The COL (Column) element is nested inside the COLGROUP element and sets SPAN and WIDTH values for cells within a column group. The same attributes applicable to the COLGROUP element are used with the COL element. Here's an example:

```
<TABLE>
<COLGROUP>
  <COL WIDTH="40"><COL WIDTH="20"><COL WIDTH="0*">
</COLGROUP>
Table body...
</TABLE>
```

THEAD (4.0)

The THEAD (Table Head) element defines a nested group of rows as a table header. This element is currently only supported by Internet Explorer 4.0 or greater.

Attributes

`ALIGN="left|center|right"`	Optional
`VALIGN="top|middle|bottom"`	Optional

TBODY (4.0)

The TBODY (Table Body) element defines a nested group of rows as the body of a table. The TBODY element takes the same attribute values as the THEAD element. This element is currently only supported by Internet Explorer 4.0 or greater.

TFOOT (4.0)

The TFOOT (Table Foot) element defines a nested group of rows as the table footer. The TFOOT element takes the same attribute values as the THEAD and TBODY elements. This element is currently supported by Internet Explorer 4.0 or greater.

UL

The UL (Unordered List) element creates a "bulleted" list. UL elements can be nested inside each other to create a multilevel bulleted list. UL elements can also be nested inside of OL (Ordered List) elements, and vice versa.

Attributes

`TYPE="disc|square|circle"`	Optional

TYPE specifies the type of bullet ("disc", "square", or "circle") to be used with the list. (The default is "disc".)

LI

The LI (List Item) element is used in combination with the OL element (and the UL element) to specify the items in a list. The LI element, despite appearances, is not an empty element, but a container element with an implied end tag (</LI>). Adding the end tag currently has no effect, although HTML 4.0 has specified that adding the end tag should cause additional space to be added following a list item.

Attributes

```
TYPE="disc|square|circle"          Optional
```

TYPE forces a bullet type for a list item and for ensuing list items.

Text Markup

The following elements are all used to "mark up" text. These elements will not start a new block and should always be nested inside of a block element (the P element, most commonly).

ACRONYM (4.0)

The ACRONYM element displays an acronym (depending on the browser) and can include the full text to which the acronym refers, which might be revealed by passing the cursor over the acronym, for instance. Here's an example:

```
The <ACRONYM TITLE="World Wide Web">WWW</ACRONYM> is a mighty big
show.
```

B

The B (Bold) element is used to turn bold on and off.

BIG

The BIG element will display text in a font that's one size bigger than the base font. To display even bigger fonts, multiple instances of the BIG element can be nested within each other. Here's an example:

```
This is really <BIG>big</BIG>. This is really, really
<BIG><BIG>big</BIG></BIG>.
```

CITE

The CITE element is used to render a citation, typically in italics. Use I or EM instead.

CODE

The CODE element is used to display program or computer code. This element should be displayed in a smaller, monospaced font. Use the TT element instead.

DEL (4.0)

The DEL (Delete) element is used to mark text for deletion, which should then be displayed as strikeout text. How it's to be displayed is left up to the browser. At the time of this writing, only Internet Explorer 4.0+ displays this element (the attributes are not supported, however).

Attributes

CITE="*url*"	Optional
DATETIME="*datetime*"	Optional

CITE designates the URL of a source document or message that is cited as the source, reason, or authority for the deletion. DATETIME can take values in the following order: *YYYY* (year), *MM* (month), *DD* (day), T (start of time element), *hh* (hour), *mm* (minute), *ss* (second), z (Coordinated Universal Time, UCT/GMT), +*hh,mm* (local time relative to UCT; replaces z), and -*hh,mm* (local time relative to UCT; replaces z). This example corresponds to September 15, 1998, 12:00 p.m. UTC (GMT):

```
<DEL DATETIME="1998-09-15T12:00:00Z">This was inserted September 15,
➡1997, at 12:00 UTC.</DEL>
```

DFN

The DFN (Definition) element is used to display the defining instance of a term. Internet Explorer displays it in italics, but Navigator entirely ignores it. Use I or EM instead.

EM

The EM (Emphasis) element is used to emphasize text, displaying it in italics. This element should always display in a browser identically to the I element—the only difference being that the EM element is a *logical* element, whereas the I element is a *literal* element.

FONT

The FONT element allows you to set font size, color, and face properties. Although it has been deprecated in HTML 4.0 in favor of Cascading Style Sheets, it's just too handy to ever go away.

Attributes

`SIZE="n" or "+n|-n"`	Optional
`COLOR="#rrggbb|colorname"`	Optional
`FACE="font[,font2][,font3]" (4.0)`	Optional

SIZE specifies an absolute or relative font size. An absolute font size is specified by a number between 1 and 7 (3 is the default font size). A relative font size is specified *relative to* either the default base font size (3) or a previously set BASE-FONT element value. Using relative font sizes, you can use the BASEFONT element to shift all following font sizes up or down, rather than having to change each one. COLOR sets the font color, either with a hexadecimal color code (*#rrggbb*, corresponding to red, green, and blue) or a color name (black, white, aqua, blue, fuchsia, gray, green, lime, maroon, navy, olive, purple, red, silver, teal, and yellow). FACE specifies a font name or a comma-separated list of font names (`FACE="courier new,arial,avantgarde"`, for instance) that can be used to display the font.

I

The I (Italics) element is used to turn italics on and off.

INS (4.0)

The INS (Insert) element is used to mark text as an insertion. How it is to be displayed is left up to the browser. At the time of this writing, only Internet Explorer 4.0 and greater displays this element (the attributes are not supported, however).

Attributes

For a description of the attributes that can be used with the INS element, see the DEL element, earlier in this appendix. See the DEL element also for examples of using the INS element (just substitute INS for DEL).

KBD

The KBD (Keyboard) element is used to display text to be entered from the keyboard. Internet Explorer displays it in a smaller, bold, monospaced font, whereas Navigator displays it in a smaller, not bold, monospaced font. This might be a useful element except for the fact that in Navigator it is entirely indistinguishable from the TT element.

Q (4.0)

The Q (Quote) element is a new HTML 4.0 element that's used to display quoted text. Theoretically, browsers should be able to render this differently depending on the document's language. This is also supposed to be a "smart" element that desists from inserting quotation marks if they are already present.

S (4.0)

The S (Strikeout) element renders text as strikeout. It was originally a proposed HTML 3.0 element that never made it into HTML 3.2, whereas the Netscape extension STRIKE did make it in. Both the S and STRIKE elements have been recognized in the HTML 4.0 draft specification, but as "deprecated" elements, with the newer HTML 4.0 element, the DEL element, recommended in their stead.

SAMP

The SAMP (Sample) element is supposed to be used to render "sample" text or any string of literal characters. This is rendered by both Internet Explorer and Navigator as a smaller, monospaced font that is indistinguishable from the TT element. Use TT, instead.

SMALL

The SMALL element reduces the font size by one size, relative to the base font. The SMALL element can be nested inside itself to reduce the font size down two levels (or more, if the base font size has been increased). Here's an example:

```
This is <SMALL>small</SMALL> text. This is an even
<SMALL><SMALL>smaller</SMALL></SMALL> text.
```

SPAN (4.0)

The SPAN element is similar to the DIV element, except that it's a text element instead of a block element. By itself, the SPAN element does absolutely nothing—only when you use it as a vehicle for applying styles to "spans" of text does it comes to life (see the Style element). Both Internet Explorer 4.0 or greater and Navigator 4.0 or greater support applying style characteristics to the SPAN element.

STRIKE

The STRIKE element was a Netscape extension for marking strikeout text that was included in HTML 3.2, but it's now deprecated in HTML 4.0 in favor of the new DEL element.

STRONG

The STRONG (Strong Emphasis) element marks text as "strongly emphasized" and is displayed in a bold font, indistinguishable from the B element.

SUB

The SUB (Subscript) element marks text as subscripted. Internet Explorer 3.0 and Navigator 4.0 display subscripts and superscripts in a smaller font, but earlier versions of these browsers do not.

SUP

The SUP (Superscript) element marks text as superscripted. To allow for non-supporting browsers, you might want to put superscripted text inside of parentheses, like this:

```
Try Goober's Hair Grease<SUP>(TM)</SUP>!
```

TT

The TT (Teletype) element, often referred to as the "Typewriter Text" element, is displayed in a smaller, monospaced font by all browsers and is the preferred element for rendering monospaced text.

U

The U (Underline) element marks text as underlined. Navigator 3.0 and earlier, however, ignore this element, so it's probably best to avoid it.

VAR

The VAR (Variable) element is intended for the rendering of variables, and it should be displayed by a supporting browser in an italic font. Use I or EM instead.

FRAMESET (4.0)

The FRAMESET element allows an author to define a multiple-frame Web page, where each frame contains and displays its own HTML document. Frames can be scrolled and resized by the user, unless scrolling and resizing is turned off.

Attributes

ROWS="*n,n,...*"	Optional
COLS="*n,n,...*"	Optional

ROWS specifies row dimensions in a FRAMESET element, whereas COLS specifies column dimensions. Pixel, percentage, or relative dimensions can be specified:

✿ **Pixel dimensions**—You can define columns or rows within a FRAME-SET element using absolute pixel dimensions. For instance, <FRAMESET ROWS="80,400"> defines two rows, with the top row being 80 pixels high and the bottom row being 400 pixels high. To allow for different screen resolutions (and browser window dimensions), you shouldn't set all rows or columns in a FRAMESET element as absolute pixels.

✿ **Percentage dimensions**—You can define columns and rows as percentages of the total height or width of the browser window. For instance, <FRAMESET ROWS="80%,20%"> defines two rows, with the top row filling 80 percent and the bottom row filling 20 percent of the total height of the browser window.

✿ **Relative dimensions**—You can combine either pixel or percentage row or column dimensions with the wildcard character (*). For instance, <FRAMESET ROWS="*,100"> defines the top row as a "relative" row that would expand or contract depending on the total space available in the browser window, whereas the bottom row would remain fixed at a height of 100 pixels.

FRAME (4.0)

The FRAME element is nested inside the FRAMESET element. It's used to define frames that are included in the frame page.

Attributes

SRC="*url*"	Usually
NAME="*framename*"	Recommended

`FRAMEBORDER="1|0"`	Optional
`MARGINHEIGHT="pixels"`	Optional
`MARGINWIDTH="pixels"`	Optional
`NORESIZE`	Optional
`SCROLLING="yes|no|auto"`	Optional

SRC specifies the frame document's URL. NAME names a frame so it can be targeted from hypertext links located in other frames. FRAMEBORDER turns the border of a frame off or on ("0" turns it off; "1" is the default). MARGIN-HEIGHT and MARGINWIDTH sets the amount of left and right and top and bottom margin spaces, respectively (the minimum value is "2"). NORESIZE stops the manually resizing of a frame. SCROLLING determines how scroll bars are treated in a frame. A "no" value turns off scroll bar display, even if the document extends beyond the dimensions of the frame. You might want to do this, for instance, in the case of the space that's added below an H1 element or other block element causing scroll bars to appear, even though no text actually extends beyond the frame. The default SCROLLING attribute value is "auto", which will automatically cause scroll bars to be added to a frame if they're required.

NOFRAMES (4.0)

The NOFRAMES element is used to provide content in a frame page that will be displayed by non-frames-capable browsers (or by frames-capable browsers where frames have been turned off). The NOFRAMES element is placed following the last FRAME element, either before or after any </FRAMESET> end tags (it doesn't really matter). A non-frames-capable browser will ignore the FRAMESET element, whereas a frames-capable browser will ignore the contents of the NOFRAMES element.

This is an example of using "nested" FRAMESET elements to create a frame page with both columns and rows:

```
<FRAMESET ROWS="25%,75%">
    <FRAME NAME="Top_Bar" SRC="mast_bar.htm">
    <FRAMESET COLS="25%,75%">
        <FRAME NAME="Left_Bar" SRC="left_bar.htm">
        <FRAME NAME="Main" SRC="main.htm">
    </FRAMESET>
</FRAMESET>
```

The following is an example of using one frame page nested inside of another (a "nested" frame page). This allows a single link to control the contents of both frame windows in the nested frame. Here's the first frame page:

```
<FRAMESET ROWS="75%,25%">
<FRAME NAME="Col_Page" SRC="col_page.htm">
<FRAME NAME="Bot_Bar" SRC="bot_bar.htm">
</FRAMESET>
```

Here's the "nested" frame page (COL_PAGE.HTM):

```
<HTML>
<FRAMESET COLS="85,*">
    <FRAME SRC="sidebar.htm" NAME="sidebar">
    <FRAME SRC="main.htm" NAME="main">
</FRAMESET>
<NOFRAMES>
Requires a Frames-capable browser: Please go to the
<A HREF="main2.htm">Non-Frames Version</A> of this page.
</NOFRAMES>
</HTML>
```

Controlling Frames

The TARGET attribute of the A element is used to control frame content. By itself, a link within a frame page will replace the contents of a frame with the Web page or other object (a graphic, for instance) that's the object of the link. If it's a page on your own server, then this may be what you want to do. However, if you're linking to someone else's page, he might not appreciate you pulling *his* page into *your* frame.

The solution is to always include a TARGET=_top attribute value in a hypertext link (the A element) that links to a Web page that's external to your Web site (or in any link where you want the object to display outside of the frame in a top-level window).

Other stock TARGET names that can be used are _blank, _self, and _parent. TARGET=_blank is similar to TARGET=_top, except that the _blank attribute value causes a new browser window to be launched. TARGET=_self loads the designated document in the same frame as the link (this is the default). TARGET=_parent loads the designated document into the immediate parent frame (the frame within which the current frame is nested). These TARGET attribute values (_top, _blank, _self, and _target) should not be enclosed in quotes. If you put them in quotes, they won't work.

You can also use frame names as TARGET attribute values. For instance, using the previous example of the two-row frame, a link in MENU.HTM with a TAR-GET="main" attribute value would replace the contents of the top-row frame to which the name "main" had been assigned. That's why you should name your frames—so that a link from any other frame can be used to control its contents.

HTML 4.0 General Attributes

Apart from the styles that can be applied to most HTML 4.0 elements, a number of additional general-purpose attributes can be applied to most HTML 4.0 elements.

Element Identifiers

HTML 4.0 has added two "element identifiers." These function like general attributes that can be attached to many HTML 4.0 elements. Here's an example:

```
ID="name"

CLASS="element class or classes"
```

ID assigns a document-wide name for a specific instance of an element. This must be a unique name, and it should not be duplicated in more than one element. This name should start with a letter and can be followed by any number of letters, numbers, hyphens, and periods, but nothing else. Note that the ID name will replace any instance of the NAME attribute used within an element.

CLASS assigns a class or classes to an element. A class is a group of elements that can have styles attached to the entire group. An element can belong to more than one class. In a CLASS attribute value, multiple classes are separated by spaces.

Intrinsic Events

"Intrinsic event" attributes in HTML 4.0 allow elements to trigger scripts based on specific events (such as clicking on, passing the mouse over, and so on). They can be applied to most elements. Here's a list of these new attributes along with some short descriptions of what they're supposed to do:

✪ ONLOAD="script"—Triggered when a window or frame finishes loading. (BODY and FRAMESET only.)

✪ ONUNLOAD="script"—Triggered after a window or frame finishes unloading. (BODY and FRAMESET only.)

✪ ONCLICK="script"—Triggered after the mouse (or other pointing device) is clicked on the element. (Most elements.)

⚙ ONDBLCLICK="*script*"—Triggered after the mouse is double-clicked on the element. (Most elements.)

⚙ ONMOUSEDOWN="*script*"—Triggered when the mouse button is held down on the element. (Most elements.)

⚙ ONMOUSEUP="*script*"—Triggered when the mouse button is released over an element. (Most elements.)

⚙ ONMOUSEOVER="*script*"—Triggered when the mouse is moved over an element. (Most elements.)

⚙ ONMOUSEMOVE="*script*"—Triggered when the mouse is moved over an element. (Most elements.)

⚙ ONMOUSEOUT="*script*"—Triggered when the mouse is moved out of an element. (Most elements.)

⚙ ONFOCUS="*script*"—Triggered when an element "receives focus," either via a mouse or tabbing navigation. (Used with BUTTON, INPUT, LABEL, SELECT, and TEXT AREA.)

⚙ ONBLUR="*script*"—Triggered when an element "loses focus," either via a mouse or tabbing navigation. (Used with same elements as ONFOCUS.)

⚙ ONKEYPRESS="*script*"—Triggered when a key is pressed and released on an element. (Most elements.)

⚙ ONKEYDOWN="*script*"—Triggered when a key is held down on an element. (Most elements.)

⚙ ONKEYUP="*script*"—Triggered when a key is released over an element. (Most elements.)

⚙ ONSUBMIT="*script*"—Triggered when a form is submitted. (FORM only.)

⚙ ONRESET="*script*"—Triggered when a form is reset. (FORM only.)

⚙ ONSELECT="*script*"—Triggered when a user selects text in a text field. (INPUT and TEXTAREA only.)

⚙ ONCHANGE="*script*"—Triggered after a control has been modified and has lost focus. (INPUT, SELECT, and TEXTAREA only.)

For more information on using both intrinsic event handlers and element identifiers, see the W3C's section on scripts in the HTML 4.0 Specification at **http://www.w3.org/TR/REC-html40/interact/scripts.html**.

APPENDIX B

Special Characters

The ISO 8859-1 character set is an 8-bit character set that allows for 256 code positions. Characters 0 through 31 and 127 are assigned as control characters. 32 through 126 correspond to the US-ASCII characters that can be typed in at the keyboard. 128 through 159 are designated as unused in ISO 8859-1, although both Windows and the Macintosh assign characters to many of these positions. 160 through 255 designate extended (or special) characters included in ISO 8859-1 that should be displayable on all computer systems supporting this character set.

Reserved Characters

These are the numerical and named character entities for reserved characters that are used to format HTML tags and codes.

Number	Name	Description	Character
"	"	Double quotation	"
&	&	Ampersand	&
<	<	Left angle bracket	<
>	>	Right angle bracket	>

Unused Characters

The number character entities 128 through 159 are designated as unused in the ISO 8859-1 character set. Both Windows and the Macintosh, however, assign characters to many of these code positions, of which 12 are dissimilar on the two systems. Below I've listed all the characters that are displayable in Windows, of which three are not available on the Macintosh. There is no guarantee whatsoever that any of these characters will display on other platforms. Therefore, my strong recommendation is that these characters not be used. A few of these characters have, however, been assigned character names.

Number	Name	Description	Character
€		Unused	
		Unused	
‚		Single quote (low)	‚
ƒ		Small Latin f	ƒ
„		Double quote (low)	„
…		Ellipsis	…
†		Dagger	† (not on Mac)
‡		Double dagger	‡
ˆ		Circumflex	ˆ
‰		Per mile sign	‰
Š		S-caron	Š (not on Mac)
‹		Left angle quote	‹
Œ		OE ligature	Œ
		Unused	

Number	Name	Description	Character
Ž		Unused	
		Unused	
		Unused	
‘		Left single quote	'
’		Right single quote	'
“		Left double quote	"
”		Right double quote	"
•		Bullet	•
–	–	En dash	–
—	—	Em dash	—
˜		Small tilde	~
™	™	Trademark	™
š		s-caron	š (not on Mac)
›		Right angle quote	›
œ		oe ligature	œ
		Unused	
ž		Unused	
Ÿ		Y-umlaut	Ÿ

Special Characters

The following characters, 160 through 255, are all part of the ISO 8859-1 character set. These characters should generally be available on any operating system that uses the ISO-8859-1 character set, which is most of them. However, 14 of these characters, which I have marked below, are not available on the Macintosh and should be avoided.

Number	Name	Description	Character
		Non-breakable space	[ ] (parentheses added)
¡	¡	Inverted exclamation	¡
¢	¢	Cent sign	¢
£	£	Pound sign	£
¤	¤	Currency sign	¤
¥	¥	Yen sign	¥

Number	Name	Description	Character
¦	¦	Broken vertical bar	¦ (not on Mac)[1]
§	§	Section sign	§
¨	¨	Umlaut	¨
©	©	Copyright	©
ª	ª	Feminine ordinal	ª
«	«	Left guillemet	«
¬	¬	Not sign	¬
­	­	Soft hyphen	–
®	®	Registration	®
¯	&hibar;	Macron	¯
°	°	Degree	°
±	±	Plus/minus sign	±
²	²	Superscripted 2	² (not on Mac)
³	³	Superscripted 3	³ (not on Mac)
´	´	Acute accent	´
µ	µ	Micro sign	µ
¶	¶	Paragraph sign	¶
·	·	Middle dot	·
¸	¸	Cedilla	¸
¹	¹	Superscripted 1	¹ (not on Mac)
º	º	Masculine ordinal	º
»	»	Right guillemet	»
¼	¼	1/4 fraction	¼ (not on Mac)
½	½	1/2 fraction	½ (not on Mac)
¾	¾	3/4 fraction	¾ (not on Mac)
¿	¿	Inverted question mark	¿
À	À	A-grave	À
Á	Á	A-acute	Á
Â	Â	A-circumflex	Â
Ã	Ã	A-tilde	Ã
Ä	Ä	A-umlaut	Ä
Å	Å	A-ring	Å
Æ	Æ	AE diphthong	Æ
Ç	Ç	C-cedilla	Ç

Number	Name	Description	Character
È	È	E-grave	È
É	É	E-acute	É
Ê	Ê	E-circumflex	Ê
Ë	Ë	E-umlaut	Ë
Ì	Ì	I-grave	Ì
Í	Í	I-acute	Í
Î	Î	I-circumflex	Î
Ï	Ï	I-umlaut	Ï
Ð	Ð	Uppercase Eth	Ð (not on Mac)
Ñ	Ñ	N-tilde	Ñ
Ò	Ò	O-grave	Ò
Ó	Ó	O-acute	Ó
Ô	Ô	O-circumflex	Ô
Õ	Õ	O-tilde	Õ
Ö	Ö	O-umlaut	Ö
×	×	Multiplication sign	× (not on Mac)[2]
Ø	Ø	O-slash	Ø
Ù	Ù	U-grave	Ù
Ú	Ú	U-acute	Ú
Û	Û	U-circumflex	Û
Ü	Ü	U-umlaut	Ü
Ý	Ý	Y-acute	Ý (not on Mac)
Þ	Þ	Uppercase Thorn	Þ (not on Mac)
ß	ß	Sharp s (German)	ß
à	à	a-grave	à
á	á	a-acute	á
â	â	a-circumflex	â
ã	ã	a-tilde	ã
ä	ä	a-umlaut	ä
å	å	a-ring	å
æ	æ	ae diphthong	æ
ç	ç	c-cedilla	ç
è	è	e-grave	è
é	é	e-acute	é

Number	Name	Description	Character
ê	ê	e-circumflex	ê
ë	ë	e-umlaut	ë
ì	ì	i-grave	ì
í	í	i-acute	í
î	î	i-circumflex	î
ï	ï	i-umlaut	ï
ð	ð	Lowercase Eth	ð (not on Mac)
ñ	ñ	n-tilde	ñ
ò	ò	o-grave	ò
ó	ó	o-acute	ó
ô	ô	o-circumflex	ô
õ	õ	o-tilde	õ
ö	ö	o-umlaut	ö
÷	÷	Division sign	÷
ø	ø	o-slash	ø
ù	ù	u-grave	ù
ú	ú	u-acute	ú
û	û	u-circumflex	û
ü	ü	u-umlaut	ü
ý	ý	y-acute	ý (not on Mac)
þ	þ	Lowercase Thorn	þ (not on Mac)
ÿ	ÿ	y-umlaut	ÿ

Notes:

[1] The Macintosh substitutes an unbroken vertical bar (|).

[2] The Macintosh substitutes a lower case x.

APPENDIX C

Glossary

Absolute URL. A complete path, or *address*, of a file on the Internet (such as, **http://www.someserver.com/somedir/somep age.htm**). Also called a *complete URL*. See also *Relative URL*.

Adaptive Palette. A color palette for an image that has been reduced to only the colors present in the image.

Anti-Aliasing. The blending of colors to smooth out the "jaggies" in fonts.

Applet. A client-side program, usually Java or ActiveX, that is downloaded from the Internet and executed in a Web browser.

ASCII. American Standard Code for Information Interchange. Defines a standard minimum character set for computer text and data. ASCII files are sometimes called *DOS text* files or *plain text* files.

Bandwidth. The transmission capacity of a network, but also the amount of capacity being consumed by a connection. A Web page containing many graphics will consume more bandwidth than one containing only text.

Bookmark. A means, in Netscape Navigator, for "bookmarking" the URLs of favorite Web sites so they can easily be returned to. It's saved by Navigator as an HTML file (BOOKMARK.HTM). A similar feature in Microsoft Internet Explorer is called *Favorites* (but these are saved as separate files rather than in a single file).

Cascading Style Sheets. A means for defining styles, using the STYLE tag, in order to control the display of HTML elements. The style sheet can either reside inside of the HTML file or in a separate file that's downloaded along with the HTML file. Current versions are Cascading Style Sheets, Level 1 (CSS1) and Cascading Style Sheets, Level 2 (CSS2).

CGI. Common Gateway Interface. An interface to a gateway through which a Web server can run programs and scripts on a host computer.

Client. A computer on a network that makes a request to a server.

Definition List. A glossary list in HTML that's created using the DL (definition list) element.

Domain Category. A major grouping of domain names (such as .com, .org, .net, .edu, .mil, and .gov), as well as many national domain categories (.us, .uk, .ca, and so on).

Domain Name. An alphanumeric alternative to an IP address that is registered with InterNIC (Internet Network Information Center).

Download. To transfer files from a server to a client. Also see *Upload*.

Dynamic HTML. Various means of providing dynamic Web content that respond interactively to user actions, such as producing on-the-fly Web pages, starting and stopping animations, and so on.

End Tag. The end of a nonempty HTML element (...</P>, for example). See *Start Tag*.

Extension. An nonstandard extension to HTML, implemented by a particular browser (as in *Netscape extension* or *Microsoft*

extension), that may or may not be displayable in other browsers.

Fragment Identifier. A string at the end of a URL preceded by a "#" character, used to identify a target anchor name. Allows a hypertext link to jump to a specific location in another or the same Web page.

Frames. An extension to HTML pioneered by Netscape that has since been incorporated into HTML 4.0. Allows HTML documents to be presented inside of multiple frames within a browser window.

FTP. File Transfer Protocol. The protocol used for downloading or uploading both ASCII and binary files on the Internet.

GIF. Graphic Interchange Format. A graphics format developed by CompuServe that has become one of the standard image formats for displaying graphics on the World Wide Web. A GIF can include up to 256 colors, transparency, interlacing, and multiple frames (GIF animation). See also *JPEG*.

GIF Animation. A GIF format image file containing multiple images, usually only viewable in a Web browser.

Gopher. A menu-driven system, predating the World Wide Web, for sharing files over the Internet. Developed originally by a graduate student at the University of Minnesota.

HTML. Hypertext Markup Language. A markup language for preparing documents for display on the World Wide Web. The current standard version of HTML is HTML 4.0 (previous versions were HTML 1.0, HTML 2.0, and HTML 3.2).

HTML Editor. A software program that edits HTML files, usually with the aid of pull-down menus, toolbars, and wizards.

HTML Element. May be a standalone tag (such as <HR>) or everything between a start tag (such as <P>) and an end tag (such as </P>).

HTML Tag. May be a standalone tag (such as <HR>) or an HTML start tag or end tag.

HTTP. Hypertext Transfer Protocol. The protocol used to exchange Web pages and other documents across the Internet. A Web server, for instance, may also be called an *HTTP server*, in contrast to an FTP (File Transfer Protocol) server.

Hypertext. Described by Ted Nelson, inventor of hypertext, as "nonsequential writing." Hypertext links allow nonsequential linking of information within a "docuverse."

Hypermedia. Another term coined by Ted Nelson. Generally refers to the interlinking of multiple media (text, images, sound, animation, and video).

Hypertext Link. A means, using the A (anchor) element in HTML, for jumping from a location in an HTML document to another Web page or object file on the Web, to a location in another Web page, or to a location in the same Web page. Also called a *hot link*.

Image Link. An inline image inserted inside of a hypertext link, usually displayed with a blue border to show that it's an active link.

Image Map. An image displayed in a Web browser that has hidden "hot spots" that can be clicked to link to their designated URLs. Older browsers only supported server-side image maps (image maps executed from a server), but newer browsers also support client-side image maps (image maps executed from the desktop, or *client*).

In-context Link. A hypertext link insert "in context" within a paragraph or other text.

Inline Image. An image (GIF, JPG, or PNG) that's displayed on a Web page.

Internet. A set of protocols for transmitting and exchanging data among networks.

IP Address. Internet Protocol Address. A unique number, such as 185.35.117.0, that is assigned to a server on the Internet.

IPP. Internet Presence Provider, also often called a *Web host* or *Web space provider*. A company that rents out Web space.

ISP. Internet Service Provider, also often called an *access provider*. A company that provides dial-up access to the Internet.

JPEG. Joint Photographic Expert Group. Besides GIF, this is the most common graphics format for the display of images on the Web. Images can select from a palette of up to 16.7 million colors. Unlike GIF images, however, JPEG images cannot be transparent, interlaced, or animated. These are often referred to as *JPG format images*, because the file extension for JPEG images under DOS/Windows is ".JPG." See also *GIF*.

Link List. A list of hypertext links, sometimes also called a *hot list*.

Link Text. The text displayed in a hypertext link, usually in blue and underlined.

MathML. Mathematical Markup Language. The proposed standard for displaying equations and mathematical symbols on the Web.

Netscape Palette. A color palette composed of the 216 colors utilized by Netscape Navigator to display images on a computer displaying 256 colors. Also called a *safety palette*.

Offline Browsing. Browsing HTML files on a local hard drive, without connecting to the Internet.

Ordered List. A numbered list in HTML.

PNG. Portable Network Graphics. The newest standard graphics format for the display of images on the Web. Supports up to 48-bit true color (JPEG supports up to 24-bit true color), as well as transparency and interlacing. So far, PNG is only supported by the latest browsers.

POP3 Server. Post Office Protocol, Version 3. An "incoming mail" server (e-mail is received from a POP3 mail server). See also *SMTP Server*.

Relative URL. A Web address stated in relation to the current (or linking) page (such as **images/mypic.jpg** or **../frames/myframe.html**. Internal links within a Web site should always use relative links, which allows the linked files to be uploaded onto a server or moved to another location, without the links having to be changed.

Server. A computer on a network that responds to requests from clients. See also *Client*.

SGML. Standard Generalized Markup Language. The parent markup language of HTML—although a parent that's probably tearing its hair out!

SMTP Server. Simple Mail Transfer Protocol. An "outgoing mail" server (e-mail is sent to an SMTP mail server). See also *POP3 Server*.

Start Tag. The start of a nonempty HTML element (<P>..., for instance).

TCP/IP. Transmission Control Protocol/Internet Protocol. The standard protocol for transmissions across the Internet.

Target Anchor. A hypertext anchor that defines the "landing spot" for a link.

Unordered List. A "bulleted" list in HTML.

Upload. To transfer files from a client to a server.

URL. Uniform Resource Locator. An address on the Web.

Web Browser. A software program that browses (or *surfs*) HTML and other files on the World Wide Web.

World Wide Web. A "wide-area hypermedia information retrieval initiative aiming to give universal access to a large universe of documents," according to Tim Berners-Lee, inventor of the World Wide Web. Also, "the universal space of all network-accessible information" (a more recent definition, also from Tim Berners-Lee). To put it as simply as possible, a "docuverse" (Ted Nelson, inventor of hypertext).

XML. Extensible Markup Language. Slated as the next-generation markup language for the display of documents and data on the Web. Likely to be a highly utilized alternative to HTML.

APPENDIX D

What's on the CD-ROM

The CD-ROM that accompanies this book contains all the example graphics and Web pages you'll use in the tutorials and exercises, plus a good deal more. Here's a rundown of the contents:

- ⚙ All the example graphics and files used in the HTML and software tutorials

- ⚙ A wide assortment of software tools (HTML editors, graphics editors, and utilities for creating forms, frames, image maps, GIF animations, and more)

- ⚙ A Web art sampler, including backgrounds, icons, graphic rules, and decorative letters

- ⚙ A collection of freeware and shareware fonts for further enhancing your Web graphics

- ⚙ A selection of Web page templates I created (including two-frame/

387

three-frame, newsletter, resume, calendar, genealogy, plus other basic and generic templates)

Running the CD-ROM

To make the CD-ROM more user-friendly and take up less of your disk space, I've set it up so that no installation is required. This means that the only files transferred to your hard disk are the ones you choose to copy or install.

CAUTION   ◆
The CD-ROM has been designed to run under Windows 95, 98, or NT. It should also run under Windows 3.1, but you may encounter unexpected problems. If you have a Windows 3.1 system running in 256 colors and you get an error message when trying to run the interface program (PRIMA.EXE) for the CD-ROM, you'll need either to reduce the number of colors that Windows 3.1 is using to 16 or increase the number of colors—if your system can display more than 256 colors—before you'll be able to run the interface program for the CD-ROM. Alternatively, you can also access the files on the CD-ROM using File Manager. All the sample graphics and Web page files used in the tutorials and exercises are also available for download from this book's Web site at **http://www.callihan.com/create2/**.

◆ ◆

Windows 3.1

To run the CD-ROM, follow these steps:

1. Insert the CD-ROM in the CD-ROM drive.
2. From File Manager, select File, Run to open the Run window.
3. In the Command Line text box, type **D:\prima.exe** (where *D* is the CD-ROM drive).
4. Select OK.

Windows 95

Because the CD-ROM has no install routine, running it in Windows 95 is a breeze, especially if you have Autorun enabled. Insert the CD-ROM in the CD-ROM drive, close the tray, and wait for it to load. If you've disabled Autorun, perform the following to run the CD-ROM:

1. Insert it in the CD-ROM drive.
2. From the Start menu, select Run.
3. In the Open text box, type **D:\prima.exe** (where *D* is the CD-ROM drive).
4. Select OK.

The Prima User Interface

Prima's user interface is designed to make viewing and using the CD-ROM contents quick and easy. It contains four category buttons—Examples, Web Tools, Multimedia, and Utilities—that allow you to install, explore, view information on, or visit the Web site for any of the example files or tools included on the CD-ROM. To install any of the example files or software tools included on the CD-ROM, select these options:

○ **Examples.** You'll find here all the example files contributed by the author, including example graphics and files used in the tutorials, a Web art sampler, a collection of Web page templates, and a font library.

○ **Web Tools.** You'll find here a wide assortment of Web publishing tools for creating and editing HTML files, including several HTML editors, plus tools for creating image maps, forms, and frames, as well as an HTML 3.2-compliant Web browser.

○ **Multimedia.** You'll find here a selection of multimedia tools, including paint and draw programs, graphic viewers and converters, and GIF and Java animation tools.

○ **Utilities.** You'll find here a miscellaneous selection of other tools, including FTP programs, zip/unzip utilities, file managers, and other utilities.

When you select any of the examples or tools from the category windows, you can execute the following options:

○ **Install.** Selecting this option allows you to install the example or tool on your hard drive.

○ **Explore**. Selecting this option allows you to explore the folder for the example or tool on the CD-ROM.

○ **View Information.** Selecting this option allows you to view any README text file or, alternatively, any Help file that accompanies the example or tool.

○ **Visit Web Site**. Selecting this option will launch your Web browser (Internet Explorer or Navigator only) and go to the associated Web site (Windows 95/98/NT only).

On the left panel of the CD-ROM interface screen are five additional options:

○ **Navigate.** This provides options to return to the main menu, go to any of the category windows, or visit the Prima Web site.

○ **Explore.** This lets you explore the current folder on the CD-ROM.

⚙ **Exit.** This lets you exit the CD-ROM interface.

⚙ **< and >.** These options move you backward or forward between the different windows in the CD-ROM's interface.

Using the Examples Section

The Examples section contains all the example graphics and files that are used in the book's tutorials and exercises. It also contains additional author-provided resources you can use to further enhance your Web publishing efforts, including a collection of Web page templates, a Web art sampler, and a font library.

Tutorials Option

Selecting the Tutorials option will let you install all of the example files that are used in the tutorials in the book. Selecting Install will copy all the example files to C:\HTML. You can also select Explore to view the contents of the \EXAMPLES\TUTORIAL folder.

Web Art Option

The Web Art option lets you access a Web art sampler on the CD-ROM that contains many background images, icons, graphic rules, and decorative letters that you can use to enhance your Web pages. Selecting Install will copy all of the folders in the Web art sampler to C:\HTML\WEBART. You can also select Explore or View Information.

A good way to view the Web art sampler is to install Paint Shop Pro from the Multimedia section of the CD-ROM and then to use its browse feature to view thumbnail images of all the graphic files in any of the folders included in the \EXAMPLES\WEBART folder on the CD-ROM. To load an image into Paint Shop Pro, just double-click the thumbnail image. You can then easily save the selected graphic to your hard drive.

Template Option

The Template option lets you install a selection of author-created Web page templates from the CD-ROM. Selecting Install will copy all of the Web page template folders to C:\HTML\TEMPLATE. You can also select Explore or View Information. Following are the Web page templates that have been included on the CD-ROM:

⚙ **Basic templates.** This is a collection of basic Web page templates that can be used in setting up a basic Web page. To preview the templates, use the Explore button and then double-click BASIC-1.HTM, BASIC-2.HTM, or BASIC-3.HTM.

✿ **Calendar template.** Use this table-based template to create events and other schedules in a calendar format. To preview the calendar template on the CD-ROM, use the Explore button and then double-click CAL-ENDAR.HTM to view it in your browser.

✿ **Frames templates.** These are two templates—one for creating a two-frame Web site and the other for creating a three-frame Web site that uses "nested frames" (this feature allows you to update the contents of two frames from a single hypertext link without using any JavaScript). To preview either the two-frames template or the three-frames template on the CD-ROM, use the Explore button and then double-click INDEX.HTM to view it in your browser.

✿ **Genealogy template.** Use this template to create your very own genealogy Web site for your family. It includes sample photo gallery pages, as well as general instructions on how to use a shareware software tool available on the Web, GED2HTML, to add HTML GEDCOM files for your different family lines to your Web site. To preview the genealogy template on the CD-ROM, use the Explore button and then double-click INDEX.HTM to view it in your browser.

✿ **Generic templates**. This is an assortment of generic templates that use a variety of different features, such as background images, background text, link colors, font size, color changes, transparent banners, vertical banners, drop caps, icon bullet lists, and styles. To preview any of these templates on the CD-ROM, use the Explore button and then double-click any of the included HTML files to view them in your browser.

✿ **Navigation bar template**. This template includes an image map navigation bar that you can use on any of your Web pages. This is the same navigation bar created in the Sunday Evening Graphics Tutorial. Editing instructions are included. To preview this template on the CD-ROM, use the Explore button and then double-click NAVBAR.HTM to view it in your browser.

✿ **Newsletter template.** This template allows you to create your very own online newsletter. It uses a two-color background image and a table to create a Web page that's laid out like a newsletter, including a masthead at the top, a sidebar table of contents along the left side, and a front page with summaries and links for the articles. To preview this template on the CD-ROM, use the Explore button and then double-click NEWSLTR.HTM to view it in your browser.

○ **Résumé template**. This template allows you to create your own online résumé. To preview this template on the CD-ROM, use the Explore button and then double-click RESUME.HTM to view it in your browser.

Fonts Option

The Fonts option lets you access a library of freeware and shareware TrueType fonts on the CD-ROM. You can use any of these fonts to further extend the kinds of text effects you can create in your graphics editor. Selecting Install will copy the included fonts to C:\HTML\FONTS. Select View Information for instructions on how to install the fonts in either Windows 95/98 or Windows 3.1. You can also select Explore to copy any individual zip files for the fonts onto your hard drive.

All Examples Option

The All Examples option lets you copy all of the example files included in the previous four options to your hard drive. The install folders will be the same as shown for the other options.

Software on the CD-ROM

A wide range of different freeware, shareware, trialware, and demoware programs and utilities has been included on the CD-ROM. You're expected to register any shareware programs or evaluation versions if you wish to continue using them beyond their evaluation periods. Some programs will stop working after their evaluation periods are up (anywhere from 14 days to 90 days), whereas some will just pester you with nagging screens. Freeware programs are free to use as long as you wish, as are some demo programs (although they may have some reduced functionality). There may also be some restrictions on the commercial use of freeware—check the individual license agreements for details.

NOTICE

Any shareware distributed on this disk is for evaluation purposes only and should be registered with the shareware vendor if used beyond the trial period.

Here are brief descriptions of some of the software that you'll find on the CD-ROM:

○ **Animagic GIF.** A powerful animation tool that not only creates GIF animation files but optimizes them to minimize file size.

- ✿ **Browse And Zip**. A plug-in for viewing zip files in Navigator and Internet Explorer.
- ✿ **CoffeeCup HTML Editor++.** A full-feature HTML editor that includes forms, frames, and color wizards.
- ✿ **Frame-It.** A great freeware program that allows you to almost effortlessly create frame-based Web sites. (See the Sunday Morning session, "The Frames Tutorial," for additional information.)
- ✿ **GIF Construction Set.** This program's Animation Wizard makes creating GIF animations a breeze. (See the Sunday Evening session, "The Graphics Tutorial," for additional information.)

NOTICE

The **GIF Construction Set** software included with this publication is provided as shareware for your evaluation. If you try this software and find it useful, you are requested to register it as discussed in its documentation and in the About screen of the application. The publisher of this (book/magazine/etc.) has not paid the registration fee for this shareware.

- ✿ **HTML Power Tools.** A collection of powerful HTML utilities, including a spell checker, syntax analyzer, rule-based editor, and more.
- ✿ **HTMLed Pro**. A powerful HTML editor.
- ✿ **Lview Pro**. A great graphics editor/viewer/converter.
- ✿ **Mapedit.** An image map editor that makes creating both client-side and server-side image maps a breeze. (See the Sunday Evening session, "The Graphics Tutorial," for additional information.)
- ✿ **Paint Shop Pro 5.** A great photo-paint program with features rivaling programs costing hundreds of dollars more. (See the Sunday Evening session, "The Graphics Tutorial," for additional information.)
- ✿ **WebForms.** A great program for creating and managing both client-side and server-side forms. (See the Sunday Afternoon session, "The Forms Tutorial," for additional information.)
- ✿ **WinZip.** One of the most popular file compression utilities around. WinZip makes working with zip files and many other file compression formats in Windows a breeze.
- ✿ **WS-FTP LE.** A great freeware FTP program for transferring your Web pages, graphics, and other files to and from the Web server hosting your pages. You can also use it to manage your files and folders on your Web server.

INDEX

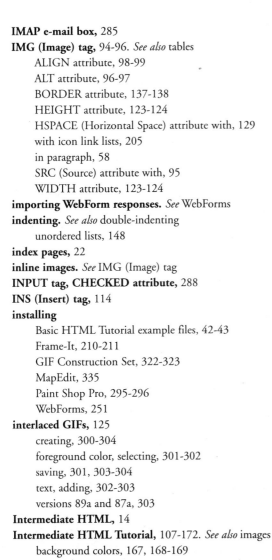

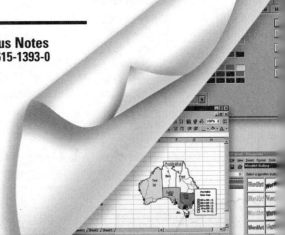

License Agreement/Notice of Limited Warranty

By opening the sealed disk container in this book, you agree to the following terms and conditions. If, upon reading the following license agreement and notice of limited warranty, you cannot agree to the terms and conditions set forth, return the unused book with unopened disk to the place where you purchased it for a refund.

License:
The enclosed software is copyrighted by the copyright holder(s) indicated on the software disk. You are licensed to copy the software onto a single computer for use by a single concurrent user and to a backup disk. You may not reproduce, make copies, or distribute copies or rent or lease the software in whole or in part, except with written permission of the copyright holder(s). You may transfer the enclosed disk only together with this license, and only if you destroy all other copies of the software and the transferee agrees to the terms of the license. You may not decompile, reverse assemble, or reverse engineer the software.

Notice of Limited Warranty:
The enclosed disk is warranted by Prima Publishing to be free of physical defects in materials and workmanship for a period of sixty (60) days from end user's purchase of the book/disk combination. During the sixty-day term of the limited warranty, Prima will provide a replacement disk upon the return of a defective disk.

Limited Liability:
THE SOLE REMEDY FOR BREACH OF THIS LIMITED WARRANTY SHALL CONSIST ENTIRELY OF REPLACEMENT OF THE DEFECTIVE DISK. IN NO EVENT SHALL PRIMA OR THE AUTHORS BE LIABLE FOR ANY OTHER DAMAGES, INCLUDING LOSS OR CORRUPTION OF DATA, CHANGES IN THE FUNCTIONAL CHARACTERISTICS OF THE HARDWARE OR OPERATING SYSTEM, DELETERIOUS INTERACTION WITH OTHER SOFTWARE, OR ANY OTHER SPECIAL, INCIDENTAL, OR CONSEQUENTIAL DAMAGES THAT MAY ARISE, EVEN IF PRIMA AND/OR THE AUTHOR HAVE PREVIOUSLY BEEN NOTIFIED THAT THE POSSIBILITY OF SUCH DAMAGES EXISTS.

Disclaimer of Warranties:
PRIMA AND THE AUTHORS SPECIFICALLY DISCLAIM ANY AND ALL OTHER WARRANTIES, EITHER EXPRESS OR IMPLIED, INCLUDING WARRANTIES OF MERCHANTABILITY, SUITABILITY TO A PARTICULAR TASK OR PURPOSE, OR FREEDOM FROM ERRORS. SOME STATES DO NOT ALLOW FOR EXCLUSION OF IMPLIED WARRANTIES OR LIMITATION OF INCIDENTAL OR CONSEQUENTIAL DAMAGES, SO THESE LIMITATIONS MAY NOT APPLY TO YOU.

Other:
This Agreement is governed by the laws of the State of California without regard to choice of law principles. The United Convention of Contracts for the International Sale of Goods is specifically disclaimed. This Agreement constitutes the entire agreement between you and Prima Publishing regarding use of the software.